By Words Alone

P9-CLE-622

BY WORDS ALONE

The Holocaust in Literature

Sidra DeKoven Ezrahi

With a Foreword by
Alfred Kazin

The University of Chicago Press

CHICAGO AND LONDON

Some of the ideas developed in chapters 5 and 6 appeared in much abbreviated form in *Confronting the Holocaust: The Impact of Elie Wiesel,* ed. Alvin H. Rosenfeld and Irving Greenberg (Bloomington: Indiana University Press, 1978).

THE UNIVERSITY OF CHICAGO PRESS, CHICAGO 60637
THE UNIVERSITY OF CHICAGO PRESS, LTD., LONDON

© 1980 by The University of Chicago
All rights reserved. Published 1980
Phoenix edition 1982
Printed in the United States of America

89 88 87 86 85 84 83 82   2 3 4 5 6

LIBRARY OF CONGRESS CATALOGING IN PUBLICATION DATA

Ezrahi, Sidra DeKoven
    By words alone.

    Bibliography: p.
    Includes index.
    1. Holocaust, Jewish (1939–1945), in literature.
2. Literature, Modern—20th century—History
and criticism.   I. Title
PN56.H55E9   808'93358   79–56908
ISBN: 0–226–23335–9 (cloth)
        0–226–23336–7 (paper)

For My Parents

And yet had not the very hand of God gripped and crushed this city deep in the ground, we would have disappeared in darkness, and not given a theme for music, and the songs of men to come.

Euripides, *The Trojan Women*

Contents

Foreword

Gerald Green's television drama "Holocaust" was not much appreciated by survivors of Hitler's death camps and by serious students of what I seem to remember Winston Churchill calling "the worst episode in human history." Gerald Green is a "middlebrow" writer with access to a large built-in public. The television "industry" and its assorted writers, producers, directors—to say nothing of the network officials who had finally consented to "unleash" something "controversial"—are used to headlining documentary material. The murder of six million Jews has for some time been conveniently packaged under the name "Holocaust." So it is not to be wondered at that people with direct experience of the Hitler horror felt "violated" by this "production."

But here is a startling fact. The main German television channels were reluctant to show "Holocaust," and apparently many did not. The most lofty contempt for "Holocaust" was expressed by certain German and Austrian intellectuals. Yet an amazing number of Germans confessed that the film had awakened them to the full extent of Hitler's destruction of European Jewry. They were now less disposed than before to retain the statute of limitations on the punishable crimes of Nazi officials.

What are we to make of Germans, even of the war generation, who needed "Holocaust" to arouse them to the "extermination" of a million Jewish children? What are we to make of the young German student who, on leaving the now-famous house in Amsterdam where Anne Frank and her family hid out from the Germans, was heard to say, "I simply never knew this!" What, when it comes to that, are we to make of Fidel Castro's declaring before the General Assembly of the United Nations that the plight of Palestinian refugees duplicates the Nazi massacre of the Jews?

Intellectuals still feverishly debate Hannah Arendt's "banality of evil" thesis. One distinguished literary critic affirmed that all literature had become meaningless after Auschwitz. Another reproached the poet Sylvia Plath for arrogating the word Dachau in poems expressing her deeply troubled personal situation. My own life experience since Hitler came to power in 1933 has been dominated, in more ways than I can count or measure, by the horrors that did not come to an end in 1945. Since there are Jews even of my own generation who would find this claim excessive, it is obvious that there are many more people who regard *the* Holocaust as just another of life's many tragedies. W. H. Auden wrote in "Musée des Beaux Arts,"

> About suffering they were never wrong,
> The Old Masters: how well they understood
> Its human position; how it takes place
> While someone else is eating or opening a window or
>   just walking dully along...

When millions were gassed, stabbed, shot, buried alive, cast alive into the furnaces, when Western "civilization" became a fantasy, and S.S. doctors of philosophy spoke wryly of Auschwitz as *anus mundi*, there were just as many who knew but could not face what they knew, who could not allow themselves to think about it, who could not bear to "get involved..." It is truly amazing to recognize how many people around us respond to nothing, see nothing, hear nothing. As a visiting professor of American literature in Germany I met a distinguished savant who declared that discussion of the death camps had become "unseemly."

It is surely people like that who plaintively ask why there is so little "beauty" in twentieth-century literature and art. To relate "art" to the Holocaust is frivolous, heartless, esthetically stupid. But what the Church calls "invincible ignorance" is so pronounced in our age of mass propaganda and narcissistic anxiety that one can see the connection between widespread reluctance, still, to confront the Holocaust and the strange idea that "Art" is a supreme good that can be made to order out of the most terrible materials and at any time. Our age will be remembered less for its art than for its technology. And one of the most terrible mementos of our technology will always be Hitler's factories of death.

The great virtue and service of Sidra Ezrahi's *By Words Alone* is that more than any other book I know on this literature, it helps us to see the terrible events that formed it. Although her book is essentially a literary history, and displays the kind of quiet judgment that literary history requires, Mrs. Ezarahi makes us see the Holocaust itself as inevitably more real, urgent, terrible, than the writing that came out of it. That is as it should be. In the history of Jewish literature generally, the creation comes before the word and transcends it. Properly speaking, there is no word for God, though our lives are at every moment full of Him and His creation. To be a Jew is to know that words strive after the reality but can never adequately capture the human situation.

The letter strives after the spirit, but will never be equal to it. Life is always more than the sum of our words. David the psalmist despaired that he could find the word, the deep deep word still lacking to human speech, that would convey the *fact* of God. And if this was true for a Jew in an age when he could escape condemnation by becoming a Christian, what is the word in an age when Jews were condemned to death as a people, condemned simply because they were Jews? Where is the "word" then? What does "literature" signify in the face of such total condemnation?

Actually, literature served and serves the condemned. Literature alone remembers so many of the victims and the particular "situation" of being a victim. Every true writer knows that whatever the final justification, writing itself is a matter of the deepest personal urgency, almost a biological task. Some of the most moving passages in Sidra Ezrahi's book relate to the age-old Jewish *need* of literature. She tells of talented writers, children among them, actually smuggled out of the ghettos so that they could continue their work. One reads with amazement that in 1942 the Vilna Ghetto awarded its "Literary Prize" to the Yiddish poet Abraham Sutzkever for his poem "The Grave Child." Their own literature, whether sacred or "modern," meant so much to Jewish writers that Sutzkever spoke of words as "a kind of link between the living and the dead." Hebrew writing in Palestine, in the early years "separated from its European parent," reclaimed its Jewish patrimony "through language that resonates with collective memory even as [the writer] may rail against its grasp upon his imagination."

The great Hebrew poet H. N. Bialik, who died in 1934, anticipated the predicament of the writer in the face of the Holocaust. "Man arrives at speech out of the magnitude of his fear of remaining even one moment in the abyss, face to face with unmediated nothingness." Yet the poet's language still leaves gaps between the words which allow for a "glimpse of the abyss." Presenting Bialik's haunting theme Sidra Ezrahi sums it up by saying that words at best are like ice floes, the great sea churning beneath and below them.

Nowhere was this disproportion of the word to the "event," of the word to some terror-stricken recognition of ultimate meaninglessness, more acutely realized than by those very writers who in the Hitler maelstrom desperately needed the word in order to convince themselves that *they* would live, and if not they, the Jewish people. Sidra Ezrahi's book is movingly full of this vital connection between the

Jewish writer and his history, the Jew and his collective ancient existence, the Jew and his God. The heroic partisan fighter and memorable poet Abba Kovner said: "When I write I am like a man praying. I inherited many things from my ancestors. One is the teaching that a man should not say his own prayer before the prayer of all the people." Despite the many outcries against God's "silence" and the understandable reproaches and curses, like those of Job himself, many a Jewish writer trapped by Hitler found that he could no more give up the idea of "God" than he could give up his identity as "Jew." "Jew" and "God" were indissolubly linked.

The brilliant Galician-born writer Manès Sperber, who fortunately was saved from the burning and in his novel . . . *Than a Tear in the Sea* wrote one of the most affecting memorials to those who were not, noted in his introduction that traditionally, the survivors of each catastrophe in Jewish history "discovered their invincibility anew. It was the invincibility of their faith: God was just, for he condemned their enemies to be transformed into murderers, while to the Jews he gave the grace of being victims only, who thereby died sanctifying the Almighty . . . .

"Now this had ceased to be true . . . they were no longer inclined and prepared to die for God. If, for the first time on Christian soil, Jews were going to be murdered *en masse* without any demands being made upon them in the name of Christ, European Jewry itself was *going to perish for nothing, in the name of nothing.*"

This is the agonizing theme, rather than the purely literary, that Sidra Ezrahi's book confronts in all courage and openness. The problem that it presents to Jews—and in view of the desperate secularization of twentieth-century life, hardly to them alone—is to what extent the imagination nourished on literature can present us with an *opening* to this problem. There is no "solution" possible, but there is a way of thinking about it that literature is somehow at home with. Literature, as the German refugee philosopher T. W. Adorno said bitterly, cannot accept "artistic representation of the naked bodily pain of those who have been knocked down by rifle butts." It cannot contact, in the face of so much agony, to "squeeze out pleasure." But as Camus recognized, a totally despairing literature, one that pretends to offer itself as such, is a contradiction in terms. Sidra Ezrahi says that the Holocaust is by definition "all-consuming." Literature, we have learned too well, is not. But it does point, in some manner more persistent than we can ever fully recognize, to the intermittency of our despair.

ALFRED KAZIN

October 1979

Acknowledgments

It is a pleasure to acknowledge the contribution, in a myriad of ways and at various stages of this book, of the following people: Sacvan Bercovitch, Alfred Kazin, Elie Wiesel, Milton Hindus, Chaim Brandwein, Gershon Shaked, David Roskies, Mona Fishbane, Michael Fishbane, Hillel Levine, Robin Becker, Miriam Sonn Raabe, Irvin Yalom, Renate Gross, Kate Hughes, Machtsha Zabner, Aryeh Zabner, Sara Dery and Irene Rosenholtz. I wish especially to thank the Center for Advanced Study in the Behavioral Sciences at Stanford for generously providing me with the facilities to complete the editing of the book; and my students in Jerusalem, for their probing questions and for the sense of urgency they have brought to our encounter with the literature.

To my family my debt is the greatest. To Talya, Ariel, and Tehila, whose innocence and laughter come daily as a counterpoint to the muted cries of murdered childhood that the poets will forever struggle to recover. And to Yaron, my life's companion, who has accompanied me with his wisdom and encouragement into the darkest regions of my long and arduous search for the art rescued from death.

Sidra DeKoven Ezrahi

Jerusalem 1979

ONE

Introduction

> Had I but rhymes rugged and harsh and hoarse,
>   Fit for the hideous hole on which the weight
>   Of all those rocks grinds downward course by course,
> I might press out my matter's juice complete;
>   As 'tis, I tremble lest the telling mar
>   The tale; for, truly, to describe the great
> Fundament of the world is very far
>   From being a task for idle wits at play,
>   Or infant tongues that pipe *mama, papa*.
>   Dante Alighieri, *Inferno*

The great illumination that the Enlightenment cast on the image of man faded and flickered during the dark years of this century and projected long shadows into the future. The habitations of death which the Nazis devised for the Jews and some of Europe's other "undesirables" may have become a trauma for modern consciousness such as only the incarnation of fantasies of absolute evil could still produce in a secular world. Sartre describes the prewar consciousness in which "the notion of Evil...had been abandoned"; by 1945, however, we had "been taught to take it seriously...Châteaubriant, Oradour...Dachau and Auschwitz have all demonstrated to us that Evil is not an appearance."[1] The implementation of the Final Solution—not an eruption of the chaotic forces of violence but a systematized, mechanized, and socially organized program—was a mockery of the very idea of culture that had survived into the twentieth century. No symbolic universe grounded in humanistic beliefs could confront the Holocaust without the risk of being shaken to its foundations.

Yet in a broad sense the subject has become as pervasive as it is elusive; the symbols of the events that began with Hitler's accession to power in 1933 and ended with the defeat of the "Thousand Year" Reich in 1945 have been inflated and diluted over the years by loosely

1

analogous application to any abject human condition and by the oblique responses of those who cannot face the subject directly. Simultaneously, a need for some sort of containment is manifested in the evolution of an abstract system of concepts and terminology which tends to distance and tranquilize. Even the rubric under which the horrors of those years are subsumed—the *Holocaust*—may be regarded as something of an evasion through verbal encapsulation. It is derived from the Greek word for whole-burnt and is meant, presumably, to suggest the extent and even the "manner" of the death of the Jews of Europe. Yet the word *hŏlŏkautōma,* which refers in the Septuagint to the "burnt offering" in the Temple of Solomon, raises problems through the sacrificial connotation that it attaches to the death of the Jews of Europe and which is, unfortunately, consistent with a prevailing Christian reading of Jewish history. (The nomenclature that has been adopted in the Jewish world does not carry the same affirmative theological overtones but, rather, signifies the enormity of the rift in Jewish history and culture brought about by the destruction of the European Jewish community.)[2] Minimally, the diffuse imagery and the facile and associative vocabulary reflect a tendency in European and American culture to circumscribe the events, to allocate to them a place and a function in human history, and to confine the madness which threatens to impinge on a "reconstructed" world.

The writer who touches such events with his inheritance of words appears to be reaffirming if not the sanities then the forms of civilized existence. Still he may be disarmed by the resistance of the matter to any attempts at discipline and by the notion that the extremes of human experience can hardly be contained within the delicate frames of art. He may be accused of uncovering the monstrous, culturally illegitimate shapes embedded in recent reality—of polluting human discourse with the language of horror and of forcing the tongue which reverberates with the infant's "mamma" and "papa" in the higher spheres of civilized society to echo the inhuman sounds produced in the "fundament" of the world—in what the Nazis themselves referred to as the "anus mundi." There is a basic tension within the artistic enterprise between the instinctive revulsion against allowing the monstrous creatures to emerge and the base sounds to be heard—as if by exposing them to the light of day the artist were somehow affirming or legitimating the deformities of man's nature—and the equally compelling instinct against repressing reality, against the amnesia that comes with concealment. The ambivalence which these opposites generate in any portrait of evil evolves here within a unique kind of cultural discourse.

The distorted image of the human form which the artist might present as but a mirror of nature transformed can hardly be contained within the traditional perimeters of mimetic art, because although Holocaust

literature is a reflection of recent history it cannot draw upon the timeless archetypes of human experience and human behavior which can
render unlived events familiar through the medium of the imagination.
Harry Levin argues, in his study of realism in literature, that "art can
be viewed and judged as imitation only when men are in confident
touch with the realities that have been imitated."[3] Stephen Crane could
write about war with convincing verisimilitude before he had ever set
foot on the battlefield, in part because war is, to the sorrow of the
generations, a familiar paradigm of human experience. The soldier-
writers of World War I still marched into battle under the cover of what
were thought to be invincible literary conventions reflecting the fixed
challenges and virtues of combat. They returned under a different banner, bloodied irreparably by a new kind of mechanized and brutal
warfare.[4] The violence committed on the meliorist visions of society,
as well as on the fortress of the self and the surviving traditions of
chivalry, which would begin to find an idiom of its own in the literature
that appeared after the Great War and that culminated in the literature
of World War II, is carried to an all but inarticulable extreme in the
Holocaust.

It may be possible, simply by piling on image after bloodcurdling
image, to convey the atmosphere of terror that prevailed under
National Socialism. Yet whereas factual reportage can add to our
knowledge of what actually happened, in fiction the realist's or the
naturalist's respect for details which comprise the fabric of historical
processes is defeated by facts which can hardly be integrated into any
preexistent system of ethics or aesthetics—facts which, in the words of
the London *Times* correspondent accompanying the British troops who
liberated the concentration camp at Belsen, are "beyond the imagination of mankind." As I shall try to show, precisely where it is most
confined to the unimaginable facts of violence and horror, the creative
literature that has developed is the least consistent with traditional
moral and artistic conventions. Even the most vivid presentation of
concrete detail and specificity, the most palpable reconstruction of
Holocaust reality, is blunted by the fact that there is no analogue in
human experience. The imagination loses credibility and resources
where reality exceeds even the darkest fantasies of the human mind;
even realism flounders before such reality.

The disjunction between generic memory and conventional forms on
the one hand, and "millennial"[5] subject matter and the literary forms
which have evolved to contain the new reality on the other, is a measure of the shifts in the boundaries of art beyond which the imagination
becomes inarticulate and form disintegrates altogether. As representational art reflects not just nature but the images of nature that
have accrued over the centuries, so the representation of the Holocaust

in art is, essentially, an oscillation and a struggle between continuity and discontinuity with the cultural as well as with the historical past.[6]

One manifestation of the writer's poverty of resource when dealing with a subject that, in exceeding the bounds of recorded experience, could not draw upon familiar models of human behavior and values, has been the heavy reliance of certain artists on psychologists or social historians to provide new touchstones. The social scientists have, it would seem, succeeded to some extent in fathoming and taming the horrors of that period by deducing theories of human response to extremity from the Holocaust experience. The very presentation of a systematic *explanation,* or the assignment of one form or another of social or psychological "meaning" to the camp experience constitutes a code by which writers, in particular those who did not share the experience, can reconstruct it.[7] Yet for others, primarily those who were close to the events themselves, it may be precisely in its *resistance* to conceptual abstraction, to psychological reductionism, that art as a version of historical memory can provide form without fixing meaning, insight without explanation, for the recovered events. For the writer to whom art is a form of resistance to death, and the fictional restoration of character and private fate a defiance of the anonymity of life in the shadow of the Swastika, no less than for the writer whose writing is in itself an act of acquiescence to the ultimate power of the system over the imagination, the creation can hardly be mediated by the claims of the analytical mind to comprehend or to instruct.

With respect to the structural metamorphoses that have taken place in response to historical discontinuities, the visual arts appear to be more amenable than the literary medium to the representation of violent disruptions in human affairs and distortions of the human image. Picasso's innovations have provided the visual vocabulary for the representation of horrors even greater than those that took place at Guernica; Jean Cayrol, in his essay on Holocaust art, writes that "Picasso is the painter *par excellence* who could have installed his easel on the 'Appel-Platz' at Mauthausen or Buchenwald."[8] Cayrol, himself a survivor who has written a number of novels and poems reflecting the concentration camp experience, collaborated with Alain Resnais in producing the film *Nuit et brouillard* (1955), which employs techniques of juxtaposition that assault the senses with an immediacy and a brutality that can hardly be matched in any other medium.

Literature like music is a sequence, not a simultaneity, of events; as Erich Auerbach has written of the contrast between the literary and the cinematic arts, a concentration of space and time such as can be achieved by the film . . . can never be within the reach of the spoken or written word. To be sure, the novel possesses great freedom in its command of space and time [and] the novel in recent decades has made use of this freedom in a way for which earlier literary periods afford no models . . . . At the same time, however, by virtue of the film's existence, the novel has come to be more clearly aware than ever before of the limitations in space and time imposed upon it by its instrument, language. As a result the situation has been reversed: the dramatic technique of the film now has far greater possibilities in the direction of condensing time and space than has the novel itself.[9]

Yet even if the arts do not develop congruently, given their structurally inherent differences, it can be argued that they do evolve along parallel lines in response to cultural or historical shifts.[10] Thus we can trace both the initial resistance and the stages of accommodation of the novel and other literary forms to the experience of social disruption and brutality which had begun to be manifested long before their encounter with Auschwitz. Frederick Hoffman's study of nineteenth- and twentieth-century fiction, *The Mortal No,* analyzes the gradual breakdown of the novel of manners as a vehicle for representing the proliferation of violence in society: "The result was to challenge the novelist in a curious way: he had in all conscience to produce a 'novel of manners of violence'; that is, he had to account for violence in a literary form that was not prepared to accommodate it."[11]

The structural responses that the forces of violent reality had begun to exact from the literary imagination are exemplified in this century not only in the ironic mode in the literature of two wars but also in the dislocations and distortions of focus in the fiction of Joyce or Gertrude Stein, in the poetry of Eliot or Pound. The shift is from violence as a passionate crime of the self to automated, socially enforced, and diffuse violence as the general backdrop for human endeavor. Holocaust literature appears in this context as the culmination of a well-advanced literary process. And if the new literary forms come not only to reflect but in some sense to anticipate current events, Kafka is the writer whose fiction so fully expressed the logic of modern technology, mechanized sadism, and bureaucratic depersonalization that Auschwitz appears almost as the realization of the fantastic world blueprinted in *The Penal Colony.* Still, the next stage, even in the literary history of violence, seems to test or transgress the boundaries of the admissible in art. When Hoffman reaches this stage in his analysis, he poses the ultimate question of whether the "circumstance of violence" in the world of concentration camps is not "so overwhelming that it is impossible for any literature to comprehend it adequately . . . . It is true that literature has never been silenced by calamity; it has not been especially nourished by it either. Catastrophes in the past . . . either have been ignored or have only temporarily been introduced into the margins of literature."[12] Nevertheless, contemporary writers persist in their attempts to extend the limits of the imagination, to devise a "strategy of the mind" which could encompass even the most violent extremes of human experience: "Wallace Stevens describes the mind as containing a 'violence from within that protects us from a violence without'; [presumably] he means that the imagination can and does meet the full force of reality, and that an act of mind must and should apply to any occasion of external violence, that it must be equal to the occasion."[13]

Yet again the basic tensions that are generated in an art grounded in monstrous reality emerge in the form of a challenge; literature which meets the "full force . . . of external violence" can be accused of engaging in a kind of complicity with the evil forms it bodies forth. Edmund Wilson, in his controversial article on Kafka in the *New Yorker* in 1947, called Kafka's representation of the forces of human cruelty and irrationality a "rather meaching compliance . . . in the presence of the things he would satirize," and argued against the tendency to compare him to a Proust or a Dante: "You cannot have a first-rate saint or prophet without a faith of a very much higher potential than is ever to be felt in Kafka." The implication is that art should provide a refuge from reality, and that "prophetic" art should at least aim at a vision of moral fortitude in the face of human suffering. Wilson's position in regard to Kafka presupposes, in other words, that the artistic representation of social disintegration or anomy denies itself as art if it does not transcend the abyss through the force of a moral vision; his attitude relates to the concept of culture as a striving toward perfection and refinement: "What are we writers for if it is not to cheat the world of its triumph? The denationalized, discouraged, disaffected, disabled Kafka, though for the moment he may frighten or amuse us, can in the end only let us down. He is quite true to his time and place, but it is surely a time and place in which few of us will want to linger."[14]

T. W. Adorno, with far less faith in the redemptive pretenses of art, also considers the danger that the very reconstruction of intolerable reality can somehow contaminate the writer, and alludes to the dissonance between aesthetic or formalistic conventions of order and beauty and the chaos and ugliness which were the essence of Auschwitz. His assertion that it is "barbaric" to write poetry after Auschwitz, made in the context of a discussion of "engaged" versus "autonomous" literature, raises the issue of whether the cultural and social degeneration that culminated in Auschwitz commands a literature that is commensurately degenerate. Yet throughout Adorno's deliberations resounds the echo of Pascal's warning, "'on ne doit plus dormir,'" and the conclusion that such an "abundance of suffering permits no forgetting," that even if art is constantly in danger of betraying the victim, there is almost no other place where suffering still "finds its own voice." Adorno also considers the options that Kafka explored in his fiction and implicitly rejects the refuge that Wilson seeks: "He who was once run over by Kafka's wheels has lost his peace with the world."[15]

For some scholars and writers the ambiguities and dangers inherent in the enterprise are submerged beneath what they conceive to be a clearly hortatory or didactic imperative. A. Alvarez has suggested that only art can restore the moral values which would make further totalitarian atrocities impossible.[16] Sartre, in the impassioned postwar treatise, *What Is Literature?* that initiated the polemic to which Adorno was addressing himself, assumed the position of spokeman for his generation when he wrote: "We are now forced by circumstances to discover the pressure of history.... We have undertaken to create a literature of extreme situations."[17] Both Sartre and later Camus, like Stevens and other writers who have touched the "flowers of evil" from one side or another, suggest that the creative writer, by expanding the boundaries of his art to incorporate unprecedented violence and despair, may in fact conquer or at least discipline them: "Despairing literature is a contradiction in terms," Camus was to write; "even if the novel describes only nostalgia, despair, frustration, it still creates a form of salvation. To talk of despair is to conquer it."[18]

In the following chapters we will be focusing our attention on the various ways in which the writers who "talk of despair" reflect degrees of submission or of conquest. The writer's very effort to "communicate," even within a system of altered perceptions, to account for the violence that had been committed on the notions of personal and collective survival, on moral and ethical values, and on aesthetic traditions which serve a continuity of cultural perspectives, is one mark of his trust in certain linkages between the past and the future. As Frank Kermode has pointed out, "the forms of art—its language—are in their nature a continuous extension or modification of conventions entered into by maker and reader, and this is true even of very original artists so long as they communicate at all."[19] Again, the manipulation of reality within the unmapped regions of human experience becomes a measure of the writer's invocation of a world beyond the barbed wire: the form of creative literature that is most "unconventional," morally as well as aesthetically, is that which stays so close to fact, which is so bound by the internal perspective of life in the lowest spheres, that all attempts to communicate with the uninitiated reader or to provide an escape route for reader, or victim, into the verities of the past or the possibilities of the future are precluded.

Intensifying with the reader's familiarity with the Nazi system, and shifting with the degree of authorial intervention, a relationship evolves between maker and reader which is probably unprecedented in the history of Western literature. However his purpose is perceived—as testimonial, elegiac, confessional—the writer is, in some sense, held accountable to whatever form of historical memory his reader subscribes to. The very act of writing is often regarded, especially by survivors and even by the writers themselves, as presumptuous. There is an unarticulated but uneasy sense that a different logic pertains in regard to "reality" when one crosses over from history or autobiography into imaginative literature; the suspicion that fiction must be somehow subversive of truth is repeatedly manifested in the insistance on the part of those who write memoirs that what they are writing is not "a fiction." It is this claim on which the documentary writers whom we will consider also base their authority. Beyond the "telling," that is, speech is perceived by such writers as an intrusion into the monumental silence of a memorial. Robert Jay Lifton, in his book on Hiroshima, refers to a "creative guilt" among the writers of A-bomb literature which is equally applicable to Holocaust writers: "What happens with the A-bomb is that the event becomes rendered so historically sacred that recreating it in any form can be psychologically perceived as hubris by both artists and their audiences."[20]

Because of the unique interaction between the reader and the written text, dictated by both the new historical condition and the commemorative impulse, the ultimate impact of much of the literature of the Holocaust lies not in the explicit resolution of the reconstructed events, but in the privileged position of the post-Holocaust reader. This is especially true of those works in which the action extends only to the edge of darkness, the reader's prescience serving to underscore the irretrievable innocence of victims who died in a distant world in which the absolute evil that came to be named Holocaust was not yet an integral part of human consciousness. In a novel like *The Shop on Main Street,* by the Czech-Jewish writer Ladislav Grossman, the real tragedy is felt not in what takes place before our eyes—the death of deaf old Mrs. Lautman in her buttons-and-lace store—but in the glimpse that the reader has of the roundup of the Jews outside her window. By comparison with what the reader knows to be their destination, the old woman's deafness, and even her death, in full dignity and innocence, appear blessed:

> Mrs. Rosalie Lautman . . . had found such favor in the eyes
> of the Lord that she had been granted seventy-eight years of
> blameless life and the precious gift of deafness, thanks to
> which she preserved unspoiled to the very end the illusion
> that the world was full of kind, friendly people.[21]

The reader who knows what the inevitable fate of every Jew was to
be in this deterministic world becomes, then, a "collaborative" witness to the events. This is especially evident in novels in which there is
no morally detached narrator to act as cicerone. In *A Prayer for
Katerina Horovitzova,* by another Czech-Jewish writer, Arnošt Lustig,
the reader enters into a kind of collusion with SS Commandant Fried-
rich Brenske in understanding the literal underpinnings of his speech to
twenty-one unsuspecting victims, which *they* choose to understand
metaphorically: "Everything will turn out just as we said it would. The
final solution is at hand. . . . Your worries will all go up in smoke."[22]
Similarly, a short poem by the Polish poet Tadeusz Różewicz, "The
Massacre of the Boys," evokes a kind of conditioned response through
the austere language that contains only the bare, unexplained signals of
a new reality:

> The children cried: 'Mommie,
> I was a good boy, really . . .
> Oh, it's so dark—so dark.'
>
> Look—they are going to the bottom
> See their little feet
> They have reached the bottom. Do you see
> these marks
> tiny footprints here and over there.
>
> Their pockets were full
> of bits of twine and pebbles
> and little tin horses.
>
> The vast plain is closed off
> like a geometric figure
> and a tree of black smoke
> rises vertically
> a dead tree
> with no star on top.[23]

The economy of language dispenses with all the physical details of
violence; the informed reader knows that —and in what manner—little
boys were massacred during the Nazi regime. The second stanza is
intelligible only to one who can visualize the shooting of children at the
edge of a mass grave. The blank margins of this poem are, as it were,

the unspoken forces of violence and oblivion that ultimately engulf and silence the civilized poetry of childhood's "twine and pebble and little tin horses."

As the Holocaust is by very definition all-consuming, a historical imperative which predetermines the fate of every individual, regardless of his merits, in a closed universe where there can be no appeal and no grace, the decisions of the victim can, at the very most, affect the quality of his "sentence"—they can never effect a reprieve. The post-Holocaust reader can, then, arrive at the fate of any given character by a process of deduction. If he does not die, his survival is, simply, an aberration. Even epic war novels such as *War and Peace*—or the less epic but more fatalistic novels of World War II—do not present war as the sole and totally predictable factor determining the lives (and deaths) of all of the protagonists. War in fiction, as in life, is a game of roulette, and survival is at least a logical possibility.

The Vocabulary of the Holocaust Universe

Perhaps the clearest evidence of the predictability and uniformity, as well as the perversity, of the genocidal system, and of the degree of its penetration into the very fabric of human intercourse, with far-reaching implications for literature, is the manipulation of language within its borders. The concentration camp, first described by David Rousset as *"l'univers concentrationnaire,"*[24] was a self-contained world which both generated its own vocabulary and invested common language with new, sinister meanings. The terms *Sonderkommando, Kapo,* and *Appel*—untranslatable because there is no precedent for them in human experience—signify not only the functions and the routine of the inmate, but also a new hierarchy of human relations, values, and expectations. The idiom of *l'univers concentrationnaire* encompasses all aspects of the Nazi operation which were a part of the master plan of annihilation and therefore common to most of the ghettos and camps. Certain terms which appear in the literature convey a specific status and a predictable fate: *katzetnik* is an inmate of any of the concentration camps, while *Häftling* has the more general connotation of *prisoner.* The adjective *concentrationary,* used here as in the English version of Rousset's memoir as a rough translation of *concentrationnaire,* is not necessarily limited in its reference to the geographical confines of the camps but may allude to the general condition of the Jew in Europe during World War II, who, whether incarcerated in a ghetto or a concentration camp, posing as an Aryan, or hiding in a barn, an attic, or a forest, was marked for extermination.

The Jews were not, of course, the only victims of Nazism, and a number of works written by non-Jews reflect the different logic of death and survival that distinguished the fate of the political from the Jewish *Häftling* in the concentrationary universe. The former were, in general, treated with less brutality and could find strength in the fact that they had in large measure chosen their own destiny; the Jews and the Gypsies were the only peoples singled out by *racial* criteria for extermination, and arrested, deported, interned, and gassed simply because of the biological fact of their ancestry. Yet the concentrationary idiom informs the literature written by all the prisoners and binds them in a common linguistic universe.

Of course, no single language was so transformed by the operation of the Nazi system as was the German language, whose syntax, style, and symbolic associations were profoundly and abidingly violated by what came to be known as "Nazi-Deutsch," the perverse rhetoric that signified the collective actions of the National Socialists. The ideological premise, with its totalitarian extension into every area of cultural expression, coupled with the incompatible goals of maintaining precise written records of Nazi deeds while camouflaging them in euphemism for the outside world, created a complex of verbal acrobatics which subsequent generations of linguists would strive painstakingly to sort out.[25] Perhaps the most absurd yet intransigent paradox can be found in the links which the fascists claimed between contemporary politics and art, hailing the Fuehrer as the successor to the artist in his possession of a transrational vision and even arrogating to Hitler the function of the "poet." Some of the major postwar writing in Germany has been read as an attempt to purge, through subtle parodies and ironic reversals of traditional literary modes and forms of speech, the language and the literature of their implication in the crimes of Nazism.[26]

Predictably, though ironically, the language most affected, next to German, by the abuses of National Socialism was Yiddish, which registered the barbaric terminology as an inseparable part of the national consciousness of the Jewish victims. Yiddish has been studied as a "record of Jewish history," accreting idiomatic expressions that have their origins in generations of persecution;[27] by the same process the terms of the most recent barbarity have been absorbed into the collective memory. And even as the language records the specific historical coordinates of the twentieth-century slaughter, the experience of catastrophe is absorbed into a cyclical reading of history that links ancient and modern forms of *hurbn* ("destruction").

The literatures of the perpetrators and of the victims remain, then, discrete organisms indelibly branded with the emblems of genocide. Questions of continuity and discontinuity with pre-Holocaust structures and values can, therefore, be considered here with reference to specific cultural contexts.[28] By a similar logic, English, in its very remoteness from the events, retains a kind of autonomy and purity that only a language which was not spoken in the concentrationary universe, and was therefore never tainted by the Holocaust vocabulary, could claim. Jakov Lind, who recapitulates the dislocation of many a young Jew growing up in the Europe of the 1930s and 1940s (his native tongue was German but, by his own admission, "I had to speak Dutch at eleven, Hebrew when I was eighteen, English when I was twenty-seven and French when I was thirty-four"), relates the mystical appeal that English had for him as a teenage refugee in Holland:

> Strange or not so strange, I began learning English with a fever I had never known for any other subject at school. I just wanted to know as soon as possible everything that had anything to do with my personal British and American allies. (The BBC wartime program "Here is London..." sounded, even to those who didn't understand a single word of it, like a message of hope for passengers of an aeroplane that had lost both wings.) English, after May, 1940, was simply the sound of defiance, the language of reason.[29]

The status of English as the language of the "outsider" and, eventually, of the "liberator" is reflected especially in the American literature which has evolved since the war; for the native American writer, as well as for the European victim, English represented not only the "sound of defiance" but also the very existence of another world and a different hierarchy of human values. Yet for one who had survived the Holocaust, even the adoption of the English language could not provide a shield against private memory. Holocaust novels written in English by survivors from Europe are differentiable from indigenous American literature by the salient marks of a translated idiom. They are examples of a literature of displaced persons who remained after the war without specific cultural citizenship, exchanging their native tongue, but not their vocabulary of experience, for the language of their adopted country. The literature that many of the survivors produced shares certain unique qualities of cultural dislocation and of crosscultural perspectives precisely because it is a literature of uprooted persons, most of them writing in acquired languages: Anna Langfus and Piotr Rawicz in French; Jakov Lind, Jerzy Kosinski, Ilona Karmel, Zdena Berger, and Elżbieta Ettinger in English; and so on. It may be, as Albert Memmi suggests, that language for the Jew is anyway a very provisional possession which the vagaries of history force him periodically to assume and then to abandon.[30] If so, this may just be an accelerated instance of a process that has become "normal" for the Jew. Nevertheless, the interchangeability of language seems to be a specific characteristic of the massive displacement of the Holocaust experience. Even when a displaced writer does not exchange what Arnold Mandel calls one's "literary nationality"[31] (Paul Celan and Nelly Sachs continuing to write in their native German while exiled in Paris or Sweden), he is at best cut off from the literary mainstream of his native land. In certain important ways the work of any of these writers can be located more firmly in the idiom of Holocaust fiction and poetry in other languages than in the literary traditions of either his native or his adopted country; and the interaction of themes, styles, and structures can be studied as part of what is primarily a transnational literature which derives from a common experience and vocabulary. The ashes that congeal as black milk in one poem and as hovering clouds in another are the hideous substance of the new order underlying variant images. The pervasiveness of the Holocaust as an experience that transcended national borders creates the possibility of a literature whose reference is, then, both personal—indeed, irrevocably traumatic—and international at the same time.

The distinction between a collective literature and a "displaced" literature is not merely linguistic but broadly cultural. The lamentation literature encompasses Hebrew, Yiddish, and European works which reflect the specific threat to Jewish civilization that accompanied the attack on Jewish existence; it draws upon a unique and continuous tradition of Hebraic response to catastrophe, invoking specific historical memories and an ongoing dialogue with Jewish destiny and theodicy. For the heirs to this tradition, which dates back to the Bible, the center of reference is the people and history of Israel; the ultimate assault of Nazism is on the survival and values of the community; and the Holocaust is perceived as a formative historical event. They locate the individual within the historical and valuational continuum of the community of which, in his extremity, he still remains a part, even if the whole no longer exists and even if his own life is fractured beyond repair. The use of historical values in the search for signification does not, as we shall see, ensure the continued reaffirmation of those principles, but it does, at the very least, inform the quest. By contrast, for the writer set adrift by the Nazis from the sources of his life's continuity, the reference is usually private experience rather than the more generalized historical questions of collective identity and destiny. The Holocaust represents for such a writer and his characters the experience of total anomy and the defilement of the integrity and dignity, as well as the body, of the individual. What emerges from a comparative evaluation is that the existentialist perspective, which focuses on the individual *in extremis,* placing the exposed self at the center as the irreducible source of meaning, and viewing biography as the limit of history, generates symbolic responses which are profoundly different from the historical vision which relates to a chapter in the martyrology of a people, anchoring the meaning of the life of the self in the fate and the cultural resources of the group.

The search for an orientation to the Holocaust from within either the collective or the existential purview encompasses a wide spectrum of stages in the relationship of art and human consciousness to cataclysmic history. Documentary literature can be seen as an intermediate stage between testimony and imaginative literature, which preserves a kind of sacred attitude toward broad historical processes that precludes, as it were, artistic "interference." The next level, at which history operates less as a specific record than as a creative resource but still reflects the artist's primary sense of loyalty to fact, is what I call "concentrationary realism," a form of fiction which places the exposed individual at its center and traces the degrees of submission to concentrationary reality, the erosive effects of brutal reality on the autonomy and integrity of the self. Another form of fictional realism, the "survival novel," constitutes the first breach in the tyranny of fact over imagination, employing memory, fantasy, and metaphor as a manner of escape from and denial of reality within the private soul of the victim. Similarly, Hebraic literature explores the possibility of a way out of as well as a way into the concentrationary universe that in turn generates a provisional attitude toward that reality—but, again, it is collective Jewish history rather than personal biography which constitutes the link between past and future by which the present is endured or tested. Finally, the most radical form of absorption of the historical events into the imagination is the myth created by the writer who is totally liberated from "facticity" but subject to the pervasive, transcendental reality of Holocaust.

Each of these stages constitutes one chapter of this book, with representative authors exemplifying the different patterns of literary response. It is still too soon to judge which of these works of art will endure—which are, in Northrop Frye's terms, "redeemable" and which "irredeemable."[32] I have tried, nevertheless, given allowances for subjectivity in matters of taste, to establish critical distinctions between works of "high seriousness" and the more popular literary productions, incorporating some admittedly middle-brow writers who may prove to be worthy of consideration in the long run more as forerunners or apprentices than as masters of a literary genre.

The writers who will be considered in the following chapters are either survivors or men and women who never lived through the Holocaust; that is, they are all writing *after* the events, and the literature they have created differs significantly from that which evolved in the ghettos and camps themselves. The most obvious distinction is the hindsight that the "completed event" offers the post-Holocaust writer; the full extent and the systematic quality of the genocide could be appreciated only after the war. Literary activity in the ghettos or camps was often a desperate attempt at self-immortalization, at leaving some human record to defy the degradation and finality of the death that surrounded and awaited the writer; on the other hand, much of the literature that has been written since by survivors is both an account of the price one had to pay for personal survival and an effort at commemoration, at resurrection of one's own dead—a process in which the survivor serves as a kind of scribe. Most significant of course in terms of the artistic process is the element of time; the literature that was coeval with the experience did not benefit from the distancing necessary for a relatively tranquil perfection of aesthetic forms or for even a temporal distinction between the "man who suffers and the mind which creates."

In order to highlight such distinctions, and to provide an internal point of cultural reference for the literature that followed, I wish to focus briefly on some aspects of the life of art in the concentrationary universe itself which are particularly worthy of attention because they represent not only active literary efforts, but also evidence of the spiritual transformation of elements of Western culture in a society sentenced to collective extinction.

Literature in the Concentrationary Universe

Some of the cultural effects of Nazism in the Jewish world could be identified even in the earliest stages of National Socialist rule. Before the policy of extermination had been systematically implemented, the impact of the Nuremberg Laws on German-Jewish culture was already considerable. Even the assimilated Jews suddenly found themselves exiled from German culture, and many began to turn back to a tradition from which they had been estranged for years or, in some cases, generations. One of the more public manifestations of this new orientation was the flourishing of a new kind of Jewish theater; plays with biblical themes were written and produced and a *Kulturband* formed with the purpose of reconstructing Western drama from a Jewish point of view.

An alternate route of escape was exile, and many of those who still could fled, whether in response to a threat to life itself or to the Nazi pollution of German culture, of which the curtailment of Jewish participation in "Aryan" civilization was just one manifestation. The *Exil Literatur* created by German emigrés to America and other countries

provides a rich resource for reflection on the implications for German
culture of the voluntary expatriation of so many of Germany's Jewish
and non-Jewish artists.[33]

Among those who were unable or unwilling to leave, and who eventually found themselves incarcerated in ghettos and then in concentration camps, art provided an important medium of defiance and escape.
Clandestine literary efforts produced numerous manuscripts which
were distributed by underground methods and served as a primary
spiritual resource for the prisoners in the ghettos and camps. Where
paper was scarce, the inmates inscribed their messages on logs, which
were often transferred from camp to camp. Underground organizations
such as the Warsaw Ghetto's YIKOR (Yiddish Cultural Organization)
sponsored literary projects and dramatic performances. Here again, as
in the early stages of the German-Jewish response to Nazism, many of
these dramas were adaptations of biblical themes with clearly contemporary connotations. This was as much for the purpose of camouflaging
references to current events as for the resuscitation of indigenous
Jewish culture. Literary creativity was so valued that in rare instances
gifted writers, including children, were smuggled by the underground
out of the ghettos and even out of concentration camps so they could
continue their work.[34]

Of the literature that was rescued from the ghettos and camps, considerable attention has been paid to the poems written by children in
Theresienstadt, which were published together with a sampling of their
drawings. Theresienstadt was unique among the concentration camps
in that it was constructed as a showplace for members of the Red Cross
and of other humanitarian organizations who might inquire into the
Nazi treatment of the Jews. Cultural activities were encouraged. The
reprieve, however, was deceptive; of the 15,000 children under the age
of fifteen who passed through Theresienstadt between 1942 and 1944 on
their way to one or another of the extermination camps, only one
hundred remained alive at the end of the war. The poems they left
behind, which are valuable as a whole primarily for the rare human
testimony they represent, are uneven in quality, but some of them
show not only a maturity born of suffering but also a mastery of form.
There are recurrent themes and stylistic patterns in this poetry that are
surely unique in the history of children's writings: nostalgia for the
world that is already lost to them (a theme reserved for aging poets in a
normal world), the contraction and diminution of the images of nature
and civilization that are available to them, the struggle between the
unbridled imagination and the constriction and inexorability of present
reality. Some of these poems illustrate the transformed images of comparison that will signify new parameters of metaphor in the more

accomplished post-Holocaust literature which we will consider.[35]

The reading as well as the writing of literature took on social dimensions which can be studied as an example of the unique cultural functions that art may assume among people living under a death sentence. A number of testimonies have survived which attest to the fact that, contrary to what one might perhaps expect, the demand for literature intensified as conditions worsened. Finding correspondences and premonitions in the books at hand, Jean Cayrol admits that, reading in a lonely cell that Julien Sorel had been condemned to death, he did not believe that he would outlive him.[36] War novels, it seems, were especially in demand in the ghettos. In one of the entries in his Warsaw diary, Emmanuel Ringelblum wrote that, along with other classics, "Tolstoy's *War and Peace* is enjoying great popularity among people who have already read it more than once.... In short, unable to avenge themselves upon the enemy in fact, people are trying to do so in their imagination, in literature." Through Tolstoy many readers seem to have taken comfort in historical analogies; in the fall of Napoleon some saw the inevitable defeat of any dictator—although the comparison between Napoleon and Hitler was of course resolved in Napoleon's favor. Whether it furnished historical parallels or simply a momentary escape from the imminence of death, literature helped to maintain the individual's self-image: "they [the outside world] can say that we did not lose our human characteristics; our minds are as busy as they were before the War," writes Ringelblum.[37]

Library facilities and the leisure time and energy to read were of course more available in the ghettos than in the concentration camps. Yet even in the camps some prisoners managed to obtain books, often under the most unlikely circumstances. Ernst Wiechert, the German writer who was interned in Buchenwald for his outspoken criticism of Nazi policies, managed, after a time, to receive permission to have copies of the books he had written sent to him in the camp. The irony of this fact, which he relates in his autobiographical novel, *Forest of the Dead,* is that his arrest could be at least partly attributed to the "subversive" nature of these books;[38] as a society of total control, Nazi Germany systematically gathered all the "refuse"—human as well as cultural—in certain designated areas. Another inmate of Buchenwald who benefited in his incarceration from the cultural controls imposed by the Nazis was Eugen Kogon, who writes in his memoirs of retrieving literary masterpieces that had reached the camp as wastepaper:

> For months on end I volunteered [for the nightwatch in the
> bread stores], taking the shift from three to six o'clock in the
> morning. It meant sitting alone in the day room .... What an
> experience it was to sit quietly by a shaded lamp, delving

into the pages of Plato's *Dialogues,* Galsworthy's *Swan Song,* or the works of Heine, Klabund, Mehring! Heine? Klabund? Mehring? Yes, they could be read illegally in camp. They were among books retrieved from the nationwide wastepaper collections. The Nazis impounded many libraries of "enemies of the state," and turned them over to these collections, part of which found its way into the camps as toilet paper. The prisoners carefully retrieved what was of value.[39]

While the Nazis were engaged in their systematic attempt to dismantle Western civilization, the inmates were deriving solace from the fragments of civilization shredded into toilet paper for the "anus mundi."

Another testimony of the capacity of the victim to transcend, through art, the agony of physical and spiritual degradation appears in Primo Levi's memoir on Auschwitz. Levi, an Italian Jew who was arrested while engaged in resistance activities, begins with an account of the initiation into camp life, and describes the slow process by which the Nazis achieved the "demolition of a man": "Nothing belongs to us anymore; they have taken away our clothes, our shoes, even our hair. . . . They will even take away our name."[40] Then one day, as the narrator, now nameless as *"Häftling* 174517," is trudging to the kitchens with young Pikolo, the messenger-clerk of the Chemical Kommando, to bring the soup ration to their group, he suddenly begins to quote from *The Divine Comedy*—to teach his unlettered companion those verses from the "Canto of Ulysses" which his memory has retained. He acts out of the urgency of one who knows that he may not live until tomorrow; one of his final gestures, then, will have been the civilizing act of the transmission of the human vision which might still somehow redeem him and his friend from the brutality of their fate. Perhaps, he thinks to himself,

> Pikolo . . . has received the message, . . . has felt that it has to do with him, that it has to do with all men who toil, and with us in particular; and that it has to do with us two who dare to reason of these things with the poles for the soup on our shoulders. . . . I must explain to him . . . something gigantic that I myself have only just seen, in a flash of intuition, perhaps, the reason for our fate, for our being here today. [Pp. 103–5]

Levi's memoir focuses on this moment as the point at which *Häftling* 174517 begins to rediscover his humanity, to combat by the powers of imagination and analogy the absurdity of his condition. In the literature of survival, which we shall discuss, such a moment represents the transition from "Darwinian" to "human" survival.

The Czech novel by Josef Bor, *The Terezin Requiem,* is another story of the role of art as the medium of spiritual struggle in the camps. It is a semifictionalized account of the performance of Verdi's Requiem—again in Theresienstadt, the showcase of Jewish culture in the Third Reich—in the presence of Eichmann and a number of his henchmen. The story is narrated from the point of view of Raphael Schächter, the conductor, who succeeds in molding the Requiem into a prism reflecting the individual miseries, and the one final triumph, of a group of camp musicians. Schächter conceives of the performance of the Requiem out of the realization that the Nazis had

> assembled in one camp the greatest Jewish artists from a large part of Europe; and they had created conditions that force men to ponder deeply the fundamental questions of life and death.... Here everyone hungered and thirsted after art, longed feverishly for every tremor of deep human feeling, all the more passionately as the world in which they had been forcibly imprisoned became more unthinkably repulsive and barbarous.[41]

The Requiem is, on the night of the performance, transformed by these artists into a cry of protest: Schächter takes the liberty of amending the libretto by answering the four pianissimo notes of the finale—the conciliatory "libera me"—with a defiant, fortissimo 'libera *nos,*" delivered by the entire orchestra and choir as four fighting blows (the three short and one long strokes of Beethoven's Fifth Symphony). "O Saint Verdi in heaven, forgive me my sin," pleads Schächter. "If you had been in a concentration camp you, too, would have composed your finale differently" (p. 83). By the end of the performance, Schächter has dropped his baton and is conducting with his fist. The entire cast of performers is shipped out on the very next transport to the death camp—but that event is so inevitable as to be almost insignificant. The real victory is measured in the confused response of Eichmann, who finally admits that the performance was "very interesting" (p. 112); his obtuseness—and even more so that of his associate Moese, who "understood music" (p. 102), but obviously did not comprehend the power of music to subvert the concentrationary system—underscores this modest triumph of the spirit. A. Alvarez has called this short novel a "real-life allegory of art poising itself precariously against destruction."[42] Like Primo Levi's recital of the Canto of Ulysses in Auschwitz, it illustrates the ways in which the significance of some of the classical elements of European culture were completely transformed in the context of the camps.

A thorough analysis of the life of art in the concentrationary universe, which is beyond the scope of this study, could also include a discussion of the uses of and attitudes toward literature, music, and the plastic arts on the part of some of the culturally more sophisticated Nazis such as Eichmann's assistant, Moese. George Steiner has for some years been engaged in a polemic over the implications of the failure of art to civilize in what was perhaps the most civilized country in Europe ("why did humanistic traditions and models of conduct prove so fragile a barrier against political bestiality?"). His conclusion, that after Auschwitz we have "passed out of the major order and symmetries of Western civilization" and find ourselves in an era of "post culture," is of a piece with the apocalyptic temper with which many contemporary writers confront the times.[43] Another writer who, as a member of Europe's political and intellectual elite and as a citizen of a country allied with Germany, was in a unique position to observe at close range the process by which the Nazis attempted to subvert Western culture, was the Italian journalist Curzio Malaparte. His rhetoric is far less inflated than Steiner's, his conclusions more affirmative of the continuity of the human vision and spirit, and yet his pain is far more real. His four-year odyssey through the wasteland of Europe during the war is recorded in one of the most sensitive and thorough accounts of the devastation. He demonstrates repeatedly the coexistence of art or aesthetic sensibility and sadism in the Nazi mind, even highlighting a peculiar form of aesthetic repugnance which the German officers demonstrated toward acts of violence or the sight of blood; Kurt Franz (commandant of Treblinka), for example, confides to Malaparte that "vomit and blood are two things that disgust me the most."[44]

Art remains, of course, intrinsically independent of the uses or abuses to which victim or victimizer subjects it, and there is more to be learned from the life of art under the Third Reich about the spirit's endurance and its elevation or perversion of the resources of cultural memory than about the inherent value of "humanistic traditions" as a "barrier against political bestiality."

After Liberation: The Testimonial Imperative

When the nightmare finally came to an end and the camps were liberated all over Europe, a surprisingly large number of manuscripts were found in the possession of the survivors. Of those who did not survive, many had managed to bury their writings or to smuggle them out of the ghettos and camps. For years after the war, friends were still digging among the rubble of the ghettos to unearth a tin can or a bottle with a manuscript. Events had turned Warsaw, Lvov, Cracow, Lublin, Vilna, and thousands of small towns into instant "tells" and the survivors into archaeologists of the immediate past. Often fragments turned up years later in the custody of peasants or nuns. The Yiddish writer Mendel Mann describes the concentrationary poetry and his reaction to it: "This was in most cases a desperate poetry, but passionate and sacred. At the time I read these creations . . . I admired not so much their literary form, but their faith, their confidence in the eternity of the Jewish word."[45]

The creative and testimonial literature from the ghettos and camps was supplemented in the postwar years primarily by the memoirs of survivors. For most of these writers, the compulsion to record their experiences could be attributed to several motives: the desire for some sort of revenge; the need to bear witness "so that the world will know what we suffered"; the desire to commemorate the dead; the impulse to absolve oneself or one's companions of aspersions of passivity or complicity; the sense of mission, to warn humanity of its capacity for genocide. But the real victory to which these documents attested was the very fact of personal survival; the written records provide the evidence of the occasional lapses in the Final Solution. As Mendel Mann has testified, "I write to prove that I am alive, that I exist, that I too am still on this planet. The world condemned me to die. I write because, through my books, I bear witness to my existence. I try to banish my solitude, to demonstrate to the world that I am here."[46]

The need to bear witness, then, seemed to many to be the primary reason for which they had been spared. The survivor, often the only one of his family or community to remain alive, almost invariably prefaced his account with a formulaic assertion of his vocation as a survivor: "And I only am escaped alone to tell thee." There is a fragment which has survived from the Hebrew lamentation literature of the fourteenth century, written by a man who returned to his hometown after a trip only to discover that a pogrom had wiped out every inhabitant and destroyed all the holy books, except one Bible. This one remaining man, who refers to himself as the "last ember," wrote a brief account of the destruction of his town on the pages of the one remaining Bible.[47] That act is a prototype of the frenetic activity that was repeated after the war in communities all over Europe, which was now "*Judenrein*" of all but a handful of survivors. The sense of urgency was intensified by the tenuousness of their own survival and the knowledge that the passage of time would be marked by the diminishing presence of the historical witnesses. In the words of the Polish-Jewish writer Piotr Rawicz, when the survivor dies or his memory fails him, his hometown "dies for a second time."[48]

Yet this body of memoir literature produced only a small ripple in the public consciousness. Beyond serving the personal needs of the writers, such testimony was meant, primarily, to serve the cause of knowledge, which is usually regarded as somehow redemptive. But again, with no system of metaphysics, of social justice or human morality or aesthetics to relate the information to, the uninitiated reader floundered in a morass of excruciating detail. Eventually such readers, numbed by the onslaught of sordid accounts and by the guilt of their own record of passivity in the face of such crimes, began to lose interest in this literature. Finally this growing disregard influenced the writers themselves, and in most countries in Europe the first frenzied years of memoir writing were followed by a decade or more of silence. Even in America, where the Jewish community was neither inconsiderable nor traumatized by firsthand involvement, the initial shock of discovery was followed by a long period of introversion, which we will explore in some detail.

Ultimately, however, even though the memoirs and diaries did not enjoy a large immediate readership, they were to have a measurable impact on creative writers, especially on those who had been remote from the events themselves. And it may be significant, in recognizing the preeminent role of Holocaust art as testimony, to note that a number of survivors have written memoirs or histories as well as fiction, as if to establish the historicity of the subject before admitting it to the imagination. Elie Wiesel followed the contours of the memoir in his first book, *Night,* in which he presented many of the autobiographical events that were to resonate, in various guises, throughout his fiction. The evocative power of art beside the imperative of autobiography is dramatized in the apposition of Henryk Grynberg's personal memoir, *Child of the Shadows,* with his brief fictional story "The Grave"; the short fictitious "epiphany" stays with the reader long after he has forgotten the chronology of events that structures the memoir.[49] Jacob Presser, a Dutch historian, published in 1968 a monumental study of the history of the Dutch Jews during the German occupation.[50] Ten years earlier he had written a short novel, *Breaking Point,* which may have been based on one of the personal testimonies that had reached him in the course of his research. The authority of his historical work derives from the accretion of comprehensive data and testimonial material; as a novelist he distills the conflicts and the agonies into one man's battle with his conscience.

Leib Rokhman is another writer whose first book is a close, autobiographical account of the struggle for survival; his second work is a visionary Yiddish novel in which all the components of the former realism are fractured into a surreal narrative of the inner life of the victim—a version of history reorganized by the creative mind which has been freed from chronology and the fortuitousness of biography.[51] A useful distinction has been drawn by Ruth Wisse between certain forms of Holocaust literature and French symbolism, which are at least technically similar, "except that the inner and outer landscapes have been inverted":

> In the works of the symbolists, the imagination repudiates
> conventional reality, skimming into its own fantastic voy-
> ages of light and discovery. Here [in the Holocaust
> literature], the events are so "fantastic" as to strain the
> resources of fiction; the suspicion of madness is never *in* the
> poet, as it is in most modern fiction, but in the events to
> which he bears witness. These selections record the tension
> between history and art—history as the wanton destructive
> chaos, art, the creative synthesis of one interpretive imagi-
> nation.[52]

In order to escape from the *finality* as well as the chaos of history, to commune with the dead through whatever transhistorical means the imagination can muster, it seems that many writers must first pay their debt to history; for the act of commemoration, however fanciful, to be compelling, and for the madness to be perceived as a property of the "outer landscape," these writers would first establish their credentials as reporters or historians whose data can then become the pliable matter of their art.

In some cases, however, the testimonial imperative so controls the artistic impulse that the boundary between the memoir literature and the fiction (the *histoire* as history and as story) seems hardly distinguishable. This is most evident in the first person novel. Paul Fussell asserts, especially in relation to the novels of World War I, "the impossibility of ever satisfactorily distinguishing a memoir from a first-person novel," since the former is also a "kind of fiction," differing from the latter primarily in its "continuous implicit attestations of veracity or appeals to documented fact."[53] There is, however, an important distinction in the claim to credibility or legitimacy that different forms of historical literature make. Documentary art is a hybrid genre between fact and fiction. In the next chapter I will discuss various examples of documentary fiction, drama, and poetry which are characterized explicitly by a deferent attitude toward history that rejects any "violation" or mitigation of reality by the mediation of the creative imagination, but that often contains implicit premises about the transcendent significance to be extracted from historical processes.

TWO

Documentation as Art

Beyond the actual testimonies of survivors, the genre which presents, ostensibly at least, the most faithful historical reconstruction of the Holocaust is the documentary novel, poem, or drama. The accommodations that documentary art has made to the imperatives of an extreme and unprecedented historical experience can be seen as part of the general trend toward fictional journalism which came to be known in the sixties as the New Journalism. Referring to A-bomb literature, Kingsley Widmer wrote that such a "fusion of journalism and fictional art now provides the stock genre for exceptional events—invasion, the fall of a city, technological exploits, rural murder, and other man-made catastrophes."[1] For the survivor of the A-bomb or the Nazi Holocaust, the documentary approach suggests a faith in memory over imagination and a loyalty to one's dead over the creations of one's mind. It reflects the sacred attitude toward history and toward the imperative of transmission that I have already alluded to as the major challenge that cataclysmic history poses for the artist. It may be seen as an extension of the regard for the primacy of the *report* that was exemplified during the war years by Thomas Mann and other writers who served as broadcasters or journalists devoted to publicizing the little-known facts of the atrocities.

Structurally, the documentary novel is usually distinguishable from the memoir by the absence of a first-person narrator who is identical with the author and by a reduced urgency of presentation, as well as by a variety of literary methods. Most of the documentary fiction of survivors is, in fact, memoir or *témoignage* which assumes a historical perspective, an overview of events achieved by dramatic means that invests them with more general significance than usually attaches to the personal confession.

For the writer or reader who was not close to the events, documentary fiction provides access to a world to which he has no empirical

24

key. The fictional process that can be generated by a glimpse at reality which, though unfamiliar, still resonates with the universal patterns of human experience is epitomized in Henry James's classic anecdote about an English novelist of his acquaintance who once passed a group of young Protestants at dinner in the home of a French pastor in Paris and later wrote a novel about French Protestant youth: "She got her direct personal impression, and she turned out her type. She knew what youth was, and what Protestantism; she also had the advantage of having seen what it was to be French so that she conveyed these ideas into a concrete image and produced a reality."[2] But in the imaginative exploration of reality which is nonanalogous, documents may be regarded as the only substitute for generic memory and documentary literature as the logical first stage at which the physical landscape and the operation of the system are established. For the writer whose primary loyalty is to historical accuracy, the assumption is that documentation lends authority as well as credibility to the representation of the unimaginable.

Nearly every documentary writer prefaces his narrative with the claim that nothing in his story is invented. Pierre Julitte insists, in the introduction to his novel *Block 26: Sabotage at Buchenwald,* that "it is, from the first word to the last, a true story,"[3] and Joseph Kessel, in a preface, goes so far as to guarantee that *Block 26* "does not include the smallest imagined detail, that nothing of the work derives from fiction, and that everything is true—even, so to speak, the commas" (p. xi). The subtitle of Anatoli Kuznetsov's book *Babi Yar* is "A Document in the Form of a Novel," and in his preface the Soviet writer maintains that "the word 'Document' which appears in the subtitle of this novel means that I have included in it only facts and documents, and that it contains *not the slightest element of literary invention*—of what 'might have been.' . . . This book contains nothing but the truth" (emphasis mine).[4] The assumption, again, which is shared by so many memoirists and historians, is that only "facts" tell the truth and that fiction somehow lies. Nevertheless, however ironically, the ultimate value of these experiments located in the interface between fact and fiction will not be measured by any strict historiographical tests of factual accuracy—although historians will continue to approve or condemn them on the basis of their presentation of evidence. The aesthetic and moral implications of what amounts to the author's abdication of creative responsibility rest not in the verifiability of individual facts but rather in the premises which underlie an ostensibly undoctored reconstruction of historical events. The very claim to historicity lends such works a certain authority. A critic commenting on Truman Capote's *In Cold Blood,* which ushered in the "nonfiction novel" of the sixties, referred to Capote's claim that the book was based entirely on fact, and argued that

> by insisting that "every word" of his book is true, he has made himself vulnerable to those readers who are prepared to examine seriously such a sweeping claim. In the long run, however, Capote's presumption will be forgotten. The living people who were involved in the case will no longer testify to another version of the story. The documents will have been pushed to the back of the files by other, more urgent, matters and crimes. Future literary historians and scholars will undoubtedly place Capote's discrepancies of fact as well as his pretensions and rationalizations in perspective, and they will join with the present and future public in enjoying the work for its own sake.[5]

Whatever durability Capote's novel may have, this reader's attitude underscores the likelihood that the genre of documentary fiction will ultimately be regarded—or discarded—on grounds other than the reliability of its factual presentation. Whatever the claims of truth may be, they are not subject in literature to scientific tests; inasmuch as fiction naturally possesses the integrity of conception which engages a reader's senses and emotions as strict documentary cannot, and facts still retain an authority vis-à-vis history that fiction cannot claim, this hybrid literature commands a unique power. Yet a critical exploration can recover the hidden contours of historical interpretation beneath the reconstructed image of reality.

Documentary Fiction as Camouflaged Memoir

Pierre Julitte survived Buchenwald as a political prisoner; as we have seen, his documentary novel, *Block 26: Sabotage at Buchenwald,* claims to be a "true story" which owes nothing—not even its punctuation—to invention. Julitte admits that he used "fictitious names" for his characters and cast the narrative in the impersonal third person primarily because he does not want the survivors (himself included) to be singled out for the usual accolades for heroism or accusations of cowardice ("the trials that we endured together . . . have made me love, rather than glorify, those who went out so courageously to battle—and understand, rather than blame, those who chose to remain behind" [p. viii]). Unlike the documentary fiction of writers who "were not there," for whom documents provide the authority of historical names, Julitte's narrative represents in this respect a partial escape from the haunting memory of real persons into the safety of a "fiction" which safeguards anonymity. The story, which is an account of the sabotage of the rocket-producing Mibau factory at Buchenwald on August 24, 1944, initiated by a small group of political prisoners, is, then, essentially a memoir which appropriates the conventions of fiction. Clearly, the countless dialogues are not an exact replay of what actually took place among the inmates of the camp, and the descriptive language owes more to invention than to memory. The distance between straight testimony and documentary fiction can be measured by comparing Julitte's description of the arrival of a group of twenty Frenchmen at Buchenwald with Eugen Kogon's factual presentation of a similar scene. Julitte's narrative opens with a passage that conveys not information but a mood:

> Snow had started to fall at the beginning of evening rollcall. By now, it had wiped out the footprints along the paths, smoothed over the line of the rooftops, weighed down the branches of the pine trees beyond the electrified fence, where naked bulbs marked a line of yellow dots across the ghostly, deserted backdrop of the camp which lay crusted beneath the dark and empty sky.
>
> A projector at the top of one of the watchtowers went on and lazily swept the night. It seemed to swallow up the shadowy patterns of the camp even as it sculpted them against the darkness. Its beam picked up a prison van that was approaching the entrance, and accompanied it as far as the gate. Snow-muffled voices momentarily broke the silence. The metallic grill clinked open, and the vehicle entered the camp. A group of about twenty men, numb with cold, struggled awkwardly with their suitcases and leaped down from the back.
>
> Paul Genteau stretched gratefully. "This doesn't look so bad," he said. [Pp. 5–6]

A short time after his arrival, the new *Häftling* is given a taste of what life is really like in Buchenwald: "The long bludgeon—a piece of heavy electric cable—whistled downward. Alain threw himself forward to escape it, but he was not fast enough. The blow caught him full across the back.... A stream of curses came from the *kapo* who had struck him, and he felt panic-stricken" (p. 11). The rhythm of this narrative and the attention to details do not add significantly to the reader's "knowledge" but heighten his interest and focus his empathy on the fate of single prisoners. Compare Eugen Kogon's description of a similar scene—weather conditions and the treatment of prisoners on their arrival at the camp—in his eyewitness account of Buchenwald:

> The arrival in camp was followed by "welcoming ceremonies." A horde of loitering SS noncoms would greedily hurl itself at the fresh game. There was another barrage of blows and kicks, reinforced by stones and cold-water hoses. Men were thrown to the ground by hair or beard. Those who

wore ties were choked. Next, hours had to be spent waiting
outside the Political Department, arms laced behind the
head in the so-called "Saxon Salute," often in a deep knee-
bend. This took place regardless of heat or cold or rain,
without food or water, without a chance to go to the toilet.
All the while any SS man might vent his spleen on the
exhausted men.[6]

Kogon's narrative distance illuminates the functioning of the system
with almost scientific detachment; Julitte documents the general conditions of camp life through the behavior and the fate of specific individuals. Yet where the imagination assumes no authority for the
created figure, the distillation and organization of experience within a
fictional framework may be no more than a technical contrivance
which is meant to be more engaging than straightforward reportage; in
his preface, Joseph Kessel attributes Julitte's choice of the novel form
to his "fear of causing the action to drag by recounting every detail of
the routine of days and nights" (p. xii). Again, unlike the report, which
is often characterized by an abrupt confrontation with unyielding
"facts," the novel can trace the initiation of the individual prisoner into
the system—the process by which consciousness gradually yields to
inexorable reality. But beyond this, the conventions of the novel may
be harnessed to the dramatization of a particular reading of history.
Each of the characters in Julitte's novel is, finally, less an individual
than a prism of the political activities which eventuated in his incarceration and of the attributes that will carry him through to the end.
This a story, then, of collective survival and the triumph of a small
group of political prisoners over a major Nazi military operation, and
everything else is subordinated to these historiographical principles.

Like Julitte, A. Anatoli (Kuznetsov) was a participant in many of the
events he describes. He admits to the same compulsion to record what
he experienced and what he observed that most of the survivors express: I have to write what happened, says Kuznetsov, because, "as it
says in *Till Eulenspiegel,* 'Klaas's ashes are knocking at my heart'" (p.
17). *Babi Yar* is based on the notes that Kuznetsov took as a teenage
boy while Nazi atrocities were being committed in the nearby ravine
and later in his own village. The novel was written twenty-five years
later, but manages to preserve fairly faithfully the perspective of the
child (except for the interpolations between chapters in which the
author repeatedly admonishes the reader that the events he is describing must not be dismissed as "literary fantasy," that this is not an
"ordinary novel," that if we are to understand the present and anticipate the future we must accept the bitter truth of the past and of the

human potential for evil [pp. 294, 65]). The first-person narrative is a deviation from the distanced perspective of most documentary novelists; it can still be distinguished from straight autobiography or memoir, however, in that, like the other novels we are considering here, the focus is not on the fate of the individual ("I am going to talk a lot about people, of course," the narrator admits, "but the intention is least of all—and I underline this— *least of all* to tell a story about all sorts of personal misfortunes" [p. 58]) but on a system and a moment in history. The author is anxious to engage the reader, to bring him to project himself into the fate from which, it is emphasized, only an accident of history spared him. The episodes which the young Kuznetsov did not experience are scrupulously attributed to the people who did, and the narrator becomes their scribe.

In an interview which appeared in the American press in 1967, Kuznetsov explained his method, which he naively claimed to have invented:

> Whenever I tried to write a "literary" chapter based on the precise facts of Babi Yar, the facts themselves would lose their sharpness, somehow become colorless, even banal.... So I wrote out the bare facts, from beginning to end, just the way it happened.
>
> The result is not a novel in the conventional sense of the word, but a photographically accurate picture of actual events. To define the genre of my book I even had to coin the term "documentary novel."[7]

Aside from the cultural isolation that this statement demonstrates—the writer's lack of conversance with what was then already a well-established form of literature—the disclaimer of artistic responsibility is instructive, especially coming from a Soviet writer. Kuznetsov's description of his writing as "photographically accurate" ignores the art of selection and interpretation inherent even in photography. His claim that his own literary tools are blunted on the hard, unyielding surface of reality, that "facts" constitute an imperative which subjugates the imagination, can be challenged by the history of the publication of his own book. *Babi Yar* first appeared in Russian and in English translation in 1967. It was warmly received by Soviet reviewers and hailed by Western critics as symptomatic of a softening in the official Soviet attitude toward the victims of Nazism. George Feifer, in a review of the book, wrote that now, with the publication of Kuznetsov's novel, the Soviet Union was finally willing to acknowledge that Jews had in fact died at Babi Yar; the book, Feifer continued, heralded "the new Soviet concern for historical accuracy."[8] In 1970, Kuznetsov defected to England and, much to the chagrin of those who had hailed the "historical accuracy" of *Babi Yar,* he published the unexpurgated edition of the novel—which included all the sections that the Soviet censors had deleted. The claim of historical accuracy remained the same in both versions, however, and the unexpurgated edition of *Babi Yar* shows as much concern with documenting the past as, if less propagandistic fervor than, the earlier version. The 1967 edition was a diatribe against fascism; the 1970 edition is a diatribe against all oppressive social systems ("the world was just one big Babi Yar.... Two great forces had come up against each other...and the wretched people were in between" [p. 204]).

Whether a documentary work of art is smuggled out of the Soviet Union to be published in the West or is published in censored form in the USSR and only later published in the West in its entirety, the very stance of "factuality," far from representing a softening of official Soviet attitudes, may signify the very opposite—the author's defiant loyalty to the individual's perception of reality over the official reality of socialist realism.[9] In this respect Kuznetsov's novel, though clearly the lesser of the two, resembles Aleksandr Solzhenitsyn's *Gulag Archipelago.* While covering much of the same territory that he had explored in his earlier fiction, Solzhenitsyn in this later work permits the reader no escape from the oppressive reality of the Russian penal system. The author insists that "in this book there are no fictitious persons, nor fictitious events...it all took place just as it is here described"; more respectful, perhaps, of literary boundaries, he refrains from calling his work a novel, referring to it rather as "an experiment in literary investigation."[10] It is an extreme example of the artist's demand for the freedom to be a historian of concentrationary reality.

The history of the publication of Kuznetsov's novel, then, which in some respects is limited to problems of censorship in a totalitarian regime, in other respects dramatizes the ways in which facts, like fiction, are ultimately cultural constructs. The documentary art of the Holocaust demonstrates different approaches to and uses of reality as a cultural category.

Documentary Fiction as the Heroic Version of History
Jean-François Steiner is another writer in whose fiction a particular reading of history underlies the claims of objectivity. In his novel *Treblinka,* he tailors the evidence of a revolt in the death camp to a rigid procrustean concept of Jewish history. Whereas in *Block 26* and *Babi Yar* it is the author's memory which serves as the primary source material of the events described, in Steiner's *Treblinka* it is documented evidence and interviews with survivors—which places the author at one remove from the subject he is treating. Steiner's avowed

purpose is similar to Julitte's; he wishes to document the heroic uprising which took place in the camp (in this case, Treblinka) in order to
counter the repeated charge that the inmates allowed themselves to be
led meekly to the gas chambers like sheep to the slaughter. Julitte's
novel focuses on the behavior and the beliefs of political prisoners; the
fact that many of them were former Resistance fighters in his view
accounts for their spirit and acumen in sabotaging the V-4 rocket factory. Steiner, in turn, concentrates on the characteristics and heritage
of the Jewish inmates, to which he attributes, paradoxically, both their
initial passivity and their ultimate resourcefulness and courage. Simone
de Beauvoir explains in a preface that in writing the story of Treblinka,
Steiner "restored his self-respect"; his own father had perished in
Treblinka and in commemorating him he needed, evidently, to exalt
him or those like him who had managed the revolt. "Self-respect" for
Steiner is synonymous with heroism; Beauvoir explains that "what
they [the rebels] passionately desired by massacring the German
'masters' was to overcome their condition as slaves."[11]

The major distinction between Steiner and the Hebraic writers we
will discuss later is that the latter appeal to the authority of Jewish
values embedded in a tradition which is their primary frame of reference, whereas Steiner invokes the authority of events or behavior from
which he extrapolates a system of values that he identifies as peculiarly
Jewish. His primary concern, that is, is with documented reality which
is made to yield certain truths, rather than with the struggle of conflicting values within a given historical context.

Steiner's ideological commitment directs the organization of his
material; he attempts to trace a progressive emergence out of slavery to
a point where the Jews are to be seen as masters of their own fate. If
Jewish history is characterized by passive resistance and martyrdom,
Steiner is saying, the revolt at Treblinka marks a crucial turning point.
The "facts" which the author himself adduces are not always amenable to such a reading, however, and occasionally lead to editorial ex-
cesses which seriously undermine the claims of historical reconstruction. In accounting for the rash of suicides that prevailed in the early
days of Treblinka, for example, Steiner defines this phenomenon as the
first step in the schema of regeneration, since it limited the ultimate
power of the Nazis over the lives of Jews. Nearly every event is interpreted as another stage in this process of emancipation. Even the
instances of macabre humor (such as the banter between two inmates
over what form their meeting will take in the hereafter—we may inhabit
the same shop window, says one, but from me they'll make toilet soap,
from you only cheap laundry soap [p. 258]) seem meant to serve here as
examples of "gallows humor" through which the prisoner triumphs

over the certainty of imminent and hideous death by relegating it to the quotidian and denuding it of its terror and strangeness.

In nearly every case, the resources which enable the victims to withstand inhuman treatment are defined as peculiarly Jewish traits. These traits, which Steiner affirms as functional or even redemptive, present, in the composite, an overcompensatory, sentimentalized portrait of a mythic being who, supposedly by virtue of his heritage, is egregiously spiritual, immune to despair, and extraordinarily inventive. The revolt that is planned and executed by members of the camp is, in the words of one of its leaders, "not only intended to save lives; it is to be an event of historical importance. It must appear as a symbol of the destiny of the Jewish people, whom no earthly power has ever been able to defeat" (p. 203).

That there are a large number of historical inaccuracies and omissions in Steiner's story can be ascertained by a close comparison with Yankel Wiernik's diary, *A Year in Treblinka,* with Vassili Grossmann's *L'Enfer de Treblinka,* or with testimonies deposited with the Jewish Historical Commission in Warsaw. Yet again it is not the highly subjective selection or distortion of facts *per se* but the composite stereotype, a simplistic reductionism in the portrayal of character and situation, which calls attention to the contradictory and unresolved premises of the genre. What emerges in this novel is a glorified sense of Jewish superiority and revisionist nationalism. It is an extreme example of a quality inherent in the literature, something which R. J. Lifton calls the "documentary fallacy"—an overriding loyalty to the dead which generates a kind of hagiographical excess, denying them the "dignity of their limitations."[12]

Because of his ideological bias, Steiner refuses to make a conscious choice between the authority of fact and fiction, never quite submitting either to the ambiguities and contradictions of actual history or to the unities of fictionalized history. He has gone so far to preserve historical authenticity as to incorporate quotes from eyewitness accounts such as Wiernik's diary and to retain the real names of his characters. These characters, however, appear as interchangeable pawns in the great flow of history; as one person dies, another takes his place, and the community, rather than the individual character, appears as the basic component and ultimate source of meaning. Of course, Steiner, like any omniscient narrator, even of documentary fiction, has invented numerous scenes, detailed descriptions and dialogues which, even where witnesses remained alive after the war, no one could have remembered with such total recall. Yet he does not legitimate his own prerogative as novelist, does not admit his subject to the imagination. Uneven in pace and tone, his narrative leaps from factual history to pure invention and back again. The scrupulous presentation of testimony ("no one remembers his name; the oral tradition of camp Treblinka has kept only the memory of a round face that seemed made to smile, two eyes with a lost expression and a short and weary silhouette" [p. 91]) backfires in the passages which are clearly fictitious.

The failure lies in his imposition of aesthetic forms on historical events rather than transforming those events through the imagination. And the incongruities which are typical of the genre intensify as reality becomes more incredible. That a writer tries to validate through the public credibility of testimony what is usually authenticated in art through the inner logic of the constructed form may derive, as I have suggested, from the fact that the Holocaust is discontinuous with common cultural experience, and suggests the kind of difficulties which the "testimonial" imperative of cataclysmic history poses for certain writers. It may be necessary to establish the facts about Treblinka before fiction is possible; in any event, in a novel such as *Treblinka,* there is an inherently incompatible yoking of two modes of perceiving human experience.

Steiner attempts to capture a slice of unimaginable reality in an art form which another writer of Holocaust fiction, Piotr Rawicz, dismisses as "pseudo-literature."[13] The incompatibilities are perhaps nowhere more evident in the popular arts than in "Holocaust," the TV documentary drama written by Gerald Green and broadcast in America and in nearly every European country in 1978 and 1979. From among the historical personae, such as Heydrich and Eichmann, who form the backdrop of this drama, a fictitious Nazi, Erich Dorf, is credited with masterminding the entire program of genocide, from *Kristallnacht* to Auschwitz. Unlike either the historical figure in a straight documentary or the character who is conceived, lives, and dies in the house of fiction, the fictitious villain in a historical context is a kind of ghostly figure who commands little or no moral attention.

With respect to the victim, the hybridization of fact and fiction creates different problems; the clarity demanded by a story tailored to mass consumption tends to generate simplistic ideological categories to cope with the elusive and spiritually unedifying subject of large-scale physical suffering and submission to death. The glorification of heroic behavior in documentary fiction or popular drama as an attempt to redeem the dignity of the victim entails a narrow reading of Jewish history and values which is shared by a number of other popular writers, including John Hersey and Leon Uris. Hersey and Uris, both Americans, have written documentary novels on the Warsaw Ghetto uprising which use the medium of the journal as their narrative frame; in the case of Hersey's *The Wall* it is probably Hillel Seidman and his diary on which the fictional Noach Levinson and his diary are based, while Uris in *Mila 18* seems to have borrowed both theme and structure from Hersey. Both writers appeal to the general authority of history, at the same time disclaiming the historicity of the details. Their novels are well researched; it is particularly evident that Hersey, a gentile journalist who came upon traces of the Jewish massacre while on assignment in Europe, spent a number of years studying his subject, perfecting the method of scholarship and the manner of fiction he had used in his work on Hiroshima.

There does seem to be a tendency on the part of middlebrow writers such as Steiner, Green, Uris, and Hersey to attempt to compel the reader's interest by the use of the documentary imperative; the "true story" commands a kind of automatic reverence and attention that the truly creative writer has to marshal all the powers of the imagination in order to achieve. But these writers are, additionally, catering to an attitude in which the ambiguities of history and the challenge to ethnic pride are resolved by heroic epic, and the documentary form, accommodating itself to ideological postures and minimal creative responsibilities, easily lends itself to such purposes. This popular version of the heroic epic is an affirmation of a simple causality in Jewish history. Like the insistence on the part of one of the leaders of the revolt in *Treblinka* that the uprising "must appear as a symbol of the destiny of the Jewish people," Alexander Brandel's final words in the bunker of Mila 18 affirm the naive confidence that by armed revolt "we Jews have avenged our honor as a people," and that the scales of history will be balanced when the state of Israel is reborn out of the ashes (p. 539). These novels which dramatize the heroic uprisings in the ghettos and camps tend to ignore or to dismiss lightly the traditional response to collective catastrophe that constitutes the dominant resource on which the Eastern European Jew could draw in his hour of suffering, and can be contrasted with the agonizing internal clash of opposing Jewish values and orientations in the fiction of the Hebraic writers who will be considered later. The Jewish historian Salo Baron identifies the heroic concept of human dignity as deriving from Roman rather than from Judaic (or Judeo-Christian) tradition. He admits that, although he personally has struggled for years against the "lachrymose conception of Jewish history," he would nevertheless warn against the widespread tendency to "misunderstand the true realities of life and psychology among the still predominant orthodox and traditionalist East European Jewish masses during the Nazi era" and to dismiss the "traditional Jewish acceptance of the divine will and the emphasis on the ultimate victory of meekness and passive resistance." Baron emphasizes the fact, frequently overlooked by historians as well as by popular novelists and the general public, that for nearly two thousand years it was not the Maccabean warriors, Mattathias and his sons, but the Maccabean martyrs, Hanna and her seven sons, who were exalted in Jewish as well as Christian literature.[14]

The challenges that the Holocaust presented to a traditional Jewish world view and theodicy were not automatically resolved by such actions as the Warsaw uprising or the Treblinka revolt, even if these are viewed as preludes to the establishment of the Jewish state. What distinguishes most of the Hebraic writing is the *internal* struggle with traditional responses to catastrophe. The varying interpretations of Jewish history which Hebraic writers offer delineate the boundaries of cultural experience and shape the very form of their art. For all of them, again, the ultimate appeal—and the ultimate recourse—is to Jewish principles of order and faith, not to objective "history."

But the unambiguously heroic reading of history, based on the claim to factuality, is more palatable to popular sentiment which is a reservoir of faith in the triumph of courage over meekness, of progress over stasis. The commercial success of the novels of Steiner, Uris, and Hersey was a phenomenon not limited to the vagaries of popular fiction but, like the dramatized version of *The Diary of Anne Frank* and the television "docudrama" "Holocaust," can be seen as an index of the penetration of the Holocaust into the consciousness of those who had not experienced it. The raging controversies that these and other documentary novels and plays touched off were generated by the recognition that, for the present at least, these works were being read as historical documents: Wiernik's diary and Vassili Grossmann's historical study were overlooked by the readers of Steiner's account of the revolt at Treblinka; Seidman's and Ringelblum's and Kaplan's diaries were passed over for Hersey's fictionalized chronicle of events in the Warsaw Ghetto, which, appearing in 1950, remained for many years uncontested as the definitive work on the subject not only in America but also, in translation, in Germany. Thus the interpretations of events or presentation of character, especially by writers like Uris or Hersey who had little or no background in the folk culture of East European Judaism, became crucial vehicles of historical consciousness. "Here, for a change, was the story of Jews who did fight unto death," wrote Ernst Pawel, in a critique of *The Wall;* " [the novel] and its success strikingly demonstrate the mechanism of denial by which the pre-Auschwitz mind sought to incorporate a radically altered and wholly unacceptable reality into a conventional frame of reference."[15] Because of the appeal to the authority of history, of objective veracity rather than the imagination as the channel and arbiter of reality, this borderline art form becomes a component in the cultural perception of major events, ultimately resisting the application of literary standards just as it resists the judgment of historical accuracy. According to

Maurice Samuel, such a novel as Hersey's cannot be read as an isolated fictional episode but as an incident along a historical and cultural
continuum; the ultimate question, for Samuel, is how the story of the
Warsaw Ghetto is "establishing itself in the Jewish People."[16] The
fictional "documentation" of Jewish history provided in these novels
stereotypic responses which were compatible with a general avoidance
or attempted redress of "unacceptable reality."

Legal Records and the Literary Documentation
of Anonymous Crimes

Documentary drama, the direct presentation of evidence unmediated
even by the digressive course of the fictional narrative, has found its
most radical expression in Peter Weiss's German play, *The Investigation*. Produced originally in 1965, it is a condensed version of the proceedings of the trials, held in Frankfurt from December 20, 1963, to
August 20, 1965, of twenty-one of the people who were responsible for
the operation of Auschwitz.

The trials themselves could have suggested the form of the play.
Susan Sontag, who claims that a trial constitutes in itself an art form
which preserves the classical dramatic contest between protagonist
and antagonist, concludes that if "the supreme tragic event of modern
times is the murder of the six million European Jews, the most interesting and moving work of art of the past ten years is the trial of Adolf
Eichmann in Jerusalem in 1961."[17]

The only logic that seems to dictate the organization of the material
in *The Investigation* is the strict logic of the legal procedure. A number
of dramatic, cinematic, and poetic interpretations of the Eichmann and
the Nuremberg trials that appeared in the sixties and seventies were
cast in the same legal frame, as if to provide a kind of decorum to defy
or reform the criminal order of the concentrationary system. The film
Judgment at Nuremberg was one affirmation of the ultimate victory of
justice over the reign of evil. And for the American writer especially, the
Eichmann trial seems to have afforded a civilized entry into the concentrationary universe.

Yet the formal protocal of a court trial applied to the systematic
lawlessness of Auschwitz can also be seen as a mockery of the pretense
of justice. As we will see in our discussion of the reflections of the
Holocaust in the American war literature, the claims of the law to
redress the crimes of the Nazis often prove feeble next to the terrible
forces which had been unleashed. This is also demonstrated in a short
story by the Polish writer Tadeusz Borowski, in which an American
officer accompanying the liberating troops enters a camp barracks as
the inmates are tearing one of the SS men to pieces:

"Gentlemen," [the officer says] with a friendly smile, "I know, of course, that after what you have gone through and after what you have seen, you must feel a deep hate for your tormentors. But we, the soldiers of America, and you, the people of Europe, have fought so that law should prevail over lawlessness. We must show our respect for the law. I assure you that the guilty will be punished in this camp as well as in all the others."

The inmates desist and wait until the kindly American has returned to his headquarters—and then they pull their man off the bunk on which he had been held under a layer of blankets and bodies, and drag him to the floor, "where the the entire block, grunting and growling with hatred, trampled him to death."[18]

This current of irony may or may not undercut the explicitly reverent attitude toward the operations of justice in the final volume of poetry by the American poet Charles Reznikoff. As in his earlier poem-cycle, *Testimonies,* in which he documents through courtroom evidence rendered into free verse the "domestic" violence—the acts of fratricide, parricide, and filicide—in America at turn of the last century, Reznikoff in *Holocaust* transforms into poetry a series of legal documents which reflect the pervasiveness of violence as a norm in modern society. In the absence of any visible editorial hand, whatever irony is brought to bear on the notion that the legal procedure can contain or avenge the horrors of genocide must be read into the text. The condensed presentation of bare facts, the terse, forensic language give equal weight on the written page to the testimony of Jew and Nazi and assign a kind of anonymity to both sides as they appear as witnesses for the prosecution or the defense, for the victim or the victimizer—as two facets, that is, of the human condition. If in fiction the documentary method tends to depersonalize the characters, to present them as the mouthpieces of opposing ideas which are resolved by the course of events, the legal perspective in poetry or drama is an additional lens through which history is depersonalized by the artist; the depositions are presented directly in the cold factual rhetoric of the legal report.

Like Reznikoff's poems, Weiss's *Investigation* omits one important aspect of the actual trials, which makes the artistic reconstruction even bleaker than the trials themselves: the emotions with which the testimonies were delivered by the witnesses. In a prefatory note to the text of his play, Weiss states that "the confrontations of the witnesses and the accused, as well as the addresses to the court by the prosecution and the replies by the counsel for the defense, were overcharged with emotion. Only a condensation of the evidence can remain on the stage." He goes on to explain that "this condensation should contain nothing but the facts."[10] "Facts," then, must be sanitized of emotion before they can constitute the evidence that Weiss will submit. They are meant to yield their inherently dramatic power as dispirited forces contending on the historical plane. With regard to the characters, although the nineteen defendants bear their real names whereas the witnesses are identified by numbers (Witness #1, Witness #2, and so on), Weiss is not insisting on the personal guilt of the accused. He has, rather, singled them out as representatives of the system which perpetrated the crimes: "the bearers of these names should not be accused once again in this drama. To the author, they have lent their names which, within the drama, exist as symbols of a system that implicated in its guilt many others who never appeared in court" (p. xi).

The performance of *The Investigation,* when it is faithful to the playwright's stage directions, powerfully executes his stated purposes. There are no histrionic aids—the stage is bare, emotion has been eliminated, and there is neither punctuation in the free-verse text nor stage business that would allow for a change in pitch or shift in position. Most performances are delivered in straight-faced monotone. The abrupt commencement of the drama *in medias res* and conclusion without catharsis or resolution of any sort give the impression of an unedited slice of testimony; the only apparent organization is the division of the depositions into eleven "songs" which describe the design and operation of the camp.

The facts or evidence presented in this drama serve as statistics, not as means of individuation. Weiss is concerned neither with the commemoration of the dead nor with the establishment of guilt and the meting out of punishment (the verdicts handed down at Frankfort are not shown), but rather with the indictment of a social system, specifically, of fascism viewed as a form of capitalism; Auschwitz, Weiss claims, would not be possible in a "Socialist society."[20] However debatable this conclusion would otherwise be, the facts are carefully selected to make it seem inevitable. The endless recitation of numbers and measurements not only delineates the physical landscape and the routine of Auschwitz, but also mocks the capitalistic/bureaucratic concern with measuring life in incremental quantities and disposing of it through mass technology: "For 2,000 people in one chamber / about 16 pounds" of Zyklon B gas was needed; cremation took "approximately an hour / Then [the crematorium] could take a new load / In crematoriums II and III / More than 3,000 people were cremated / in less than 24 hours"; the "Black Wall" where executions were held was "about 10 feet high / 13 wide" (pp. 238, 259, 159). The text bears the impersonality of a clinical report, detailing how many

calories the inmate received each day and how many he expended,
what rare diseases developed among the prisoners, and so on. As such
it is both a reflection and an attempted exorcism of the "Nazi-
Deutsch" that survived in the language long after the Nazi defeat. The
horror in the drama is, then, inherent in the language itself as well as in
the information that is being transmitted. The tone of scientific detachment is also a quality of the postwar psychological and sociological
studies of the prevailing conditions in the camps and the generic responses of the victims. The portrayal of emotions on stage, like the use
of specific names, would restore personality to the witnesses; Weiss
prefers to retain the anonymity they shared as victims. More radically
even than Steiner, Weiss views his art as the expression of historical
moments and political movements. "I think audiences are ready to
become concerned with the real world rather than with the private
loves and hatreds of individuals," he says; "my plays do not have
conventional lead roles. The lead roles are played by history and
ideas."[21]

When he refers to the primacy of history and ideas, Weiss is not
ascribing importance to specific events any more than he is singling out
specific individuals for blame or pity. Unlike Reznikoff, he does not
even identify the Jews as victims; in the dialectical reading of history, it
is relatively unimportant that one group has been chosen for suffering
at a given moment. Weiss insists that, although he himself is half
Jewish, he has never thought of himself as a Jew and that *The Investigation* is not meant to be an exclusive portrayal of Nazi inhumanity to Jews:

> The Nazis did kill six million Jews, yes, but they killed
> millions of others. The word "Jew" is in fact never used in
> the play . . . . I do not identify myself any more with the Jews
> than I do with the people of Vietnam or the blacks in South
> Africa. I simply identify myself with the oppressed of the
> world . . . . *The Investigation* is about the extreme abuse of
> power that alienates people from their own actions. It hap-
> pens to be German power, but that again is unimportant. I
> see Auschwitz as a scientific instrument that could have
> been used by anyone to exterminate anyone. *For that mat-
> ter, given a different deal, the Jews could have been on the
> side of the Nazis. They too could have been the exter-
> minators. The Investigation is a universal human problem*
> (emphasis mine).[22]

This perception of the roles of the Nazi victimizer and the Jewish
victim as, essentially, interchangeable is not unique to Weiss among
German writers (and Weiss clearly considers himself at least as much a
German as a Jew—as he says, "some [of my friends] may even have

obeyed orders at Auschwitz. Might I not, too?")[23] and indicates the way in which certain artists deal with the burdensome issue of German responsibility. Such a controversial perspective is, of course, especially credible in the documentary drama which purportedly derives the authority for its interpretation of history from the facts themselves. Erwin Sylvanus's play *Dr. Korczak and the Children* uses certain theatrical techniques to convey the interchangeability of roles. As a documentary artist, Sylvanus first seeks to establish credibility by claiming that "the author has not invented the events depicted in this play; he has merely recorded them."[24] He then proceeds to dramatize the emotion-charged story of Janusz Korczak's fidelity to his orphaned wards which extended as far as the gas chambers. By the subtle Pirandellian device of having one actor play more than one role—the chief nurse of the Krochmalna Street Orphanage also playing the Nazi officer's wife, one child playing both an orphan and the officer's child—he implicates all of humanity as potential accomplices. Although in several cases the actors resist the roles they have been assigned, they ultimately comply and eventually *become* the persons they are playing. The involvement of the audience in the mechanics of selecting theatrical roles may be intended, as George Wellwarth suggests, as a way of "shocking the audience into attention"—they are meant to watch what appears to be an ordinary group of people (the actors) become part of the machinery of mass murder.[25] Weiss provides for similar effects in his play, and following the example of Ingmar Bergman's production of *The Investigation* in Stockholm in February 1966, most directors have harsh spotlights trained directly into the audience throughout the performance, thereby involving the spectator in the general responsibility for the system that made Auschwitz possible—or, Weiss seems to be saying, inevitable. Wellwarth claims that the dramas of Sylvanus and Weiss are "attempts to erect expiatory wailing walls."[26] The psychological effect may, however, be exactly the opposite—that is, the basic premise of a universal human tendency to respond uniformly to certain social stimuli can serve to dissipate the moral load that comes with particularity and historical accountability.

Documentary Literature as the Moral Reconstruction of the Past
The conceptions of history and of the function of drama underlying Rolf Hochhuth's play *The Deputy* generate a very different manipulation of documentary material from that of his compatriots. *The Deputy* was first produced in Germany in 1963. It has been estimated that, if produced in its entirety, the play would take from seven to eight hours to perform; it is therefore subject to abridgement at the whim of the

director, so that the versions differ in significant ways. Nevertheless, the governing premises are carefully explicated by the playwright in a sixty-page essay, on the historicity of the events portrayed and the principles of artistic manipulation of documentary records, which is appended to the written text.

By virtue of the public nature of the medium and the controversial nature of the subject matter, *The Deputy* became, overnight, a cultural "event." The American Nazis picketed the theater on the opening night of the Broadway production, and the play's indictment of Pius XII for criminal silence touched off a controversy which was probably unprecedented in the history of drama.[27] The Pope appears only in one scene, but the central theme of the play is Father Riccardo Fontana's discovery of the destination of the Jews who are being rounded up and deported from their homes in Europe, and his doomed efforts, in cooperation with Kurt Gerstein, the anti-Nazi who penetrated the ranks of the SS, to demand a statement of protest from the Pope; the Pope's failure to respond leads to Riccardo's voluntary deportation and eventual death in Auschwitz.

Few have disputed the facts which Hochhuth dramatizes, and which he supplements with additional evidence in his appendix. His emphasis on factuality may even be somewhat deceptive, leading some of his critics to claim that he has done little more than juxtapose edited documents. Certainly he is dramatizing a moment in history and isolating the actors who made history at that moment, but the insertion of additional historical evidence in elaborate stage directions and in the lengthy appendix seems designed less to add information than to erect a fortress of authority against any accusations of historical inaccuracy, so that the historical *vision* which the facts are meant to comprise will be unassailable. The playwright himself admits that "aside from the Pope, the Nunzio, Gerstein, Hirt and Eichmann, all characters and names are fictitious."[28] Of course, in the best tradition of documentary art, even the "fictitious" characters are for the most part modeled on real persons, and other characters are stereotyped representations of categories of actual victims. But Hochhuth's objective is not to present data which, in the aggregate, would constitute a deterministic overview, to present historical logic in place of moral autonomy—as, in a sense, Weiss does; it is rather, as he states in the appendix, to "pick his way through the rubble and incidental circumstances of so-called events in order to reach the truth, the symbolic meaning." The dramatist, Hochhuth continues, quoting Schiller, "cannot use a single element of reality as he finds it; his work must be idealized in *all* its parts if he is to comprehend reality as a whole" (pp. 287–88).

The reality which Hochhuth constructs is a distilled conflict between moral absolutes; for all the accumulation of facts, ambiguities of character and situation have been eliminated. Kurt Gerstein, that enigmatic figure who insinuated himself into the SS in order to sabotage it from within, but who was nevertheless compelled in the end to supply the Zyklon B that was used in the gas chambers, appears here far less tortured and compromised than he was, by other accounts, in real life; Saul Friedlander's biography of Gerstein, written a few years after the appearance of *The Deputy,* was called *Counterfeit Nazi: The Ambiguity of Good.*[29] Only a hint is given in *The Deputy* of the role he is to play as supplier of the poison gas, and his "capture" in act 5 at the hands of the Doctor suggests a martyr's death; in reality he committed suicide in 1945 and was posthumously indicted by the de-Nazification tribunal in Tubingen in 1950 for his SS-linked activities. Finally, fifteen years later, the indictment was reversed and he was acquitted after a review of the evidence. Gerstein might be seen as one of those shadowy figures who, in the language of one version of the Cabbala, enters the dark regions of evil in order to redeem the "sparks" but cannot emerge undefiled. Yet Hochhuth, while insisting on the historicity of his character, minimizes the complexities in order to place him in the schematic role he has assigned him. At the very least, then, the legal history of this case, Friedlander's account, and Hochhuth's characterization represent three different interpretations of biographical "facts." The contradictions, particularly in regard to so thoroughly and reliably researched a character as this one, illuminate the ways in which documentary theater arranges certain public facts, and interprets the more obscure facts about which there is no public consensus, so as to arrive at a specific reading of historical events.

Another major character who is submitted to a kind of reductionist treatment is Pacelli himself (Pius XII). In general Hochhuth, like other documentary writers, has been criticized for creating stick characters with very little subtlety or growth. Even such stage business as the hand-washing scene contributes more to the symbolic than the historical portrait of the man. Although, unlike Weiss, Hochhuth is concerned with assigning historical responsibility and with establishing the option of free choice even in the most extreme situations, he does seem less concerned with character than with the individual as representative of moral alternatives. He goes so far in the editing of documented history as to fabricate a meeting between the Pope and Gerstein, in order to demonstrate beyond a shadow of a doubt Pacelli's knowledge of the deportations and to dramatize his decision to remain silent.

This reductionism is especially apparent in regard to the men of the Nazi high command who appear in the play. Documentary writers are nearly alone in their attempt to resurrect the murderers along with their victims. For Hochhuth it is not the psychological model nor political ideology that provides insight into evil; here the descent into the death camp is a descent from realism into a mythical realm delineated by the enormity of the crime. In this play, anyway, it appears that the architects of Auschwitz succeeded in resurrecting Satan as a dramatic possibility for the postmodern world. Sartre quotes Maritain as saying that Satan "is pure. Pure, that is, without mixture and without remission. We have learned [through the mass murders and death camps] to know this horrible, this irreducible purity."[30] Eichmann and various other SS officers are the embodiments of pure, opaque, and impenetrable evil in Hochhuth's drama, and the Doctor in Auschwitz, who is patterned after the infamous Dr. Mengele but whom Hochhuth refuses to dignify with a name, is the closest approximation in twentieth-century drama to the incarnate devil. In contrast to the other characters, he projects the same fascinating appeal—*mutatis mutandis*—that Milton's Satan projects in the company of Adam and Eve. And his half-serious, half-cynical challenge of divine justice is both an echo and a parody of Satan's challenge to man's faith, in the Book of Job:

> I've ventured what no man
> has ever ventured since the beginning of the world.
> I took the vow to challenge the Old Gent,
> to provoke Him so limitlessly
> that He would have to give an answer.

> [P. 247]

But unlike other mythic representations of the evil of the concentrationary universe, the Satanic forces are not diffused, unchecked, throughout the entire system. Along with the resurrection of pure evil, Hochhuth reaffirms the old moral equations and the fixed polarity between good and evil as options for action. Riccardo Fontana and Gerstein represent the path of redemptive acts, and the Pope is the battleground on which this psychomachia unfolds. The medieval morality play provides a schema of objective moral conflict which precludes psychological complexity or ambiguity; as Swiss critic Rolf Zimmerman states:

> For Hochhuth the only issue is the responsiveness of the human heart and conscience. The standard of good is constant, the vision undimmed. He does not want his public to recognize human subjectivity; he wants it to judge historical events with its heart.... Rather than place the individual with his relative limitations, stage center, Hochhuth, to the contrary, focuses on the residue of the absolute within each individual, the universal piety of the heart that abrogates all distinctions—including that of character—when it begins to speak.[31]

As both historian and moralist, then, Hochhuth portrays the character from the outside, judging him by standards of absolute good; the modern artist as "creator" is more likely to engage in the kind of psychological explorations that mitigate moral absolutes and allow for weakness, vacillation, and even complicity. And as a Christian, Hochhuth is not simply dramatizing the silent complicity of a Pacelli but focusing upon Pope Pius in his capacity as the highest recognized spiritual authority of Christendom at a time when the conscience of the civilized world was on trial. At such a moment there can be no mitigating circumstances or flawed characters; the morality play, as Zimmerman says, "does not demand heroes but saints."[32] The audience is meant to see, then, not just the failings of one man but the embodiment of the failure of the spirit of every human being to rise to the burden placed upon it in those dark times. In his encounter with Riccardo, the Doctor himself voices the challenge against which the entire drama struggles on behalf of civilized existence:

> The truth is, Auschwitz refutes
> creator, creation, and the creature.
> Life as an idea is dead.
> This may well be the beginning
> of a great new era,
> a redemption from suffering.
> From this point of view only one crime
> remains: cursed be he who creates life.
> I cremate life.

> [P. 248]

The boundaries of the created world shrink with every tap of the Doctor's swagger stick. It is only the righteous few—Gerstein among the executioners and Riccardo among the silent witnesses—who counter the Doctor's challenge and complete a religious perspective which, though rare in the post-Holocaust era, is an attempt to restore its sanity and its morality. Riccardo is in spirit and in deed the genuine "deputy" of Christ on earth and as a semifictitious character represents the answer that the imagination could give to history.

Although his craftsmanship is uneven, as a philosopher of poetic language Hochhuth contributes significantly to the polemic that surrounds Holocaust art by insisting that certain constraints were imposed on the image-making mind by the reality of Auschwitz. After rejecting what he calls "documentary naturalism" in art, which cannot compete for comprehensiveness and shocking effect with the daily newsreel (pp. 222, 288), he also rejects the kind of aesthetics which would transform the Holocaust into detached metaphor and the victims and victimizers into pure symbols. The dialogue, which reflects the documentary concern for accuracy in its reproduction of accent, dialect, and jargon, is almost entirely free of metaphoric language; in his elaborate stage directions for the scene which takes place in the cattle cars leading to Auschwitz and in the camp itself, Hochhuth submits that the kind of approach used by Paul Celan in his "masterly poem, 'Todesfuge,' in which the gassing of the Jews is entirely translated into metaphors," would be "perilous" if transferred to the stage:

> For despite the tremendous force of suggestion emanating from sound and sense, metaphors still screen the infernal cynicism of what really took place—a reality so enormous and grotesque that even today, fifteen years after the events, the impression of unreality it produces conspires with our natural strong tendency to treat the matter as a legend, as an incredible apocalyptic fable. Alienation effects would only add to this danger. No matter how closely we adhere to historical facts, the speech, scene and events on the stage will be altogether surrealistic. [P. 223]

This struggle with the language of metaphor has been a major concern for novelists and poets as well as playwrights. For some German writers the memory of symbols and abstractions used to forge national unity and camouflage heinous crimes is a warning against inflated rhetoric. As Günter Grass stated in a speech in 1969, he strives now to "live without symbols and banners."[33] Among documentary writers, this concern has been especially prominent. Kuznetsov, like Hochhuth, expressly regards "reality" as sovereign over image. The objectivism that Reznikoff embraced in his later poetry was the expression of his avowed belief in "writing about the object itself...; I let the reader, or listener, draw his own conclusions."[34] A comparison of the successive drafts of Reznikoff's *Holocaust* reveals the process of simplification, of objectification, that left a bare skeleton of fact without any rhetorical wraps. What these writers are saying is that the artist has been deprived of his poetry by the Nazi violation of symbolic communication and by the sur-real reality of Auschwitz. The transformation of reality into metaphor becomes, by this logic, a kind of "defense mechanism" by which post-Holocaust culture distances reality. Hochhuth, Reznikoff, and other documentary writers would force their audience to confront reality by closing off, as far as possible, the option of viewing it as fantasy. As master of the imagination the artist again becomes the historian *par excellence*.

The Documentary as Landscape for Biography

Most documentary art reflects broad ideological, moral, and political concerns and subordinates individual personality and psychological complexity to a specific reading of history. There are, however, a few writers for whom documentation provides a backdrop for the private struggles of individuals. Ultimately, of course, these individuals are also caught in the sweep of collective destiny. But from this perspective, history does not employ them as agents of scrutable ends but intrudes upon them and catches them unawares in the petty acts of self-indulgence.

For an American writer such as Richard Elman, who does not have the empirical resources, the documentary pretext is a claim to authority as well as authenticity. In a prefatory note to *The Twenty-eighth Day of Elul,* Elman demonstrates the documentary artist's typical regard for the primacy of fact over imagination when he states that a set of documents and correspondence came to his attention in 1960: "The following April I started to work on a long short story in which it soon was apparent that certain documentary characters had emerged. The more I subsequently tried to put them out of my head the more their lives crowded in on me."[35] The documents and documented biography exercise a kind of imperative over art and the created character. This experiment demonstrates the incompatibility between the probing psychological approach of the artist-as-creator and the informational, collective overview of the artist-as-historian.

The Twenty-eighth Day of Elul (1967) is the first in a trilogy of novels, each relating the same story from a different, but in each case private, perspective. *The Twenty-eighth Day* is narrated through the letters of Alexander Yagodah, survivor of the Holocaust, to the executor of his American uncle's estate, in which he tells his family's story. *Lilo's Diary* (1968) is the fragmented journal of Alex's cousin and fiancée who was left behind by the fleeing family as a ransom to the gentile who arranged their escape. The third novel, *The Reckoning* (1969), is based on the daily ledgers of Newman Yagodah, Alex's father. All three narrators reveal themselves to be rather despicable characters—only Lilo is ultimately purified by her suffering. Elman goes to great lengths to dispel the aura of sainthood which has attached itself to the martyred Jews in much of the literature. Of such people as Newman Yagodah history cannot present a sacrifice to the gods; such a burnt offering would, as it were, offend Their nostrils . . . These characters are simply run-of-the-mill, morally deficient individuals who are caught off-guard by destiny. The tragedy of their lives is that, like the inhabitants of ancient Pompeii caught in volcanic lava, these people are frozen in their present unregenerate state—with no chance for making amends. As Newman Yagodah writes in one of his last entries:

For Who is alone now will remain alone . . .
And Who has no home now will not build one any more . . .[36]

Nevertheless, the "documentary" or "historical" imperative dictates a certain symbolic logic which transforms the lives of these people into microcosms of the collective catastrophe. The passionate, violent actions of betrayal and sexual exploitation seem intended to be emblematic, the scenes of lust and rape in *The Twenty-eighth Day of Elul* rather transparently signifying the imminent violation of an entire people, and the family squabbles in *The Reckoning* (Yagodah's betrayed wife accuses him, "you are our murderer" [p. 168]) presaging—and in some sense even upstaging—the violence about to be perpetrated by the Nazis. By presuming a kind of parallelism between public events and private affairs, Elman translates the Holocaust into a nemesis for flawed character or a macrocosmic version of domestic betrayal and violence.

With Elman as with other documentary writers it hardly matters what the actual degree of invention is or what the exact proportion of fact to imagination may be. It is the very pretense of factuality that precludes imaginative transformation of events. Saul Bellow has identified as a peculiarly American trait the "desire for the real [that] has created a journalistic sort of novel which has a *thing* excitement, a glamour of process; it specializes in information . . . it merely satisfies the reader's demand for knowledge."[37] The goal of diffusion of information is probably much better served by straightforward reportage; yet what emerges from a close reading of most of the documentary literature is that behind the camouflage of "factuality" lies not merely a desire to "inform," but explicit or implicit ideological perspectives which generate specific selections and interpretations of history and different modes and logic of relating and manipulating the historical reconstruction of reality in literature. Julitte's and Kuznetsov's novels are memoirs which, in the guise of fiction, claim a larger "historical" relevance in order to demonstrate certain social and political doctrines. Weiss goes even further in exploring the artistic potential of "scientific" history which substitutes social processes for people as the villains of history and statistics for individual characters as the fabric of drama. For Hochhuth, on the other hand, as historiography becomes more of a "science," the documentary artist assumes the evocative cultural function of memory and the ethical function of accusation and absolution. J.-F. Steiner uses documented history as therapy for the ruptured pride of the victim, endorsing a view of Jewish character and Jewish history which presupposes the redemptive value of heroic acts. Elman reverses the telescopic lens to reduce historical events to a backdrop for an enlarged reflection of biography. In each case the author relies upon his adherence to documentary evidence both to establish credibility for his particular view of history and to legitimate the artistic prerogatives, language, and presentation of character which derive from this basic attitude.

Of course history provides the source, if not necessarily the authority, for all of the literature of the Holocaust; nevertheless, when the writer does not insist on the historicity of character or situation he relinquishes both the automatic credibility that accrues to a "documentary" writer and his vulnerability to criticism on grounds of historical accuracy. A comparison of two artistic adaptations of the same event or a comparison of an eyewitness account and a fictional account of the same event[38] reveals not simply discrepancies in the transmission of information but, in each case, the inner vision of the artist. It is not the event, then, that is being communicated, but the acquisition of the event by the creative mind. Two very different literary versions of the murder of Auschwitz Lieutenant Schillinger—Arnošt Lustig's novel *A Prayer for Katerina Horovitzova* and Tadeusz Borowski's story "The Death of Schillinger"—reveal the extent to which one writer maintains the polarities of good and evil and exalts the heroic impulse whereas the other merely records the tale, from the outside, without moral comment or preferred center of consciousness. These writers, who were in fact closer to the actual reality than most of the documentary writers, assume the classical prerogative of the historical novelist in modeling their fiction after the broad outlines of historical events and personalities but inventing all those circumstances which separate fact from fiction.

Documentary art is, essentially, an attempt at artistic reconstruction of the actual; the more complete assimilation of the subject into fiction is an exploration of the *possible*—of the new options for human behavior that historical precedent has generated. Piotr Rawicz begins his novel *Blood from the Sky* with the typical documentary claim: the narrator explains that he is relating the forthcoming story entirely on the basis of the papers of one survivor which fell into his hands. But the "Postscript" to the novel reveals the extent to which the subject has left the realm of human *history* and entered the realm of human (or "subhuman") *nature:*

> *This book is not a historical record.*
> If the notion of chance (like most other notions) did not strike the author as absurd, he would gladly say that any reference to a particular period, territory, or race is purely coincidental.
>   The events that he describes could crop up in any place, at any time, in the mind of any man, planet, mineral...[39]

THREE

"Concentrationary Realism" and the Landscape of Death

The encounters between the imagination and traumatic history span the spectrum from reverence for specific facts in the documentary literature to the utter transformation of reality in the mythical litera-ture. The artist who "documents" history is followed on this con-tinuum by the realistic writer who delineates the concentrationary uni-verse not through specific "facts" but through the creations of his fact-haunted mind. Both writers represent a deferent attitude toward history that would appear not to violate or mitigate reality by the medi-ation of the creative imagination. But implicit in most documentary art is the ideological premise that reality must in the end yield a transcen-dent significance as part of a discernible historical process, whereas for the writer whom I call the "concentrationary realist" the naked indi-vidual emerges as the only arbiter of a self-enclosed reality devoid of transcendental references. Further, although in their adherence to the real properties of the actual experience these writers share a loyalty to history with the documentary writers, unlike them they have re-linquished familiar patterns of response and reconstruction and em-braced the new reality; their fiction conveys a degree of engagement in and submission to the operations of the concentrationary universe from which the documentary author maintains his distance.

In this literature Auschwitz becomes not only a historical "fact" but a human option; fiction records here not merely events that actually took place (which, by the very arbitrariness of history, could equally not have taken place) but the potential, and therefore in some respects the logic, of human response to such extreme situations. In demon-strating that realism in literature presupposes, beyond the concrete details, archetypal patterns of experience and response, Erich Auer-bach describes the use of the random moment by certain contemporary realists as illuminating the "elementary things which men in general have in common."[1] The fiction which never leaves the confines of the concentration camp assumes, in effect, a new set of archetypes based on an experience that was unique in the annals of human society and that constitutes, in turn, a Darwinian mutation in the accommodation of imprisoned selves to brutal reality. The Holocaust which for the documentary writer is a function of his own or historical memory has been fully absorbed into the imagination of the concentrationary realist. And in certain ways he is even more faithful to life-as-it-was than the documentary writer. He is less concerned with footnoting historical events (although actual persons and events may be named), but he remains relentlessly faithful to the past by closing off all avenues of escape from the concentrationary universe. Just as he does not invoke the authority of "history"—which could provide him with an avenue of return (quite simply, the war began in 1939 and ended in 1945)—so this writer does not use metaphorical, metaphysical, mythological, or ideological support to help organize, analogize, or transcend the experience.

Neue Sachlichkeit and Concentrationary Realism

Erich Kahler discusses, in *The Tower and the Abyss,* the *Neue Sachlichkeit* ("New Factuality") which after World War I replaced the subjectivity of expressionist art in Europe. It differed radically from the old realism in that for the meticulous, almost loving detail which conveyed a "devout" attitude towards nature, the postexpressionist realism substituted a "cruel, indeed vicious over-stress of facts, [a] showing of objects in their inexorable suchness, in a glazed nakedness." In literature as in painting, this crass, cold precision suggests that a bitterness or profound sadness had replaced the reverent attitude of the old realists toward the external world.[2]

If, as Kahler suggests, the violence in contemporary society found its earliest and most direct expression in Hemingway's war fiction, in Eastern Europe the Holocaust and the ravages of the Second World War were to generate an even more radical accommodation of the New Factuality to the extremes of unprecedented reality. Much of the Eastern European, especially Polish, literature that was published soon after the war is written in a laconic, straightforward style that conveys a reality stripped bare of image. A formulation of the challenge that these postwar writers confronted was furnished by Czeslaw Miłosz in *The Captive Mind* when he described what might be considered the paradigmatic experience of his war-torn generation: that of the man lying on a pavement under fire from a machine gun. Literature, says Miłosz, must withstand the test of such "brutal, naked reality.... Probably only those things are worthwhile which can preserve their

validity in the eyes of a man threatened with instant death." Only
literature "based on an equally *naked* experience could survive trium-
phantly that judgment day of man's illusions."[3]

The mandate which Miłosz presents to the realistic writer concerns,
essentially, the communication of experience in terms so concrete and
unadorned that they cannot be construed as "emotional luxuries"[4]
which would betray the quality of ultimate confrontation. He does,
however, presuppose experience which can be communicated and may
even be endemic to the condition of contemporary man, as well as a
tradition of realistic literature which conveys the universal underpinnings of private experience.

Much of the fiction of the Holocaust is a version of inherited conventions of realism, using language to signify a new reality and yet to
reaffirm the old verities that are Ariadne threads directing the ultimate
emergence into a postwar world. Additionally such realism serves, like
the documentary literature, to render the experience so familiar that it
becomes a shared historical resource. There are, however, a few authors, of whom the Polish writer Tadeusz Borowski is a prominent
example, who carry Miłosz's mandate to the farthest extreme, reconstructing Nazism in terms that are concrete but do not even begin to
establish verisimilitude. The ground of this fiction, unlike that of conventional realism, is nonanalogous reality. Although this prose shares
so many of the basic features of the New Factuality, especially in its
presentation of the grotesque details of physical debasement and death,
that affinities have been drawn between Borowski and Hemingway,[5]
the differences are as significant as those between a concentration camp
and a battlefield. By Hemingway's own admission, his narrator is detached from the events he recounts, and he presents not the emotion
évoked by the scene but the formative components of the emotion—
"the sequence of motion and fact which made the emotion" and can
reconstitute it in the mind of the reader.[6] The narrative postures of
other realists of the macabre, such as Poe, Villiers de l'Isle-Adam,
Maupassant, or Jerzy Kosinski, who control and navigate through a state
of horror as both subject and object, resemble the internal perspective
of a writer like Borowski but are in some respects quite different from
it. Borowski's stories constitute a concrete realism which emanates
from within a violated universe, which lays bare the victim's own form
of adaptation to the situation in which he finds himself. The narrator is
not the architect of and in most instances does not actually espouse the
sadistic norms which prevail in this universe; even in his debasement
he may not abandon the human image altogether—nevertheless, he is a
part of his story, a prisoner of the reality he describes. Like the camps

which were isolated and for a time hidden from the civilized world, the facts of behavior are presented here with no outside moral or emotional alternative or corrective.

Borowski is the writer with whom, in a sense, Holocaust literature begins and ends. Like Kafka, about whom Nathalie Sarraute wrote that "to remain at the point where he left off, or to attempt to go on from there, are equally impossible; those who live in a world of human beings can only retrace their steps,"[7] Borowski has reached, in one direction at least, the limits of literature. His stories on the concentration camp are relentless in their presentation of "brutal, naked reality."

In the history of Holocaust literature there are relatively few stories which are actually located in the camps; most of them either reach the periphery of the concentrationary universe—the Jewish town on the even of deportation, the ghetto, the forests or other fugitive hideouts (the epilogue is an act of deduction)[8]—or relegate the camps to the contained limits of memory or imagination.[9] The concentration camp is a world without exit and, unless one clings to a chronological or ideological structure or to metaphorical or mythical forms of escape, there can be no organizing principle to point the way out. Borowski rejects the very notion of such a principle. "I do not know whether we shall survive," he writes in one story, "but I like to think that one day we shall have the courage to tell the world the whole truth and call it by its proper name."[10] "Truth" is reality which is not mitigated by any rhetorical transports that could convey the reader to a more familiar, more comfortable world. Perfection of form—for that matter, the very idea of aesthetics divorced from matter that is inherently bloody and sweaty—is to Borowski a travesty of human suffering. In a passage from the long story "Auschwitz, Our Home," the narrator in Auschwitz writes to his lover in Birkenau:

> You know how much I used to like Plato. Today I realize he lied. For the things of this world are not a reflection of the ideal, but a product of human sweat, blood and hard labour. It is we who built the pyramids, hewed the marble for the temples and the rocks for the imperial roads, we who pulled the oars in the galleys and dragged wooden ploughs, while they wrote dialogues and dramas.... We were filthy and died real deaths. They were "aesthetic" and carried on subtle debates.
>
> There can be no beauty if it is paid for by human injustice, nor truth that passes over injustice in silence, nor moral virtue that condones it.

> ... And we shall be forgotten, drowned out by the voices
> of the poets, the jurists, the philosophers, the priests. They
> will produce their own beauty, virtue and truth. [Pp. 111–12]

Somewhere, then, even in the greatest work of art may lurk the lie
that betrays the man under machine-gun fire, in the moment before
death... This is an element of the "barbarism" that T. W. Adorno
spoke of—inevitably, the

> artistic representation of the naked bodily pain of those
> who have been knocked down by rifle-butts contains the
> potential—no matter how remote—to squeeze out plea-
> sure.... Through aesthetic principles or stylization and
> even through the solemn prayer of the chorus the unimagin-
> able ordeal still appears as if it had some ulterior purpose. It
> is transfigured and stripped of some of its horror and with
> this, injustice is already done to the victims.[11]

Borowski is one of the very few writers whose art does not transfigure
brutal reality. For him literature must function as a vehicle of preservation, as a medium through which the experience of victimization becomes part of the collective consciousness; like Hochhuth, he rejects
pure aesthetics as frivolous at best and as the cooptation of evil into
culture at worst. Borowski shares this conviction with a small group of
his compatriots, of whom Miłosz is one and the poet Tadeusz
Różewicz another. Michael Hamburger calls their attitude and the
antipoetry that issues from it the "new austerity," and cites a few of
those poets "whose experience of total war and total politics has shaken them out of the assumptions... that personal feeling and personal
imagination still accord with general truths of a meaningful kind." At
its most extreme, "the new austerity is not only anti-metaphorical but
anti-mythical."[12] Hamburger quotes Różewicz as having once stated
that what he had revolted against after World War II was that poetry
"had survived the end of the world, as though nothing had happened";
his own poetry, Różewicz continues, is a poetry of "salvaged
words... uninteresting words... from the great rubbish dump, the
great cemetery." After Auschwitz, poets should no longer be concerned with the creation of aesthetic objects: "The production of
beauty to induce 'aesthetic experiences' strikes me as a harmless but
ludicrous and childish occupation." His own poetry, then, is written
"for the horror-stricken. For those abandoned to butchery. For survivors. We learnt language from scratch, those people and I."[13]

As with the poetry of austerity, it is difficult to classify the prose of
Borowski and other concentrationary realists as imaginative literature.

It is a catalogue of human responses to concentrationary society. There is no psychological analysis. Language delineates regions never before explored by the human mind, leaving little ground for the empathy which is fiction's natural province. It is an extreme example of the kind of "hammering factuality" that Irving Howe defines in Orwell's *Nineteen Eighty-four,* where "delicacies of phrasing or displays of rhetoric have come to seem frivolous." This fiction cannot be "understood, nor can it be properly valued, simply by resorting to the usual literary categories, for it posits a situation in which these categories are no longer significant."[14]

A Diminished Rhetoric

In the context of the concentration camps and mechanized mass murder, rhetoric can be regarded not only as "frivolous" or superfluous, but even as subversive. The operations of the imagination are preempted by a process whereby men were actually metamorphosed into objects. Everything in the camp was calculated to reduce the human being in the first place to the appearance, behavior, and worthlessness of a helpless animal. His head was shaved; he was deprived of his name (hereafter the status of an individual was measured by the number on his arm: "the electrician [was] a fantastically old serial number, just a bit over one thousand..." ["Auschwitz, Our Home," p. 114]), of contact with the outside world, and of adequate nourishment; and he was subject to the unrelenting threat of torture and death. But it was *after* his death that the final indignities on the human person were committed; with a thoroughness that is mildly conveyed by Bettelheim's description of the process whereby the "total person became commodity," the corpse was ultimately discarded with such care that "no salvageable material was wasted"[15]; his teeth yielded up gold for the aggrandizement of the Third Reich, his hair became the stuffing for mattresses, his skin the shades for lamps, his ashes fertilizer for the fields, and his fat—the ultimate metonymy—the ingredient for soap. A number of writers have contributed to what has become an internal discussion of the viability of metaphor in Holocaust literature. One of the interlocutors in Carlo Levi's Italian novel *The Watch* puts it simply:

> What sort of novel do you want after Auschwitz and Buchenwald? Did you see the photographs of women weeping as they buried pieces of soap made from the bodies of their husbands and their sons? That's the way the confusion ended. The individual exchanged for the whole.... There you are! Your *tranche de vie*—a piece of soap.[16]

The horror that is registered repeatedly in this literature at the realization that the concentrationary universe is the "reification"[17] of
metaphor, that the forces of chaos which rhetoric had only *signified*
before had now been unleashed upon the world, is the horror of
acknowledging that reality has reached the limits of the imaginable.
This is the process by which, as Piotr Rawicz's narrator so trenchantly
sums it up, "word became flesh, and flesh—smoke."[18] In an effort to
realign language and experience, he decides at one point to ban
"figures of speech" altogether, to "kill comparisons," and to "engage
in mere recounting, mere enumeration" (pp. 183–84). That is
essentially what Tadeusz Borowski has set out to do: to recount,
enumerate. Where he does use images of comparison they are, for the
most part, similes borrowed from the same realm of experience. Referring to the "library" located in the hospital where he works, the
narrator of "Auschwitz, Our Home" says he has not been able to
verify which kinds of books the library contains, "for the room is
always locked up as tight *as a coffin*" (p. 85, emphasis mine). (This is
not really an "Auschwitz" image; it is borrowed from a world where
death was still dignified by coffins.) In a descriptive passage in another
story, the weather conditions prevailing in the camp are likened to
instruments of torture:

> A dark, gusty wind, heavy with the smells of the thawing,
> sour earth, tossed the clouds about and cut through your
> body *like a blade of ice* .... Several bluish lamps, sawing to
> and fro on top of high lamp-posts, threw a dim light over the
> black, tangled tree branches reaching out over the road, the
> shiny sentry-shack roofs, and the empty pavement that
> glistened *like a wet leather strap*. ["The Supper," pp. 132,
> 133, emphases mine]

The story "This Way for the Gas, Ladies and Gentlemen" begins:

> The delousing is finally over, and our striped suits are back
> from the tanks of Cyclone-B solution, an efficient killer of
> lice in clothing and of men in gas chambers ... not a single
> prisoner, *not one solitary louse* can sneak through the gate.
> [P. 9, emphasis mine]

To the extent that rhetoric or eloquence serves to mitigate fact or to
integrate it into a larger scheme, the persistence in this literature of a
factuality which does not allow for transcendence through metaphor is
a reinforcement on the literary level of the brutal inexorability of concentrationary reality.

In closing off all the avenues of escape from this reality, the writer is taking a position not only concerning the violated world but also concerning the artist's privileges vis-à-vis that world. Resembling in this respect the documentary novelist who yields to history the authority for characters and events, he relinquishes the moral prerogative which places the creator above his creation. But, unlike the documentary writer, he himself appears, in various guises, as a creature. In so doing he may actually betray his own biography. Miłosz cites the reports of Borowski's fellow-prisoners which testify to his exemplary—even heroic—behavior in Auschwitz (where he managed to survive for two years) and Dachau, from which he was eventually liberated by the Americans.[19] But Borowski's first-person narrators, like the rest of his characters, are almost invariably tainted by the guilt of some form of collaboration in a system which had been devised so that one could survive only at the expense of others. "I think we should speak about all the things that are happening around us," writes the narrator of "Auschwitz, Our Home." "We are not evoking evil irresponsibly or in vain, for we have now become a part of it" (p. 93).

The characters who appear here have become part of the evil, yet they are not evil itself. There is still an important distinction between these men, forced to collaborate in order to survive, and the Nazi murderers. Miłosz writes that "in the abundant literature of atrocity of the twentieth century, one rarely finds an account written from the point of view of an accessory to the crime. Authors are usually ashamed of this role."[20] But in Borowski's case this is not merely a pose or an allegory of the diffusion of evil in the mind of the victim, along the lines of Kosinski's *The Painted Bird,* which we will consider later. Borowski's characters are *human,* and even as they collaborate, even as they adopt an attitude of indifference or even cynicism in order to get through the day's work, they cannot banish the images of human suffering that lodge in their memory. Borowski is brutally forthright in detailing the compromises with a civilized life of "good deeds" that the *katzetnik* had to make; but he refuses to abandon the human soul categorically to the powers of darkness. Although he has been regarded as the one writer in whose fiction the prisoner is totally identified with his oppressor, his conduct utterly reduced to the level of bestial instinct, there are subtle ambiguities in this fiction which militate against the tendency to interpret all the prisoners as equal collaborators in the devil's camp. Borowski consistently refrains from judging the behavior of the inmates, and in the absence of a guide through this region of moral ambiguity, the distinctions between the degraded and the inhuman remain subtle and elusive. One story is told of the mass execution of a group of Russian soldiers (narrated this time by an observer of the event). It describes the shooting and shattering of heads on the pavement—in language that might be used to describe the cracking of so many nuts. As soon as the Russians have been disposed of and the corpses dragged temporarily under the fence, the Kommandant and his SS officers withdraw—and a hitherto silent crowd of *Häftlinge* fall on the corpses with a "shrieking roar." The following day, a "Muslimized" (moribund) Jew from Estonia tries to convince the narrator that "human brains are, in fact, so tender you can eat them absolutely raw" ("The Supper," pp. 135, 136). To dismiss this simply as "collaboration" or the total pervasiveness of the cannibalistic system is to apply absolute moral categories that make no allowances for starvation.[21] Even in the "anus mundi" a distinction can still be made between those like the Jews from Estonia who would eat corpses in order to stay alive, and those who, in their strategy for survival, would kill their fellow inmates for their flesh. Curzio Malaparte, the Italian journalist, witnessed starved Russian prisoners consuming the flesh of their dead comrades and distinguished between such miserable victims and the German murderers. "The Germans are sentimental people, the most sentimental people in the world," he wrote. "The German people will not eat corpses; they eat living men."[22] Their counterpart in the camp society as represented in Borowski's fiction is Becker, the filicide. "Real hunger is when one man regards another man as something to eat," he says ("A Day at Harmenz," p. 34). It is his behavior which manifests the monstrosity of total acquiescence to the logic of the Nazi universe.[23]

There is, then, no single "persona" in Borowski's stories. The protagonist from the "Canada Commando"[24] in "This Way for the Gas, Ladies and Gentlemen" exhibits some of the diverse and conflicting responses which are still possible within a diminished arena of moral options; sitting on his bunk, he complains that "we are without our usual diversion: the wide roads leading to the crematoria are empty" and tells his buddy, Henri, that "dammit, they'll run out of people" (p. 10). Later he is gripped, as the first transport of the day recedes toward the gas chambers, with sudden compunction.

> "Listen, Henri, are we good people?"
> "That's stupid. Why do you ask?"
> "You see, my friend, you see, I don't know why, but I am furious, simply furious with these people—furious because I must be here because of them." [P. 20]

Overcome with revulsion, he nevertheless concludes: "I see the camp as a haven of peace. It is true, others may be dying, but one is somehow still alive, one has enough food, enough strength to work..." (p. 28).

The narrator of another story, "The People Who Walked On," relates, quite matter-of-factly, the progress of a soccer game which a group of inmates play in a field next to the loading ramp from which new arrivals are taken to be gassed: "Between two throw-ins in a soccer game, right behind my back, three thousand people had been put to death" (p. 64). This laconic commensuration of the tally of goals scored and of people gassed indicates the degree of this prisoner's adjustment to the operation of the system; the grim irony is only latent in the text and must be catalyzed by the outrage that the reader, secure in a world of restored symmetries, brings to it. Yet even this seemingly impervious narrator softens his tone at the end of his tale as he admits to the indelible impression that these anonymous victims have made on his memory:

> Your memory retains only images. Today, as I think back
> on that summer in Auschwitz, I can still see the endless,
> colorful procession of people solemnly walking—along both
> roads; the woman, her head bent forward, standing over the
> flaming pit; the big redheaded girl in the dark interior of the
> barracks, shouting impatiently:
> "Will evil ever be punished? I mean in human, normal
> terms!"
> And I can still see the Jew with bad teeth, standing beneath my high bunk every evening, lifting his face to me,
> asking insistently: "Any packages today? Could you sell me
> some eggs for Mirka? I'll pay in marks. She is so fond of
> eggs..." [P. 77]

And there is the story of the Jew who is an "experienced prisoner" from Majdanek who finds work in Birkenau's hospital section—but who is "selected" to be gassed after he falls ill ("The Man with the Package," p. 127). The narrator notices that he proceeds to the gas chambers naked, like everyone else—but clinging to the small package that contains all his earthly possessions (a spoon, a knife and pencil, some bacon, a few rolls and some fruit). The narrator laughs, but his neighbor, a doctor from Berlin, explains with a "shy smile" that "holding a package" could be "a little like holding somebody's hand, you see" (p. 130). The narrator concludes his tale with a reference to the curious rumor that "the Jews who were driven to the·gas chamber sang some soul-stirring Hebrew song which nobody could understand" (p. 131).

Borowski is a chronicler of the small acts of compliance, of despair, of cowardice—and, occasionally, of bravery—that myriads of men performed as they "passed through" Auschwitz; as each character is silenced by the "cremo" or removal to a different station, another comes to take his place. That each of Borowski's stories is narrated from a different point of view is reflected in the language itself. For the narrator who has not yet reached the lowest spheres, the natural world is still accessible; the opening paragraph of "A Day at Harmenz" is pure pastoral, reflecting the thoughts of one prisoner who has been in the camp only a few months:

> The shadows of the chestnut trees are green and soft. They sway gently over the ground, still moist after being newly turned over, and rise up in sea-green cupolas scented with the morning freshness. The trees form a high palisade along the road, their crowns dissolve into the hue of the sky. From the direction of the ponds comes the heavy, intoxicating smell of the marshes. The grass, green and velvety, is still silvered with dew, but the earth already steams in the sun. It will be a hot day. [P. 30]

There is no hint in the language that this narrator is an inmate of Auschwitz, working in a labor Kommando just outside the camp. The longer an inmate survives in Auschwitz, or the higher his position in the hierarchy of evil, the more his adaptation requires the kind of suspension of qualities of the mind and heart which would appear criminal or pathological to the normal person living in normal circumstances. This process is measured by a corresponding contraction in the prose. In the story "This Way for the Gas, Ladies and Gentlemen," the narrative oscillates between the straightforward, functional realism of bare description from which all rhetorical and moral projections are omitted ("the heat rises, the hours are endless. There have been no new transports for several days. We are without even our usual distraction; the wide roads leading to the crematories are empty") and the emotional remission into memory and eloquence that a full belly occasionally facilitates ("we... slice the neat loaves of crisp, crumbly bread... sent all the way from Warsaw; only a week ago my mother held this white bread in her hands...dear God, dear God..." [p. 10]). Henri, the narrator's companion who matter-of-factly admits that "since Christmas, at least a million people have passed through my hands," tells him that the "worst are the transports from around Paris: one always meets friends."

> "And what do you tell them?"
> "That they're going to have a bath, and then we'll meet at the camp. What would you tell them?" [Pp. 26–27]

We can trace in these stories, then, the process by which the laws that govern the outside world are suspended. At the most extreme end of this process of mental cooptation, the language reveals a

functional attitude toward objects and events which precludes any
generic or analogous thinking that might transport the *Häftling* beyond
this world in which survival depends on constant watchfulness and
accommodation.

Like Borowski, the German-Jewish novelist Edgar Hilsenrath explores the stark, pitiless landscape of death, and eliminates access to
the outside world and hope for the future through a constriction in the
language and frame of reference. In the novel *Night,* Hilsenrath's impersonal narrator doggedly pursues the central protagonist, Ranek,
through all the stages by which a man's soul is compromised, betrayed,
and all but destroyed as his body gradually succumbs to illness and
death. This man's prison is the small Ukrainian ghetto town of Prokov
on the banks of the Dniester. His adversaries are hunger and
disease—and the terror, though seldom the presence, of the Nazis who
are gradually liquidating the ghetto by deporting its surviving inhabitants. There is no tangible enemy here against whom one could
muster even mental opposition; there are no battles to be won. It is a
slow process by which all the trappings of civilization are stripped
away and the erosion of one's very personality is accomplished.
Although the setting is a ghetto and not a concentration camp, and the
victim is spared the pain and humiliation of slave labor and torture,
there is no escape. The concentrationary system is so pervasive that,
again, even the narrator's imagination serves the enemy through internal metaphor: "there was creaking and rustling everywhere and their
own two shadows pursued them *like guards*";[25] "when they stepped
into the yard, the sky was *as red as blood*" (p. 256). Deborah, Ranek's
sister-in-law, walks through the town park and notices that the trees
have been sawed off and the wind has blown away the few leaves that
still clung to the truncated branches: "there they stood, serried *like
naked corpses,* who diabolically, were condemned to stand upright"
(p. 454, emphases mine).

The diminution of existence to the dimensions of bare survival is
reflected in the paucity of articles of this world as well as of images that
would remind one of external reality. A handful of accessories provide
the skeletal structure of this fiction. We first encounter Hilsenrath's
Ranek as he appropriates a hat from his dead friend, Nathan. This act
in itself constitutes an initial loss of identity which is to become more
pronounced with the passage of time. The opening sentence of the
novel—"the man stepped quietly into the room" (p. 9)—establishes
the anonymity which the system has imposed on the individual. At one
point Ranek stops to look at his image in a windowpane: "It was half
effaced: an unshaven face featureless in the shadow of the hat's wide
brim. He stepped even closer to the window, but his face did not

become more distinct. Then he suddenly felt as though this were not his own face at all staring back at him, but another face, which legally belonged to the hat: Nathan's face" (p. 130).

Physical properties are emblematic and catalytic of psychological states. Their effects on the consciousness are like those of Proust's *madeleine,* but they are even more conspicuous in a landscape uncluttered by other objects or memories. The physical world which is represented in this fiction by the barest minimum of description may suddenly be invaded by an artifact from the past—and the juxtaposition is a measure of the deterioration of human society even more than the desolation itself. The effect is the same as a tiny red ball or a yellow ribbon would have if it appeared in one corner of Picasso's gray *Guernica.* One item which serves this purpose in Hilsenrath's novel, a doll, has not even managed to survive the war unscathed. But the description of the doll which the inmate keeps as a memento of his former life contains more pathos than most of the descriptions of physical suffering in which Hilsenrath's novel abounds: "He called the doll Mia. A pretty name. Mia had only one eye. Her stomach had a slit in it and the wood shavings were coming out. Still, it wasn't ugly. Which was surprising. Perhaps because the room was so bare and there was not even a single picture on the walls? The doll loaned the room a little warmth" (p. 111).[26]

The occasional intrusion of memory or dream in Hilsenrath's novel, like the image of mother evoked by the loaf of white bread in Borowski's story, can provide momentary escape. Yet because even the unconscious is in the employ of the Nazis, even momentary recall of the past is dysfunctional for accommodational survival in that it evokes the entire civilized world that has been forfeited. Nocturnal dreams appear in this literature as a palimpsest of memory half effaced by the presence of unremediable pain. Although Jean Cayrol claims that dreams provided the last refuge for the *Häftling,* a kind of *"maquis"* to which he could retreat and find familiar echoes of love, of freedom, and of happiness,[27] the concentrationary realists represent dreams as a world which has been contaminated by the horrors of present reality. In Hilsenrath's novel Ranek has a dream which is both symptomatic and prophetic: he dreams that he returns to the city of his youth, Litesty, and walks the "streets of a city no longer contaminated by Jews. No one recognized the man who had returned" (p. 78). His dream provides both a commentary on the hopeless desolation of present reality and a glimpse of the devastated future he will not live to see.

No Afterlife

All remissions prove momentary anyway. Ranek ultimately dies a slow, gruesome, unheroic, and almost unnoticed death. There is no survival in this world—even if life is prolonged beyond the liberation, it is only so that one can bear witness, that is, relive over and over again in "fiction" the life in the camps. The literature is a relentless measure of the success of the system in penetrating and controlling the imagination. An occasional prisoner in Borowski's Auschwitz is, ultimately, liberated—but only to carry the logic of life in the camp into post-Holocaust reality. The most "surrealistic" passage in Borowski's fiction is a disjunctive presentation of the concrete elements of the concentrationary experience; what reads like the hallucinations of a disordered mind or the visions of a grotesque Boschian apocalypse is merely a transference of the properties of that experience to the outside world on the part of the victim who yet remains fully aware of his loss of prospects for a normal recovery:

> Sometimes it seems to me that even my physical sensibilities have coagulated and stiffened within me like resin. In contrast to years gone by, when I observed the world with wide-open, astonished eyes, and walked along every street alert, like a young man on a parapet, I can now push through the liveliest crowd with total indifference and rub against hot female bodies without the slightest emotion, even though the girls may try to seduce me with the bareness of their knees and their oiled, intricately coiffed hair. Through half-open eyes I see with satisfaction that once again a gust of the cosmic gale has blown the crowd into the air, all the way up to the treetops, sucked the human bodies into a huge whirlpool, twisted their lips open in terror, mingled the children's rosy cheeks with the hairy chests of the men, entwined the clenched fists with strips of women's dresses, thrown snow-white thighs on the top, like foam, with hats and fragments of heads tangled in hair-like seaweed peeping from below. And I see that this weird snarl, this gigantic stew concocted out of the human crowd, flows along the street, down the gutter, and seeps into space with a loud gurgle, like water into a sewer. ["The World in Stone," p. 159]

There is no "afterlife," for the living or the dead. In both the ancient Greek and Hebrew sources of modern civilization the manner of one's dying was a signal of the value of life itself: Jeremiah warns of the withdrawal of God's "peace" from His people, in a portrait of the anarchy of death:

> High or low, they will die in this land,
> without burial or lament; there will
> be no gashing, no shaving of the head
> for them.

> No bread will be broken for the mourner to
> comfort him for the dead; no cup of consolation
> will be offered him for father or for mother.
>
> [Jer. 16: 6–7]

Cassandra describes the desolation of Troy in terms of the displacement of burial grounds and the disruption of burial rites:

> Those the War God caught
> Never saw their sons again, nor were they laid to rest
> decently in winding sheets by their wives' hands, but lie
> buried in alien ground . . .[28]

None of the rituals that have dignified life's final passage in ordered societies was available to the inmates of the ghettos and camps. Where existence was a form of living death most of them were not intimidated by thoughts of final extinction as a state of nonbeing so much as by the suffering that must precede the end and by the utter oblivion that followed it—which entailed obliteration not only of one's physical presence, but of all traces of identity and all semblance of the human form. Like the atomic bomb over Hiroshima, which was, in the understated words of one of the *hibakusha* ("survivor") writers, a death-dominated event conspicuous for the "omission of various ceremonies,"[29] the Holocaust was, in sum, the unceremonious mass production of death. Charlotte Delbo, in her sensitive and moving memoir of Auschwitz, *Aucun de nous ne reviendra,* evokes the scene of death which violates the *rites de passage* that dignify mortality; Delbo is repulsed not by the thought of death, which is almost courted as the surcease of pain, but by the sight of the unmourned, naked corpses: "I want to die but not to be carried on the small [roughly hewn] litter. Not to be carried on this small litter with legs hanging down and head dangling, naked under the tattered cover . . ."[30]

Like the tombstones that a few survivors erected after the war to the memory of their dead on the mounds of mass graves at Bergen Belsen, much of the literature is a restoration, through rhetoric, of the elegies of properly mourned death. Stephen Spender commends poets like Nelly Sachs and Abba Kovner for replacing "gross fact" with the "extreme agony of death-bed prayer," for providing a "veil between us and the dead."[31] The camp realists reject all the dignities with which other writers shroud the corpses. In a rare departure from direct iteration, the disrupted rhythms of life and death are underscored in Hilsenrath's novel, as occasionally in Borowski's fiction, by the irony of incongruence rather than by elegy. The narrator describes, in the only idyllic scene in his bleak universe, two bodies floating down the Dniester river:

Two corpses were drifting comfortably down river: a man
and a woman. The woman drifted somewhat ahead of the
man. It looked like a flirtation: the man constantly trying to
snatch the woman but without succeeding. Then the woman
drifted a little to the side and grinned at the man. And the
man grinned back at her. And he caught up with her; his
body touched her body.

Both corpses now proceeded to float in a circle; for awhile
they stuck together as if they wanted to unite. Then they
floated downstream, reconciled. [P. 311]

This *danse macabre* is the only passage in the novel which evokes
the carefree activities of a normal life—flirtation, lovemaking,
reconciliation—in an atmosphere of calm abandon. Those two, it may
be said, were among the "lucky" corpses. Even the living could never
be so lucky. Death has such dominion that the living seem to de-
compose before each other's eyes; Ranek muses on the beauty of a
young woman with whom he shares his food and bed for awhile (one
who has come "to vegetate with him for a brief period"):

She was young. But that didn't mean much. You aged
quickly here. Now he knew that she had pretty teeth, like
pearls...which would probably drop out soon because of
malnutrition. Her full mouth would crumple then; he could
imagine this process with great exactness. Her skin wasn't
grey yet. That would happen too. [P. 109]

This is a good example of fictional realism that captures the logic,
rather than the statistics, of the concentrationary universe.

Psychopathology and the Literature of Extreme Situations

These stories, which are among the very few instances of relentless
self-exposure in the literature of the camps,[32] have an internal logic and
a fixation on the concrete to the exclusion of abstract or symbolic
thinking that relate to the outside world in almost the same way that
schizophrenic or brain-damaged perceptions of reality relate to "normal" perceptions. The schizophrenic's language has been characterized as functional and concrete and intelligible only within the
idiosyncratic boundaries of his pathology.[33] The world of the *katzetnik*
is, of course, not primarily a function of his mental set; nevertheless, it
is as far removed from "normal" reality as the most pathological state.
And although, unlike the schizophrenic's, his relinquishing of self was,
at some point, intentional and therefore can be considered as extreme
accommodational, rather than pathological, behavior, the more the
katzetnik is assimilated into the camp system the more complete is his

loss of will and of memory and of all other socially connected functions.

A comparison of verbal manifestations of psychopathology and literary reconstructions of the "extreme situations" of our time may be especially reasonable in the consideration of concentrationary realism since it is the least contrived, philosophically and aesthetically, of all the literary responses to the Holocaust and the least attentive to common social symbols. It represents the almost total breakdown of the function of sign-making; Peter Brooks, defining man as *Homo signiferens,* suggests that the "psychic numbing" that was observed as a predominant response to the ubiquity of pain and death on the part of both A-bomb and concentration camp victims "might be a kind of impairment of this sign-making function itself, and could imply a psychically defenseless man who is overwhelmed by what has become for him an undifferentiated and insignificant reality." In this context "the breakdown of symbolization . . . would be the incapacity to imagine that necessary leeway in existence, an overacceptance of the literality of existence."[34]

The relentless realism of a writer like Borowski or Hilsenrath does not provide a compass by which the reader can orient himself vis-à-vis the known world. Still, the perimeters of his isolation are significantly different from those of the schizophrenic who is locked into the universe of his private fantasies; because the inmates of the camps shared a community of experience and language, concentrationary realism can be regarded as an internal literature whose signs are comprehensible and "public" to those who were there. For the sake of the outsider and out of respect for the continuity of the boundaries of art, much of the fiction of the Holocaust has been sanitized of the filthy, scabrous quality that life acquired in the camps; Borowski and Hilsenrath are among the few who, without courting sensationalism or scatology for its own sake, present the internal landscape of the concentrationary world— that is, the conjunction of a brutal reality and the degrees of accommodation that the imprisoned soul makes to that reality. This is the *terminus ad quem* of the process of inner acquiescence with coercive reality that can be traced in the fiction of other twentieth-century realists. Submission can be measured in this literature in attitudes toward time and metaphysics as well as in the use of imagery borrowed from other universes of experience.

Camus suggests that "by the treatment that the artist imposes on reality, he declares the intensity of his rejection" and that realism in art implies at least some degree of "consent" to "one part of reality."[35] Camus's own suspension of external reference and submersion in the "destructive element" in *The Plague* can be seen as a form of "consent" to a very specific self-enclosed ambience as the sum total of reality.[36] Similarly, many of the invalids in Mann's *Magic Mountain* and most of the patients in Solzhenitsyn's *Cancer Ward,* like the deluded victims in Kafka's fiction and the inmates of Auschwitz, are entrapped in what they perceive as objective, inexorable reality. In spite of the fact that in the case of the victims of tuberculosis or the plague or cancer, death attacks the organism from the inside and may be a *metaphor* for social decay, whereas in the case of the victims of Nazism death is an external, historically real force ("Death is a proud German master"—Celan), the regard for the temporal and spatial dimensions of incarceration as ontological absolutes is common to the perception of most of the doomed characters in this group of novels. Until his "escape" into the snowy mountains surrounding the sanatorium, Mann's Hans Castorp exhibits all the characteristics of a perfectly acquiescent victim—albeit enjoying the creature comforts that are geared to cheer him to his doom. Unavailable or inconceivable to other patients on the mountain or in the cancer ward, or to the plague-ridden townspeople of Oran or the inmates of Borowski's or Hilsenrath's concentration camp, it is escape—even the mere contemplation of escape—which can turn disease or incarceration into a provisional reality. Thus Joachim Ziemmsen's flight to the flatland or the nighttime swim that Tarrou and Rieux take in the sea also constitutes a momentary escape from and abiding defiance of the tuberculosis- or plague-infested reality, as do Kostoglotov's sexual fantasies and return home during the remission of his cancer.[37] These characters, who at some point resist the system and demonstrate their loyalty to and faith in the outside world and its values, even though the disease has not been entirely defeated, share a "survivalist" perspective with certain Holocaust writers who will be considered in the next chapter. The other patients share with the protagonists in Borowski's and Hilsenrath's fiction the suspension of "objective" time and reordering of priorities that represent capitulation to the system or the disease.

FOUR

Literature of Survival

They no longer felt humanity as a limitless milieu. It was a thin flame within them which they alone kept alive. It kept itself going in the silence which they opposed to their executioners. About them was nothing but the great polar night of the inhuman and of unknowingness, which they did not even see, which they divined in the glacial cold which transpierced them. Our fathers always had witnesses and examples available. For these tortured men, there were no longer any.

J.-P. Sartre, What Is Literature?

The realism of the concentrationary writers who were discussed in the last chapter is characterized primarily by the quality of containment that informs the language as well as the structure and thematics of the fiction and measures the degrees of acquiescence of the victim to the laws of the system. A different version and form of reality is reflected in the fiction in which the concentrationary experience emerges as provisional, and memories of a pre-Holocaust past and visions of a post-Holocaust future function as a promissory note to redeem the suffering of the present. These novels are structured minimally by the chronology of personal survival, which leads out of as well as into the concentrationary universe, and they are marked by much broader perspectives and a far wider range of rhetorical possibilities than concentrationary realism. Most of this fiction commences in or has reference to the prewar world; the *ancien régime* then slowly crumbles into the nightmare of ghettos or camps or fugitive hideouts. In the end, the survivor usually returns to the ruins of his former existence.

Nearly two decades after the liberation, "survival literature" began to appear, dramatizing the process by which civilized life had shriveled to bare existence and was then pitifully resurrected out of the ashes. Most of these novels have been written by women, and whereas this could be sheer coincidence, the predominance of women as writers and as characters in A-bomb literature as well[1] suggests a significant trend, especially insofar as such literature is predicated on the primacy of biological survival; two of the salient events in the concentration camp fiction are the birth of a child in the camp in one novel and the resumption of the survivor's menstrual cycle in another.

As in other novels of incarceration, a distinction should be made between the *survivor* and the *victim* on the one hand, and between the *survivor* and the *hero* on the other. The survivor (or would-be survivor—in this case the fortuity of actual survival is less significant than the psychological attitudes which determine behavior) is one who resists his condition as a victim; unlike the characters in the fiction of concentrationary realists such as Borowski and Hilsenrath, he refuses to be defined by the norms of the concentrationary universe. As Terrence Des Pres writes, in a seminal essay on the survivor-figure in the works of Camus, Solzhenitsyn and Malamud, "to be a victim is to suffer death in life, and it is this condition that the survivor would transcend." The resistance to victimhood entails not only a strategy for personal survival but also a code of morals, "for a man may live in more than one way, at his own or at others' expense. In extremity, that is, survival involves moral choice." The decisions based on his exercise of moral freedom are what distinguishes what Des Pres calls the "human" from the "Darwinian" survivor;[2] in a phrase he borrows from Solzhenitsyn, "the wolfhound is right and the cannibal wrong."[3]

It is not even necessary to recall some of the characters in Borowski's fiction in order to visualize the victim as cannibal or to call attention to the subtle distinction between cannibal and wolfhound; within the survivalist genre itself there are characters who come to adopt a Darwinian, or even cannibalistic, strategy for self-preservation.[4] And the temptations are never entirely overcome, even for the "human" survivor, who is constantly in danger of being compromised in his humanity beyond the point of no return. Whatever he did, the *Häftling* could not avoid some adjustment of pre-Holocaust ethics to his present reality; as one psychiatrist put it, "there is reason to believe that a person who fully adhered to all the ethical and moral standards of conduct of civilian life on entering the camp in the morning, would have been dead by nightfall."[5] The ability to accommodate ambiguous and relativistic attitudes without relinquishing a moral code altogether seems to have been the single most important factor in determining the quality, if not the duration, of survival in the concentrationary universe.

The distinction between the survivor and the hero derives both from the celebration in contemporary literature of the "antihero" and from the quality of death in the concentrationary universe as anonymous, ubiquitous and unceremonialized. Stephen Spender and others have pointed out that the expiatory death of the martyred hero is no longer a model for the Holocaust writer:

> The idea of the death of millions of people being a subject for poetry threatens a tradition in which tragedy concentrates on the suffering of one symbolic, exalted victim—the crucified hero—with whom audience or readers identify and in whom they recognize their own deepest sense of what is terrible. For there to be tens of thousands of tragic heroes would be to submerge Oedipus, Hamlet and Lear in massive anonymity; and the anonymous victim is, in the Western tradition, no subject for tragedy.[6]

In a society no longer sustained by the assurances that death is a corridor to salvation, in a universe in which, since the individual counts for nothing, his death cannot possibly be sacrificial or exemplary—in a universe created solely for the purpose of manufacturing death, dying is the ultimate capitulation to the system. The struggle to stay alive is the accretion of small acts of defiance; "within a landscape of total disaster," says Des Pres, "mere existence is miraculous."[7]

Beyond the popular novels that decorate Holocaust history with a symmetry of heroes and villains, an occasional serious work does exalt heroic action, the grand gesture of defiance, within the terms of classical tragedy, or adapt the Christian model of the sacrificial victim.[8] But for the most part the hero in Holocaust literature has been reduced to the dimensions of a survivor and his acts to the minimal gestures of self-preservation. And self-preservation which does not entail the total relinquishing of one's psychological and moral sanity is by no means an easy task.

Although the struggle for survival may take similar forms under different systems of oppression and in the literature that issues from them, leading to a reading of the literature as a collective record of response to the terrors of modern totalitarianism, important distinctions between the Nazi and Soviet concentration camps have informed the imaginative reconstruction of each experience. Though nearly equal in the perniciousness and scope of their operation, the camps were established to serve different purposes: the Soviet penal camps were set up primarily for internal political reasons, and the casualties are a function of a despotic policy of political homogenization; the Nazi extermination camps, on the other hand, were established as an international system to implement an explicit policy of genocide as part of a vision of a world order based on biological principles. As a result, the relationship between the concentrationary and the nonconcentrationary world which determines the survivor's prospects for the future is significantly different: the Soviet camps exist largely on the periphery of a self-perpetuating society, and their inmates are an integral part of—and even a threat to—the system, whereas the Nazi camps were the final instrument in the total destruction of a separate civilization. If he survives, the Soviet prisoner usually has a family or at least a community to refer to and return to; the Jewish survivor who returns from the camps or from his years as a fugitive has no place to go. The moment of return and the "afterlife" of the survivor are central themes in the Holocaust fiction under consideration.

An Estate of Memory, by Ilona Karmel, is a monumental story of the struggle for survival of three Jewish women—Barbara Grünbaum, Tola Ohrenstein and Aurelia Katz—and a girl, Alinka, incarcerated together in a concentration camp. The narrative, which alternately emanates from the consciousness of each of the four, traces their growing dependence on each other, the tensions and tendernesses in their relationships, their conspired efforts to facilitate the birth of a child when one of them turns out to be pregnant, and their successful attempt to smuggle the infant out of the camp. Only the baby and the girl are destined to survive the last convulsions of the Holocaust, but the concerted effort is perhaps the most moving account of the temptations, the devotions, the sacrifices, and the breakdowns in the fragile network of group survival in concentration camp literature.

A trilogy of French novels by Anna Langfus constructs a more relentless picture of the life-preserving instincts of the fugitive and the postwar nightmares of the survivor. *The Whole Land Brimstone* is the story of a young woman's minimal endurance of the war years under the pseudonym of "Maria," and the gradual stripping away of all the affective relations which anchored her life to this world: the death of her parents and finally, after a prolonged struggle, of her husband. Her futile return to her family home and the unutterable despair that attends it conclude this bleak novel. Its sequel, *The Lost Shore,* commences in that timeless aftermath of the Holocaust where the first novel left off, and traces the aimless wanderings of the anaesthetized survivor, accompanied only by the ghosts of her former life, through the streets of postwar Paris. Her association with an older man, which in the beginning affords her only financial security and minimal physical comfort, and the moments of abandon shared with a group of children on a resort-town beach ignite the slow fire of a return of emotive energies. The third novel, *Saute, Barbara,* is a variation on the theme of *The Lost Shore:* it traces the wanderings of another Jewish survivor, Michael,

through liberated Germany to Paris, haunted by memories of his
escape from the house in which his wife and daughter were about to be
shot to death by the Nazis. In the course of his guilt-ridden odyssey he
abducts a young German girl who reminds him of his daughter; he
attempts both to resurrect his daughter and to take revenge on the
murderers by kidnaping the girl and inducing in her the fear that must
have plagued his own child in the moments before her death. After
allowing himself to be lulled into ordinary pursuits, including a job and
an intended marriage, he escapes from his own normalizing impulses,
leaves his work and his fiancée, and restores the little girl to her home.
The moment of separation from this new companion is, as in the case of
Maria's forced exit from the old man's life in *The Lost Shore,* marked
by a show of emotion which reveals that a thin layer of scar tissue has
grown over the survivor-wounds.

   Tell Me Another Morning, by Zdena Berger, is, like Langfus's
novels, a first-person narrative—a fictional medium that preserves the
immediacy and authenticity of the memoir (all of these novels are
versions of autobiography) and attests to the ultimate survival of the
narrator ("and I only am escaped alone to tell thee"). Berger's narrative is, in addition, interspersed with passages which describe the same
events objectively, in the manner of a historical chronicle, adding a
broader and more detached perspective to the experiences which are
otherwise filtered through one center of consciousness. *Tell Me
Another Morning* is another story of the survival, first in the ghetto and
then in two concentration camps, of a young woman, Tania, and her
two friends. The inevitable return to her childhood home, to find it
expropriated by strangers, is accompanied in this instance by a renewal
of the life forces, symbolized by the sudden onset of menstrual bleeding.

   The uniformity of the concentrationary system and the fact that
these novels follow the basic contour of historical events account for
certain structural similarities in the fiction written in different languages by survivors of different ghettos and camps. I have already
discussed the phenomenon of linguistic mobility which the displacement of the war years precipitated. All of the writers under consideration write in adopted tongues: Zdena Berger, who was born in Czecho-
slovakia, and Ilona Karmel, who was born in Poland, write in English;
Polish-born Anna Langfus writes in French. Another aspect of
the uniformity of the experience is the fact that although each of
these authors exhibits a different degree of religious or ethnic consciousness, there is no external frame of reference to which the victim's fate is related; the essence of the survivalist perspective is the
confrontation between the naked self, stripped of all civilized supports,

and the machine which would dehumanize before destroying him. The Holocaust evolves as a condition of total anomy; for the character in a survivor-novel, who does not associate his suffering with the collective ordeal, the ultimate assault is on his integrity and dignity and his very right to exist as an individual. The assimilated Jew whose Jewish identity is more a function of Nazi legislation than of personal confession experiences incarceration as a violation of the most elemental right of self-definition.

Much critical attention has been paid to the abuses of the self that modern forms of collectivization have committed—of which the concentration camp is the most extreme example. Erich Kahler's literary and philosophical "inquiry into the transformation of man," *The Tower and the Abyss,* focuses on the debasement and disintegration of the individual who has been viewed as the ultimate repository of meaning in Western civilization. Frederick Hoffman devotes the last section of his study *The Mortal No* to the "search for a new basis of self-definition" in light of the violence that has defiled the individual and deprived him of traditional visions of grace and immortality: "The self is, in this view of it, the beginning, the source, and the responsible center of all revaluations of life and of the death that superintends and haunts it."[9]

It is in this tradition that we can locate survivalist fiction; the experience which has been characterized minimally as the search for a "miserable crust of moldy bread" is retrospectively portrayed by the survivalist writer as a struggle to maintain integrity of self, rather than as an ego-shattering submission to the system, as in concentrationary realism, or as participation in a collective history, as in the documentary or the Hebraic literature. There are, it is true, isolated instances in the survival literature of ritual responses to personal crises—Tania, for instance, anticipating imminent death, utters the doxological *Shema Yisrael* in a kind of atavistic cry exhumed from the depths of her soul. But, like Borowski and Hilsenrath, the writers of survival novels represent for the most part aspects of universal human responses to concentrationary oppression. When the assimilated Jew, represented especially in Langfus's novels, for whom only a circle of family and friends mediated between himself and the state, was deprived first of statehood and then of family, he could draw only upon whatever psychological resources he had in order to cope with the situation. This anomic condition was exacerbated for the Jew in hiding by the assumption of a false identity; a recurrent theme in this literature is the confusion of identities among fugitive Jews, and the fear that one's real self would somehow be lost in the process of survival. The actual costs of such a strategy are only gradually registered, however; the narrator of Langfus's *The Whole Land Brimstone* catches herself giving her false name to the prisoner in the cell next to hers when there is no longer any reason for doing so:

> Why give him my assumed name? To exercise caution now was ridiculous. Why, then? Perhaps to persuade myself that all this was happening only to this Maria who was not really me. And why shouldn't everyone act out this sinister comedy under a false guise? When the curtain fell on the final massacre the actors would walk away safe and sound, turning their backs on the sham corpses of the characters whom they had been playing. It was appearance that suffered and died, and their sufferings and deaths were not real. [Pp. 222–23]

That it is, finally, impossible for the survivor to "walk away safe and sound" is manifested in the fact that throughout the entire novel the reader never discovers what Maria's real name was and that in the postwar sequel, *The Lost Shore,* she appears still as Maria. Again, the restoration of identity may prove more difficult for the assimilated Jew, deprived of national citizenship yet unattached to the Jewish collective, whose definition of self has no social reference.

One of the basic premises, then, of this genre is the absence of a sense of any larger order to which the suffering of the individual can be related. In this respect I would draw another distinction between the Holocaust fiction of survival and other categories of survival novels. The fiction of Solzhenitsyn and other *zek* ("prisoner") writers from Soviet Russia is cast not only in terms of the personal endurance and survival of the protagonists, but also in terms of the ideological and social ramifications of their plight. And even in what appears to be the paradigmatic survivor-novel, Malamud's *The Fixer,* which dwells on the suffering of the Jew entrapped in a blood libel and incarcerated in Tzarist Russia, the source of the character's strength and ability to persevere is his growing sense of mission on behalf of the Jewish community whose fate could depend on the outcome of his trial.[10] By contrast, the Holocaust victim fighting for survival as represented in the literature considered here knows that he has been abandoned, forgotten and, even before his death, banished from the land of the living. The will to live and to somehow preserve the human image is, then, a dialectic between self and soul; the prisoner who has no external moral or social authority to whom he must give account is responsible for his deeds only to himself and to the desperate hope that perhaps he will survive—and then he will have saved something of the human spirit for "later."

First Stage: Collapse of the "Ancien Régime"

The survivor-novel usually begins in the time of preternatural quiet just before the German occupation and establishes the reality of the world which will furnish, during imprisonment, the material for memory and a vision of return. The process by which civilized life disintegrates is a gradual one, an initiation for the reader as well as for the protagonist which concentrationary realism, by the very limits of its horizon at the barbed wire fence, does not provide. Occasionally, in a novel such as Karmel's *An Estate of Memory,* the narrative commences in the camp itself, *in medias res:* "On that day everyone in the camp was painted."[11] But the author provides several other distancing effects such as the narrative use of the past tense to convey the provisional reality of the concentrationary universe. By contrast, in a novel of another genre, Jorge Semprun's *The Long Voyage,* the relentlessly continuous present tense serves to absolutize the experience by eliminating past and future and establishing the concentrationary universe *sub specie aeternitatis:* "There is the cramming of the bodies into the boxcar, the throbbing pain in the right knee . . ."[12]

The *ancien régime* is delineated in the survival novels largely through physical properties, and the stripping away of the objects of a comfortable, civilized life marks the gradual denuding of the human soul of all its material and affective supports. The focus on *things* in this literature signifies a palpable foothold in a world from which the individual is about to be banished and measures the transformation of his ambience. In Langfus's *The Whole Land Brimstone,* the disintegrative phase in the lives of a cultured, assimilated Jewish family living in the suburbs of Warsaw is inaugurated by the crash of their chandelier as the first bombs hit their town. And on the Polish manor where the young Jewess Barbara Grünbaum presides in Karmel's novel, the transfiguration of the known world is represented by the violation of rural tranquility as the drone of an enemy plane voices over the drone of a bee and a drop of honey metamorphoses into a bomb: "her guests . . . were sitting down to breakfast, their voices blending drowsily with a bee's drone. The drone grew loud, such a stillness fell; only in the corner the radio kept talking. She sat down. From a knife placed carelessly across the bowl a drop of honey hung, elongated like a pendant. She looked at it. The radio spoke on. And when the drop fell, this was war" (p. 78). It is perhaps an exaggerated preoccupation with the objects of this world which characterizes the self-indulgent young women who are the central protagonists in these novels. They relinquish only with great difficulty their property and accept with even greater difficulty their diminished status. These ingénues embody in the extreme the naive confidence in the perpetuation of present reality, the lack of desire or ability to prepare for contingencies, and the utter disbelief in the face of the trials that await them, which characterized the attitudes of most of the Jews of Eastern Europe. In *Tell Me Another Morning* Tania exhibits these qualities in her sulky musings as the family is fleeing by car from Prague before the advancing Germans:

> I was in my bed before. Before the old newspaper sellers shouted in the streets. Everything will be different now. I feel I would like to stop it before it happens.
> I am very sleepy now. The skin of my cheek against the cold window glass; I will sleep. Maybe I will wake up in my bed, and there will be no war.[13]

Nearly identical language marks the resistant attitude of the spoiled young bride who is the heroine of *The Whole Land Brimstone*. Shortly before the expected arrest of her family, she reviews the scenes of her childhood as if to fix the *status quo ante* in her mind as a buffer against the unknown: "that night I followed [my memories] back through childhood as one takes a final look at a familiar landscape before leaving it forever" (p. 14). She dwells for a moment on—of all things—her chamber pot, that vessel of the pampered nights of her childhood and young womanhood, carried even to her conjugal bed by the faithful Nanny. That night, following the crash of the chandelier presaging the shattering of all her porcelain and crystal dreams, young Maria cannot bring herself to thrust that "squat white piece of chinaware" under her bed, as she was in the habit of doing. "Not that night. I could not take my eyes off it, and I found its appearance at once mocking and reassuring" (p. 13).

Gradually, one by one, the artifacts of the familiar world are violated and destroyed. The attachment to objects often constitutes both an obstacle to the kind of practical adjustments a would-be survivor has to make and the symbol of an entire network of values, and the diminution or violation of the tangible world is emblematic of the step-by-step delamination of all the layers of civilized existence: during their search for valuables in the home of Tola Ohrenstein's family, one SS officer catches his heel on "a golden thread trailing from the embroidered lion on the prayer-shawl bag." The officers order Mr. Ohrenstein to wrap himself in the shawl and to pray—for their amusement (p. 52). A comparable moment occurs a short time later, in the camp. The guards enter the barracks looking for gold, and they order all the women to stretch out their hands to ensure that no wedding bands have been overlooked:

> A thin band of gold caught the flashlight beam and a woman whined that the ring would not come off—after so many years it just would not.

"Really?" said the Lagerkommandant. "Then we shall
cut the finger off."

Smacking like an infant, the woman gnawed and chewed
at her finger. Then, just as the ring fell jingling on the black
ice, wind tore her shift up, and sallow, like a plucked hen,
her body stood out in the light. [P. 67]

Intimidated by threats of torture into betraying her wedding vows, the
woman is suddenly reduced from a wife to a whore.

The beloved objects are replaced by sinister objects such as tanks
and green uniforms, yellow badges and notices of curfews and deportations. The woman who clings to her picture of an ordered world
still refuses to comply or to adapt: "I went on desperately rejecting
everything that met my eye, everything that I heard" (p. 47), states
Maria as she tells of her family's relocation in the Warsaw Ghetto.
When the ordinance stipulating the wearing of yellow badges is posted,
Tania protests: "At first, when mother brought it home, I thought—I
will never wear it. I prefer to die" (p. 13). The changes which do
eventually take place not only in Tania's environment but also in her
response to it are marked by the succession of physical objects which
are the stations of her descent: a yellow star, a stone saint, a shower.
The "stone saint" is a statue of Saint Wenceslaus staring over Wenceslaus Square with sightless eyes, ignoring the people below who are
disappearing into ghettos and camps but who leave the streets "un-
changed" (p. 20). The shower is the *memento mori* in a world which
has been utterly transformed. It is significant, though, that for a mind
such as Tania's, intent upon naming the properties of a changing world,
there are still certain objects and places which are never identified—the
ghetto and the camp and the camp "doctor" are the most salient
examples—and this may be seen as a meaningful act of exclusion, of
protest against the naming of spheres which cannot be assigned a place
in the created world.[14]

Yet even as the things of this world metamorphose into something
else and whole other areas of experience remain shrouded in the horror
of silence, a glimpse at a familiar article can touch off memories that
remind the sufferer of former times; just as a loaf of bread or a doll
offers momentary comfort to the characters in the fiction of Borowski
and Hilsenrath, so here the object catalyzes memories and a reaffirmation of the bonds with home. Under the precarious protection of a
German soldier, and hidden in a whorehouse (the home of the social
deviant provides, it seems, a natural refuge for a new breed of outcasts), Maria unpacks her suitcase; she takes out a "nightdress dating
from before the war—one of those frothy silk-and-lace nightdresses
that girls' dreams are made of" (p. 105). It is true that in Anna Langfus's

novels, as in Hilsenrath's *Night,* such memories are only rarely admissible and provide only momentary remission, and that the pain of loss outweighs the benefits derived from communing with the past. But even those who eventually lose hope cling long and hard to the remnants of their former lives, now shrunk to the dimensions of a small suitcase, now to a photograph. Later, the houses and buildings, the statues and gardens of one's hometown, the chamber pot, and even the nightdress and the photograph come to inhabit the "estate of memory," where they are hoarded by the would-be survivor, who has not surrendered herself entirely to the system, as signposts to guide the ultimate return. And even if she returns finally to find that there is nothing of her past left to help her redeem the future, memory has functioned as one of the two pillars which uphold the struggle for survival; the other is the ability to endure pain and humiliation.

Second Stage: Descent into the "Anus Mundi"

As she is evicted from her home and begins the journey that is to lead to death or minimal survival, the individual is quickly stripped not only of her material possessions but also of her standing in the world. Social distinctions rapidly evaporate and a new hierarchy of authority emerges in the concentrationary universe. The predator replaces the aristocrat in a system which is founded on the principle of mutual distrust and exploitation. The best example of this transformation is the story of Tola in Karmel's novel—Tola Ohrenstein, heiress to the wealth and prestige that her family had amassed as Cracow businessmen. At first she applies the principle of *gentillesse* that obtained in the civilized society in which she had been raised; she finds it beneath her dignity to peddle for food like the "'leeches,' the vendors whom she loathed" (p. 121). Slowly, however, she begins to understand the laws that operate in her new environment; her first act of peddling is the altruistic sacrifice of her own gold tooth to help support the group of four women with whom she has cast her lot. From that point on she serves the system with such fidelity that it eventually becomes clear that she has simply substituted one power structure for another. The process is gradual, as the sanctions of the former system are deeply ingrained.

But finally what has been a prostitution of self for the sake of the group crosses the line of altruism into Darwinian survivalism. After volunteering for and receiving the position of *Anweiserin* for her barracks—which entails the supervision and possibly the "selection" for deportation of the women under her command—she confronts her friend Barbara, who insists that "one must draw the line" even where such sacrifices of one's human dignity are made for the sake of

others. "I did it only for myself," Tola retorts, and then adds, "Why
do you look so nonplussed? Anything done for someone else is a
sacrifice, a noble deed; but try to do the same thing for yourself and the
sacrifice becomes a disgrace. Why? I too am someone; I've no contract
for survival, I too am afraid" (p. 342).

Once Tola has crossed the line, there is no turning back—at least not
until the very end when the author rescues her from the ultimate implications of her deeds. From the moment she becomes an *Anweiserin*
until that final moment, she collaborates with the murderers and becomes increasingly estranged from her companions until she disowns
them entirely. The deterioration of her character is signified first of all
by the loss of her sense of identity: "in the washroom, when she
looked into the broken mirror perched up on the pipe, the too-red
mouth it reflected, the large tired eyes struck her always as something
arbitrary, no longer hers" (p. 375). As in Hilsenrath's novel, the obliteration of self—and with it, of accountability—appears here as one of
the first signs of compliance of the victim with the system. Tola comes
to view herself, increasingly, as a *body* to be fed and cared for; her only
desires are for "safety" and "bread" (p. 381). Her actions are those of
the lowest, most predatory creature; in the final apocalyptic act of
nighttime ditch-digging which precedes the liberation, she lashes out at
the women with all the fury of a crazed animal: "Her stick struck, she
was sated; and already the blow had dropped into the dark, already she
was dashing on to the next blow, always like the first because she felt
empty as at first" (p. 423). Tola in the last convulsive moments before
the collapse of the concentrationary universe has become, like some of
the characters in Borowski's fiction, the perfect victim. Ironically, the
self-solicitude that originally motivated her actions has turned into
such total acquiescence in the system that there can be no survival
beyond its collapse; as rumors circulate about the imminence of the
war's end, Tola Ohrenstein—who has become nearly as powerful in the
concentration camp as her family was in Cracow—realizes that she is
now a creature unable to breathe outside of its element:

> Over—the war is over, Tola thought, and could not under-
> stand what this meant, as though for her, unable to see
> herself anywhere but here in this camp, there was no war. If
> the war is over there will be no work tonight, the trucks
> won't come again if it is over; the smell will lift. And now
> when she began to understand, panic gripped her; she must
> run, must find a place to be alone, at once, before everyone
> burst into a jubilant shout. [P. 403]

The gradual and psychologically plausible process of Tola's cooptation is reversed in the last hours of her life by a kind of sacramental act
of rebirth. As she collapses into the grave that the living had dug for

themselves during that long grueling night, she believes that she too is dying. And when she finally awakens, her soul as well as her body has been resurrected; like the primordial Adam she names the objects of this world as she emerges from the dust: "Whatever the hands touched were syllables which she made out and put together into words: grass was her first word, then earth, then stone; and what felt like a damp stone, what her fingers refused to touch, was an arm" (p. 433). Soon the salutary tears come—tears "for what had been done to her and for what she had done to those two with whom she would soon be together" (p. 433). She goes to them, to Barbara and Alinka (Aurelia, the fourth in their group, has died of typhus in the meantime) to try to save them or to share their death. And, in fact, she does succeed in saving Alinka, who is destined to be the only survivor among the four.

This restoration of Tola's humanity, with which the novel ends, is dramatically powerful even though it violates the psychological logic that has prevailed up to that point. It is a merciful attempt to save the protagonist from the abyss and it can be accomplished only by an act of "divine" intervention. Once Tola had decided that the other women would "pull her down" and that to ensure her survival she must go it alone, the last of the ethical constraints which still bound her to a small human community was severed. And since she exemplifies the character whose behavior is dictated by external authority, once set on a new course she had to follow the black road as far as it would take her. Only rarely in this literature, as in the reality of the camps, do we find an individual who retains the courage and the presence of mind to comply with the laws of the concentrationary universe only until he reaches the point of no return—and at the last moment to retreat and recover his soul. The other major character in Karmel's novel, Barbara, is prevented by visions of her own *largesse* from even embarking on that road—and, in fact, it is Barbara's studied altruism and her inability to "dirty her hands" that prompt Tola in the first place to defile herself for the sake of the group. The characters in the novels of Berger and Langfus never find themselves in the borderline situation which would test the limits of their humanity.[15]

"Human" Survival: The Search for Meaning
in a Meaningless Universe

We have seen, in the case of Tola, that efforts at self-preservation could change the character so radically that it could hardly survive the light of liberation day. Preservation of the spirit as well as the body is far more likely where the individual remains attached to a mutually sustaining group, even if the group comprises only one other person. The characters in most of the survival novels have at least one companion who for some period shares their struggle—and there are numerous occasions, such as illness or the long marches during which those who fall by the wayside are shot, when one member weakens and would surely perish were he not upheld by the others. The need for companionship is so great that "cousins" or "lovers" are frequently adopted—often sight unseen—across the fence that separates the men's and women's camps. Maria is sustained throughout the first part of her ordeal by the presence of her husband, Jan; after his death her minimal survival is secured by the various men who befriend her— although most of her will to live has died with Jan. The clearest expression of the strength that group solidarity affords is to be found in Karmel's novel: "The smell of damp wool lay over the barracks. From clothing spread out to dry, mud splashed down to the floor while they lay shivering in the cold. And when they huddled tighter, when their bodies, though each was frozen, lent a bit of warmth to one another, peace came over Barbara, as if this—to be still here, still together—was enough" (p. 212).

Yet companionship is not quite enough. In order to withstand the extreme moments of privation and temptation the individual must draw on resources which lie at the core of his being. In his essay "On Pain," Ernst Jünger contends that "in the great and cruel process of transformation which man is undergoing in our age the touchstone is pain and not value, pain which completely disregards all values." A person's worth, given such an assumption, should be measured in terms of his ability to confront and endure his pain by "establish[ing] distance" from it.[16] In the imaginative literature there are few examples of individuals who succeed in overcoming the tortures of the body and the degradation of the soul simply by attending to their pain. That is why the main character in Langfus's first two novels is so forlorn—because she is, ultimately, left with no reason to survive beyond the primitive instinct for self-preservation. Maria does learn to endure the pain of torture—even to welcome it as a diversion from her loneliness and bereavement; after a session with her torturers she paces her prison cell, nursing her smashed thumb as, in a normal world, she might have nursed her child: "The pain was suffocating underneath and struggling to get out. In the end it became intolerable. I got up and walked about, my good hand supporting my bad. The injured thumb rested on my shoulder like a baby's head. And I started groaning again, which seemed to calm and lull it. When I was too tired, I sat down and rocked myself as mothers do to send their children to sleep" (p. 211). Pain and filth become Maria's constant companions in prison, and her attention to them so occupies her days and mitigates her survivor-guilt that when the wounds have begun to heal and she is given a bath prior to being transferred from prison, she realizes that there is nothing worthwhile for which she would trade her pain and her dirt: "I had the feeling that I was now more vulnerable. As though I had started back towards the human condition, in which there would not be room both for me and for this pain" (pp. 238–39).

In the psychiatric literature survivors attest to the salutary effects of memory and fantasy in the struggle to overcome pain and degradation. Viktor Frankl maintains that it is the "will-to-meaning" that can provide the strength to persevere. Attributing his own endurance of a particularly difficult moment in the camp to a sudden mental vision of his wife, and claiming to have encouraged other inmates to dwell on those things—their loved ones, their work—which had given meaning to their prewar lives, he explains the beneficial effect of such memories:

> This intensification of inner life helped the prisoner find a refuge from the emptiness, desolation and spiritual poverty of his existence, by letting him escape into the past. When given free rein, his imagination played with past events.... Their world and their existence seemed very distant and the spirit reached out for them longingly: In my mind I took bus rides, unlocked the front door of my apartment, answered my telephone, switched on the electric lights.[17]

In the fiction, visions borrowed from other realms of experience serve both to structure the narrative and to measure the distance that the soul has managed to preserve from the reality that the body is enduring. As we saw in the preceding chapter, memory is not functional for Darwinian, accommodational survival, and it is seldom admitted into the minds of Langfus's characters, Maria and Michael, since it contains the tainted riches of a life which is not only past, but irretrievably lost. Maria explains the process of functional amnesia to herself even as she is experiencing it:

> I told myself that people in our position were wrong to delve into their pasts. There were too many things that revived one's taste for living. One responded to the glow of familiar sensations, of feelings that fired one's spirit and led to futile rebellion; whereas in fact one had to tell oneself that nothing in one's past had ever been of the slightest importance, that fear and gloom were man's natural lot, that once plucked from the easy life to which he had grown accustomed, he lost even the feelings that he had thought most real and most profound, becoming a malignant, panic-stricken beast with nothing to spur him on but the blind instinct of self-preservation. Logically he should have aspired only to peace. And if it were death that was to supply it, why should he not wish for death? [P. 224]

Ultimately, that is, the "blind instinct of self-preservation," accommodational survival, may metamorphose into self-destruction.

The same thing comes to be true of Tola as she becomes more and more deeply immersed in the mire of accommodation. At first she combs her past for memories that may be useful in helping her to endure her own pain and alleviate that of her sick companion, Aurelia: "Of her past only what could now be put to use remained: her sickly childhood stood by, helping her to read the signs of thirst or pain, and her mother, showing what comfort there was still to give" (pp. 294–95). But eventually, as she becomes tainted, other memories of the past, which might have served as a foothold into the future, come to serve instead as a reproach, because they invoke the moral norms as well as the comforts of her former life. And since she has violated those norms in this world, the pleasures and the beauties of that other world—once free for the asking—are now unobtainable. In Tola's imaginary "game with future and past," the future survivors are a multiplied version of her own debased character: that they have forfeited their identities through cooptation becomes obvious when the "mirror suggested that something had been misplaced: a face, their own—for it was clear that this puffy blotch could not be theirs." "They" make up their face and decide to "go away alone to the country, into the mountains. And the mountains were beautiful, and the waterfalls. *Yet, a pane of glass seemed to enclose this beauty like goods too costly ever to be reached*" (emphasis mine). These imaginary survivors return to the station full of fear for the "child" who was left behind, and "holding it tightly, they knew that here was a part of them, here one for whom they would give their all—if the time ever came and the need.

"And the time had come, and the need" (pp. 386–87).

Tola is just one of those thousands who, when the time came, and the need, did not have the courage to give their all. Her memories of an innocent, protected childhood abruptly suspended can no longer provide an avenue of return: "It was so early still; it was suddenly so late" (p. 386).

Barbara Grünbaum, on the other hand, is the archetype of the "human" survivor. She is sustained as much by her memory as by her solicitude for her companions—and when she talks about "after the war," it is in terms of her life before the war, "for her the future being the past transplanted" (p. 120). Gradually versions of Barbara's dream of return—of the embrace of her husband Stefan (a Polish soldier who, she presumes, is still alive), the reception of the servants, and even the furnishings in her manor ("the gold-rimmed cups jingling as a carriage rolled into the driveway; the lace that sun wove upon the velvety surface of the piano; or the credenza, smooth, a bit sticky under her touch, like the loaves of honeycake with which it was scented" [p. 230])—are adopted by the three other women (even by Tola, for a time) as they come to accept Barbara as their protector and guide into the future. (It should be borne in mind, however, while acknowledging Barbara's remarkable strengths, that she is the only one of the four who has—or at least can believe she has—someone and some place to return to.) The effect of memory on Barbara and on the others, to the extent that they adopt her method of coping, is to relativize present reality and provide an avenue of mental escape. Her daydreams function much like the recital of musical or literary texts that Primo Levi and Josef Bor testify to: they undermine the total sovereignty of the present.

The constant temptation to surrender to concentrationary reality, and the salutary function of memory in extricating one from that reality, can be measured in the thought images which signify despair or hope, submission or resistance in Karmel's novel. At one point Barbara is overwhelmed by the sense of the inevitability of her own death—untimely and hideous; her fear takes the form first of an instrument of torture ("a wire seemed to push through her head") and then of a monstrous creature (a "huge snail...[was] sucking her in"). These images, reminiscent of the "imprisoned" metaphors of the concentrationary realists, give way to a brutally concrete vision of concentrationary death:

> Again the snail would sway [rendering the victim totally passive], again she would know nothing until one night she would see herself—barefoot, in rags, her shoes, her clothes gone for bread, the bread too gone, only barrels left that she would lick out, like the Chinaman who had swollen from hunger, then was shot. And then...
> She bit into her fist. The pain did not help, she saw it: the O.D. men pulling at the mud-caked feet—then the crate— then the long wavering tracks. [P. 219]

Barbara's attempt at self-mutilation (biting her fist) does not provide an outlet for her mental anguish. Finally she resolves simply to sit quietly, to shrink like her shadow on the wall, and to wait. As she is sitting the images of home come unbidden to rescue her from her stupor: "A gray haze was rising around her, and her head felt like an apple with its crown pared off; upon the exposed nerves dust was sifting like sugar into the hollow where the core had been." Although the simile is meant to suggest pain no less intense than the pain represented by the wire pushing through her head (it is the pain that the pared and cored apple must, as it were, feel), the image itself provides a way out of pain; by transferring her identification from the suffering apple to the eater (herself, in better times), she can overcome her present fears: "Apples. When had she eaten such apples, sweet with sugar, with cinnamon and cloves? On the eve of her going away, Marta had baked them for her..." (p. 218). The memory has taken her outside of her suffering self just far enough to know that "she could never shrink." The process is completed when she finally asks herself, "What shall I do?" galvanizing the forces that will ultimately lead to self-preserving action (p. 219).

There are many other instances of Barbara's near-surrender embodied in acquiescent rhetoric and of the emancipation effected through memory and fantasy. We have seen that the compliant victim—Ranek or Tola—loses his identity in the process of accommodation; in clinging still to his or her memory of a distinct past and projecting it into the future, the "human" survivor preserves a sense of self. The narrator of *Tell Me Another Morning* nearly loses her hold on the past and on the future but clings desperately to her name as the last bastion of identity in the suspended present of the camp:

> Sometimes on Sunday I think of the future. I see it only as another, better camp, with more food and two blankets. The past is almost gone now. It is as if there has been no distant past. I think of the near past, the past of camps. But even that does not hold together; events unravel, and places and times pull apart. *On Sundays I repeat my name,* so as not to forget. I say it to myself: Tania Andresova, born...age... *Each Sunday I regain my identity before becoming again a blank face among other blank faces,* a pair of feet sinking in snow, a mouth gulping down a bowl of soup. [Pp. 149–50, emphases mine]

Yet memory is not only the recall of specific experiences but also a vocabulary of possible being in the world; the metaphoric language which affirms certain generic patterns of behavior in the normal world is as much a safety valve from the pressures of present reality as are specific memories. The smallest act of altruism on the part of the inmates in Karmel's novel, the tiniest improvement in their situation, is celebrated by a metaphor suggesting domestic tranquility or the pleasures of normal civilian life: when the women are transferred from the miserable Cracow camp to a camp where conditions appear to be better, the difference is signified by the fact that they are made to march not in a column but "in a leisurely crowd, *like tourists stopping at whatever delighted their eyes*" (in this case, a full moon, rows of bent bushes, clean, untrodden snow). The narrator continues: "The air was quiet except when at times—*like a hostess who, guests gone, sets her home aright and then rests*—the breeze stirred, erased the footprints, restored the road to its damask smoothness, then ceased" (pp. 103, 104, emphases mine). Later, in that same camp, and under deteriorating conditions, Tola and Barbara are among a group of women who receive a clandestine handout of soup from inmates of another sector, Werk A, who have more to eat: "Under the billows of black smoke uncoiling from the huge chimney, a crowd milled, calling, waving from behind the barbed wires. *As in a home tables for refreshments are set out at the guests' arrival,* so here stones, here bricks and planks were being piled, and the Werk A people climbed upon them so that the food they had brought could be reached over the wires" (p. 195, emphasis mine). The incongruity of tenor and vehicle is immediately apparent: a few bowls of murky soup thrust at ragged skeletons "under the billows of black smoke uncoiling from the huge chimney" become "refreshments" set out for guests in a genteel home. Such similes are in effect an attempt to establish not likeness but aspiration, to resist barbarism by clutching at vestiges of civilized behavior. At times images that suggest tranquility and normalcy are employed almost like sentries to deny grim reality access to the imagination: rumors of an imminent "selection" touch off in Barbara a "carefree mood *as of one who, suitcases packed, ticket in pocket, would soon be on the go*" (p. 201, emphasis mine).

Even illness—always so grotesque and almost always fatal in the camps—is tamed and dignified by the fantasy of civilized amenities. As Aurelia is convalescing after childbirth (a condition which was equivalent, in its dangers and usually tragic consequences, to a terminal illness), she takes a short walk past the barracks, leaning on Barbara: "She looked like all the other women after childbirth, as they stroll through the hospital corridor, the strongest visitor lending his arm in support, the others following, a hushed, watchful retinue" (p. 272). Later, when Alinka is suffering from typhus, Barbara grants the illness all the attentions of a proper bedside manner:

> Her hand meanwhile smoothing out the paper sheets, she transformed the bunk into a sickroom where the patient rests among flowers and lace, and the doctor into the great Warsaw specialist whose every word would be obeyed like an oracle's.
>
> And already he was growing into his role: "Good morning," he boomed, flicking a speck off the threadbare corduroy. "Good morning, and how is our young lady today?"
>
> Half dead, half bald, the young lady lay there... [Pp. 391–92]

Barbara's struggle, in thought and action, is against the two "tempters"—bestiality and death. Toward the end, when she works as an orderly in the camp infirmary, she marshals all her powers against those two. She beats the women who litter or who fail to wash, or who fight with each other. She struggles to keep out the devil and the beast of prey, to stem the chaos, to preserve a semblance of humanity. "Pigs! Are you?" she screams at the women who are locked in combat over a crumb of bread or a place at the stove; they shriek and pounce and claw at one another until suddenly her voice and her broom stop them and restore their identity: "'Quiet!' and the broom swung *until at last the solid mass broke up into women, the one gaping mouth into faces* startled as though they had wakened from an evil dream" (p. 395, emphasis mine).

The struggle against the temptations of death, the serenity of surrender, is much more difficult—and when the calm, satiated look comes into the eyes of one of her patients Barbara knows death has won another round.

The key to human survival, as it is represented here, lies in maintaining one's identity and humanity, one's "rebellion," in Camus's terms, even when there are no chances of changing or in any way altering the dire conditions in which one is condemned to live: "real freedom is an inner submission to a value which defies history and its successes."[18] In the end, the rebel may not succeed in preserving his own life, but at least he will not have become an accomplice to the murder of others.

In the broadly chronological structure of the survival novel the fact that there is a past engenders expectations of a future and serves to further mitigate and relativize the present. The cardinal sign of surrender is the relinquishment of that external frame of reference, signifying the obliteration of one's past and the disintegration of one's ego. Tola tries, very early, to escape her own feelings of bereavement, which can find no outlet in the concentrationary world of mass, unmourned deaths, by pretending that her parents never existed: "They had not been killed, they had simply never existed; she had always been alone—this camp, this bunk her only home, the only greeting of her mornings the hoarse 'All up!'" (p. 40).

The disorienting effect that an absence of *rites de passage* had upon the inmates of the ghettos and camps has already been noted in the fiction of the concentrationary realists. Those who acquiesced simply adopted the new measures of time: the morning reveille, the *Appel*, the soup ration. Those who resisted clung to whatever echoes of the world's clock reached them in their isolation. The Commandant of Treblinka had had the clock hands at the fake station house which stood at the entrance to the camp painted at an eternal 3 o'clock. Even nature, perennial illustrator of the passage of time, was denied access; in the absence of any vegetation, the seasons could be marked only by the fluctuations in temperature: "Until the first days of October the warm weather had stayed on and, since in the camp where nothing grew nothing could wither, it seemed as if the summer would last forever." Yet when the winter winds come the inmates take note of time's passing, sighing with bitterness that another season has elapsed, bringing no change, and yet sustained by the "undeniable hope which new air, new sky always holds out." Finally the camp commandant grants official status to the new season: "As if the Lagerkommandant wished to bestow a touch of autumn color upon the camp, the barracks were painted a dull yellow-brown." But the "survivor" has already celebrated the change and continues to find ways to express her resistance: Barbara's favorite place of refuge in the camp is a secluded spot close to the wires; tall pines stand on the other side of the fence, "their overhanging branches smuggling in the contraband scent of pine needles and of cones" (pp. 68–69, 189).

The most significant event in Karmel's novel, which affirms both the normal life cycle and faith in the future, is the birth of Aurelia's baby. It is an event which to each of these motherless and childless women symbolizes, if only briefly, the regeneration of all her unborn and her dead (p. 308). Evoking a time when mothers all over Eastern Europe—in bunkers, in attics and sheds, in the forests and most certainly in ghettos and camps—were reduced to suffocating their own babies in a desperate attempt to save their own or their families' lives, the birth and preservation of this baby represent acts of resistance and faith no less miraculous or courageous than the uprisings in ghettos and camps that are celebrated in the novels of heroism. And when these women manage to smuggle the child out of the camp, "that was how 'later' began" (p. 276).

Theodore Mundstock: "A Survivor of the Concentration Camp of the Mind"

In concluding the discussion of this phase of the survivor-novel, I would mention briefly the novel by Ladislav Fuks, *Mr. Theodore Mundstock,* which in theme, language, and structure bears all the markings of the genre. In one important sense this Czech novel actually represents the consummate execution of the form, as it is an exercise in the *imagination* of survival.[19] All the elements of trial, torture, and endurance have been distilled of historical particularity and appropriated as challenges to human behavior in extremity. It is an affirmation of faith and moral strength born of utter solitude and the clear anticipation of the full horror of the actual events.

Theodore Mundstock is a former clerk in the rope business who, with the Nazi invasion of Prague, has lost his job and is losing all of his friends to deportation and certain death. The novel spans a six-month period before the arrival of his own summons, during which Mundstock, through a series of grueling exercises, prepares himself for life in a concentration camp. The narrative contrasts the appearance of a victim with the mettle of a survivor by alternating between an external and an internal perspective: to the people on the street, Mundstock is merely "an elderly man hurrying along in a worn and dusty old coat with the six-pointed yellow star, hands in his pocket and head bent forward." But the omniscient narrator insists that "if any of the passers-by had had sharp enough ears they might have heard him whispering like tiny rustling leaves, murmuring like young wine, whistling like a dancing clarinet, chiming like a bell." His inner strength and joy are the attitudes of one who has just decided that he "would be saved." His reasoning follows meticulously from the primary question he has posed for himself: "Who could survive the concentration camp?"

> And the first methodical answer which came to his mind did not just come to his mind but was methodically thought out; it was as follows:
>   The man who went about things sensibly, with a logical method.
>   The man who was thoroughly, properly prepared for everything in a logically planned manner.[20]

The man, in other words, who adopted the insanity of the concentrationary universe as the foundation upon which to build a sane, logical, moral response.[21]

The attitude that Mundstock appropriates as a guarantee of survival is predicated on the "understanding and thorough comprehension of reality, at the same time stripping it of all fantasy, illusion and invention" (p. 116). Equipped with the knowledge—and the courage to face it—of the fate that awaits deported Jews, he begins by training himself to perform the primary tasks that will be demanded of him in the concentrationary universe: he practices holding his suitcase so that its weight will not sap his energies; he sleeps on his ironing board to accustom his body to the hard, narrow bunk that will be assigned him on his arrival in the camp; he hacks away at the wall in his apartment to prepare himself for hard labor in the quarries; he acquires several sets of false teeth to be able to produce the proper physical response (teeth falling out) when subjected to torture; he even rehearses a threatened execution by a squad of Nazis. And then, only a few days before the summons arrives for both himself and Simon Sterns, son of his close friends and the only one of his acquaintances still remaining in the town, Mundstock determines to teach Simon the method of survival which he has devised. His earlier delusions of collective salvation and of his own messianic role finally shrink to the efforts of a "human" survivor to save one other life, that of his young friend. In the final scene, as Mundstock approaches the roundup site, he glimpses Simon from afar and is about to cross the street to join him and the others— when he is run over and killed by a German military truck. The irony of Mundstock's death lies of course in the arbitrary, accidental circumstances in which it occurs; in his last moments of consciousness Mundstock asks himself frantically, "what were we doing, just practising, we couldn't prepare ourselves for everything, it was all some terrible mistake I made..." (p. 213). Death is, after all, a "proud German master"—he will get his victim, one way or another.

And yet Mundstock's death is not simply the mockery of his method by the furious fates; he has left a legacy—the lessons and the love he bestowed on Simon—which increases the chances of the boy's survival. And for this he is rewarded with a Kaddish, the ceremony of death of which he would have been deprived in the camp: "an almost inaudible voice whispered 'Yisgadal veyiskadash shme rabbo...'" (p. 214). And at the moment of his death, Mundstock's shadow, Mon, who has been the companion of his imagination during the six months of his preparation, seems to merge with the boy (Si*mon*), as if the old man's soul had found its survival in the body of his young friend. The resolution of the novel, which escapes melodrama by the matter-of-fact simplicity, wry humor, and humanity of the narrative, affirms the most basic values of survivalism even in the face of the death of the would-be survivor.

The Survivor: After Liberation

When the liberation finally did come to those who were still alive to experience it, it was different from anything the inmates had imagined in their life-sustaining dreams. As soon as the war was over and the camps opened, the survivor emerged from the mass grave and a new phase of life began. Many of the survivor-novels end at this point, suggesting that, like Job, the liberated *katzetnik* would return to his home to begin the long, but inevitably successful, process of reconstruction. And yet, for those surviving Jews who did come back to reclaim the past, there was nothing left to reclaim. In some cases the landscape had been utterly transformed, and the desolation is delineated in the literature in the same physical terms that described the plenitude of the prewar world: "Some of the people got off the trains *where no towns were* and walked away under the bend of smoke" (emphasis mine).[22] In other cases, more horrible in a way, the physical landmarks remain; only the human landscape has been transformed.

The survivor traces his way back along the avenues of memory, following, like Theseus, the threads that he left behind him on his descent: "They moved again, men and women, looking for their city: for the stone horseman on the square, the bronze clock on the tower, the bridge watched over by the headless saint, the castle whose windows of blue crystal always reflected their wonder."[23] But when the survivor, Tania in this case, mounts the stairs of her childhood home, where the mauve curtains that her mother had hung still flutter from the window, it is to discover that the only traces of her past are these objects: "I should leave," she thinks to herself, as she is about to knock on the door; "I should not go in and have the curtains explained. I want them blown over the window of my past" (p. 240).[24]

And yet it is supposed that Tania, with the return of her life energies, will find the strength to begin anew. Alinka and the baby, the only survivors in Karmel's novel, are last seen recuperating in a convalescent home. This moment, these years, whatever time the survivor is granted after his liberation, what Solzhenitsyn calls the "small, additional, added-on life,"[25] is to be regarded as the ultimate reward for the struggle. Des Pres, in quoting from Solzhenitsyn's *Cancer Ward,* adds that for Kostoglotov, "to continue to live, even for a few months, is absolutely worth it," that for the survivor who has nothing, "nothing at all but this short reprieve, this extra life free and his own . . . this is everything."[26] Here again, however, there is a crucial distinction between the survivor of the Soviet camps and of the Nazi camps, and, among the Holocaust survivors, between the anomic survivor and the one who ultimately identifies with the collective destiny of the Jewish people. The Soviet prisoner, as I have already suggested, has a place of return. The Holocaust survivor whose Jewish identity—even though it may not have been an important resource during his struggle for survival—has somehow survived the stripping away of all other civilized supports may be able to dissolve his personal grief in the collective mourning and the collective regeneration of the Jewish people in their homeland. Of course even he can never completely lay his ghosts to rest. But it is the anomic survivor, who has absolutely nothing to return to and no one to mourn with, who remains completely alone with his ghosts and his guilt. Nearly every culture has its folk myths about the soul of an unburied corpse which haunts the living, seeking repose. In Jewish folk tradition the *dybbuk* is a wandering soul which gains entry into the body of a person whose sins make him vulnerable to demonic penetration.[27] The "homeless dead" of Hiroshima are said to have burdened the conscience of the survivors who could not grant them proper burial.[28] The survivor of the Nazi Holocaust who believes, justifiably or not, that his survival was secured at the expense of those nearest and dearest to him, falls easy prey to such visitations. A prolonged period of mourning, punctuated by guilt, often ensues, finding no outlet or resolution in the ritual acts usually associated with mourning.

Another major impulse that the survivor of the cataclysm of Auschwitz or Hiroshima carries with him into the postwar world is the desire to relive, repeatedly, the experience of survival, as the most fundamental and ultimate experience of his life. The term "Lazarene" for the Holocaust survivor, as defined by Jean Cayrol in his essay "Pour un romanesque lazaréen,"[29] pinpoints the most formative aspect of the survivor's experience: his encounter with death and the dead—but obscures the distinctions between the aura of grace and miracle that suffuses the gospel story of resurrection and the wretched state into which the Jewish survivor of Nazism emerges. As long as the prisoner or fugitive is engaged in the struggle for self-preservation, the life-wish predominates, even if life has been denuded of all civilized comforts. But, ironically, once he emerges from the struggle, victorious to all appearances, his life more often than not ossifies into an interminable state of thanatopsis. The most powerful and uncompromising fictional explorations of this theme are Anna Langfus's last two novels, *The Lost Shore* and *Saute, Barbara*.

The act of return which completes the survival phase and begins the postwar phase occurs at the end of *The Whole Land Brimstone*. Maria returns to her former home to find it, of course, occupied by new tenants; despondent, she descends to the basement in the predawn dark, and finding there a familiar trunk that had belonged to her nanny, she crawls on top of it and tries to rest, the burden of her survival summed up in the moment before sleep overtakes her: "I told myself that, up above, one of those countless days that I still had to live through must already be dawning" (p. 318).

The Lost Shore begins in the same mental state. Life for such a survivor, far from being the celebration with which Kostoglotov embraces his freedom, is but a succession of days lived through in a kind of emotional stasis. Nearly every action is performed out of habit—"I got up, a longstanding custom"[30]—and only the barest necessities are deemed worthy of exertion; in fact, those activities aimed at satisfying hunger and fatigue, which secured minimal survival in the concentrationary universe, are courted by the postwar refugee in an effort to keep the ghosts away: "I reflected that soon what little money I still had would have gone—soon I should be hungry again. Fundamentally, I was relying on hunger. I knew from experience that it could be a wholesome preoccupation, and one strong enough to make a victorious assault on all the things one harbours within one, without being able to free oneself of them" (p. 16).

Yet even the most essential functions are difficult to achieve

independently, and the survivor falls into a kind of lassitude, an emotional paralysis in which he allows himself to be acted upon, but hardly
ever acts. He has, as it were, lost his right to his own biography—in the
case of Maria, she has lost not only her family and her home but her
name as well; Michael, the narrator of *Saute, Barbara,* is known to us
only by his first name, as if there can be no more patronyms where
whole families have been obliterated. Maria lets Michel Caron arrange
her life; Michael allows himself to be manipulated into a job and almost
into a marriage. These are the living dead, the displaced persons who
have no foothold on this earth. Maria spends the days after her liberation following people at random, as if to acquire a private destiny by
attaching herself to someone who has a name and a home: "Each of
them filled the universe with his or her person. I would trail humbly
after them, expecting the unworkable miracle from the first person I
bumped into" (p. 15). But she knows that her life has no substance; she
hovers above the world of the living like a shade from Hades. As she
sits down in a subway she looks around at her traveling companions:
"Generally, they did not see me—I already belonged to a different
species" (p. 10). Later she says to her benefactor, Michel Caron, to
dash his hopes of ever arousing her feelings: "Do you know what lies at
the end of your waiting? Nothing. Nothing whatever. For I myself am
nothing. It is only by chance that I am still alive. Alive to no purpose"
(p. 110).

Yet it is seldom that a survivor in a postwar novel commits suicide; it
is as if, having been inoculated with small doses of death, he is immune. Maria tries to drown herself in the sea after the suicide of a
young friend; as she is about to go limp the instinct for self-
preservation takes over and she thrashes her way back to the shore—
only to be overcome with grief at the thought that she is "incapable of
going through with anything" (p. 207).

Images of death abound in this fiction; for Maria even the subway
represents the invasion by the living of subterranean realms that should
be reserved for the dead. *The Pawnbroker* by Edward Lewis Wallant is
saturated with such imagery. Although as an American novel it is a
derivative form of the genre created by survivor-writers, leading to
simplified polarities and resolutions, it does share some of the distinct
characteristics of the form. The refugee, Sol Nazerman, does have a
surname, but it is not his own so much as an emblem in the allegory of
redemption that his life is to become. Nazerman, like Maria, is an
anaesthetized survivor who performs his daily functions—in his case
the running of a pawnshop—like a walking corpse. Each year he marks
the anniversary of the death of his family and of his own spiritual death,
and notes that "one could only die once. He had been extinct for a long

time..."[31] As he looks in the mirror he marvels that his "teeth continued to manufacture calcium, as hair and fingernails continued to
grow in the grave." When a young social worker, Marilyn Birchfield,
tries to pierce his armor he warns her against attempting to become
intimate with him in words that echo Maria's warning to Michel Caron:
"You would be guilty of necrophilia," he tells her; "it is obscene to
love the dead" (pp. 71, 162).

Langfus's Michael considers himself to be in a state of suspended
animation; for him time—and biography—stopped when he jumped
from the window of his home and abandoned his family.[32] His narrative
opens among the ruins of a German town—the natural habitat of an
extinguished soul ("I love ruins," he says [p. 7]), and even as he
performs the perfunctory tasks that life requires of him, he projects
about himself an aura of deathly stillness, as if his life were being lived
under the shimmering rays of a desert sun: he most values his fiancée
when she is absolutely quiet—"at each murdered word, at each gesture
relegated immediately to nothingness my heart swells with recognition
and sympathy for the young woman" (p. 143).

Yet Michael's very acquiescence to his fiancée's advances shows
that he cannot consign himself completely to the company of those
survivors who "do not participate any more," who have "removed"
themselves from the world of the living; he himself admits that he still,
somehow, seeks "a retreat among the shades and a home among men"
(p. 57). None of the heroes in these postwar novels ever gives himself
over completely to either realm: Michael, the most guilt-ridden of the
three, is condemned, like a sinner in Purgatory, to relive over and over
the moment of his escape; Maria is visited by the ghosts of her entire
family, who go so far as to advise her on how to manage her affairs:
"You and I will go away together," she says to the ghost of her husband, Jan, as he confronts her with her decision to go away with
Caron; "he (Caron) will be the rails and the train that will enable us to
get there. He will be the house in which we shall live together" (p. 75).
Nazerman is haunted in dreams by the visions of his wife and children
under torture.

The path back to sentience is, then, riddled with nightmare and
remorse, but by the end of each novel the protagonist has discovered in
himself a small crack in the wall of his solitude through which a ray of
feeling has penetrated. In the case of Langfus's characters, the breach
is effected very slowly and painstakingly: its only evidence is the cog-
nizance that Maria takes, in the last line of her story, of "the discordant
and *almost* painful cry of a bird" (emphasis mine) that rends the silence
as she leaves the home of Michel Caron,[33] and Michael's emotional
embrace of the child he has finally returned to its home, when he thinks

she has chosen instead to stay with him ("Minna...you have come back...Minna...Minna," he murmurs[34]). But the crack in Michael's soul is so slight that Minna's withdrawal (she had come back only to retrieve her jumprope) is enough to seal it for good: his narrative ends as a passerby stops to ask him the time—and a lassitude inhibits the movement of his hand as it reaches for the watch in his pocket, *"as if time itself slowed down before stopping forever"* (p. 261, emphasis mine).

In Wallant's novel, Sol Nazerman's withdrawal has been so complete that, as in the case of Tola, it takes a divine act to liberate him. Nazerman had, over the years, evolved an elaborate mechanism by which the "cogs and gears and ratchets" of his soul were held together and allowed him to function at the level of the barest of animal needs. His "hopes had long ago been amputated," and he prays ("in what would have been a prayer had it been addressed to anyone outside himself") only that the fragile machine holds "until I'm dead." If it breaks down while he is alive, he is aware that he will "have to live in the chaos" (p. 138). His final emergence into the "chaos" of feeling is so drastic that, even more than Tola's rescue, it is psychologically implausible. Using the prototype of Christian sacrifice that redeems the suffering soul, Wallant stages a latter-day crucifixion: the pawnbroker's assistant, *Jesus* Ortiz, is killed while attempting to save Nazerman during a holdup; dying, Jesus releases the floodgates of Nazerman's love and grief. It is a sacramental transformation which Wallant repeats in *The Tenants of Moonbloom* and *The Children at the Gate,* and it is so complete and cathartic that it accentuates the writer's existential remove from concentrationary memory which, survivor-novelists like Langfus seem to be saying, can never be totally resolved or eradicated.

Another survival novel written by an American which demonstrates the irrecoverability of cataclysmic history is Saul Bellow's *Mr. Sammler's Planet.* Sammler is the "Lazarene" who literally crawled alive out of a mass grave and then hid in a mausoleum until the war's end. Even after having been stripped of all material comforts and having learned to attend only to the barest minimum of needs, however, he does not emerge as the anaesthetized survivor whom we have come to recognize as typical of this genre. The two luxuries which he still allows himself are the luxury of thought and speculation and the luxury of feeling. His feelings are not the effusive "potato love"[35] of Bellow's Herzog, but the simple acceptance of man's duty to his fellows; in the private eulogy over the body of his nephew, Elya Gruner, with which his story ends, Sammler acknowledges that Gruner "did meet the terms of his contract. The terms which, in his inmost heart, each man knows. As I know mine . . .''[36] It is a more dramatic and resolute form of the pledge that recurs in survivalist fiction.

Minimal commitment to one's fellow men appears in this literature, then, to be the only possible escape from the anomy and destitution which attend the survivor's reentry into the stratosphere of the living. The commitment which Langfus's characters make is far more fragile than that pledged by Bellow's survivor, their feelings far more tentative than the flood of emotion experienced by the transformed hero of Wallant's novel. But once physical survival has been secured there must be some force beyond attention to one's personal needs to keep a man going. I have suggested that the victim who had a more defined sense of identity as a Jew and located his death or his survival in the spectrum of a community and a history of fellow-sufferers may have been sustained by the sense that his struggle was part of a process larger than himself. The next chapter is an exploration of the literary forms which are built upon the perception of the Holocaust as a confluence of personal and collective destiny.

FIVE

The Holocaust as a Jewish Tragedy 1: The Legacy of Lamentations

"Many Jews mourned the destruction of the First Temple, but only the writer of Lamentations transformed the mourning into eternal tragic poetry."[1] Many writers have mourned the slaughter of Europe's Jews, but a few have transformed private mourning into the jeremiads that may endure within an ancient Hebraic tradition. The literary modes considered up to this point derive from a cultural perspective that is primarily Western and secular, and even a cursory comparison with the Hebraic literature suggests that major distinctions in theme and form can be traced to basic differences in underlying attitudes.

The literature of survival posits the self as the ultimate source and referent of meaning; personal survival as the ultimate goal; and death, disintegration of the self, or acquiescence to the system (the degrees of which are explored in detail in the fiction of the concentrationary realists) as the ultimate defeat. The substance as well as shape of the fiction of both the survivalists and the concentrationary realists is, then, the struggle for or abdiction of personal integrity and autonomy.

If there is a way out of as well as a way into the inferno for the individual survivor whose physical and moral preservation provides him with a private and an ethically normative link to his pre-Holocaust past, for the Hebraic writers not personal but collective biography, not the odyssey of the self but the history of the people constitutes the matrix of continuity between past, present, and possible future. This literature, like most of the documentary literature, locates the center of meaning in the community or in general historical, moral, and theological principles. But unlike documentary fiction, drama, and poetry, which draw primarily on Western literary forms and themes, and which adopt the fictive documentation of history as a kind of contrivance by which the imagination can tentatively enter the concentrationary universe while paying homage to the primacy of "historical facts," the Hebraic literature is rooted in a different literary and philosophical tradition, in which centuries of persecution and a codified system of beliefs have shaped specific cultural responses to collective catastrophe, and historical events are absorbed into an inherited valuational framework. Whereas most of the documentary writers view the Holocaust as a monumental clash of social or moral values on the plane of universal history, and the survivalists are motivated largely by the need to convey and legitimate their own sufferings and commemorate the particular lives and deaths of their companions, the Hebraic writers write out of an additional impulse—to place the Holocaust within the spectrum of Jewish suffering and, frequently, to commemorate the cultural universe that was destroyed along with the people.

Yiddish Literature: A Return to the "Themes of the Fathers"

This orientation dominates the Yiddish and much of the Hebrew literature written in the shadow of the Holocaust. The *ḥurbn*, as it is referred to in Yiddish, was a blow to Yiddish civilization which all but obliterated former schisms in thought and form among Yiddish artists. Writers who had worked hard at establishing their independence and autonomy vis-à-vis the community, who had assimilated modernist ideas, who had declared themselves "Introspectivists" (*InZikh*) and denounced the collective imperatives that had bound their predecessors found themselves reclaiming the scorned perspectives, if tempered by irony or even despair. The poetic responses to the pogroms of the early part of the century had already begun to recover the links with the centuries-old tradition of Yiddish folksong and threnody. In balancing what David Roskies calls the "poetic [or private] voice" against a background of communal devastation and distress, some of the poets of the twenties even risked being charged by their contemporaries with betraying the Introspectivist commitment and regressing to a "nationalistic" perspective.[2] But World War II caused a far more drastic upheaval in the poetics of these writers and a severe constricting of thematic options. As Irving Howe has observed, after the Holocaust, "every Yiddish writer felt himself under the most sacred of obligations.... In the end, the luxury of choice would be denied [to the Introspectivists]...quite as much...as to the more traditional poets.... There was no choice but to come back, with blessing or curse, to the themes of the fathers."[3]

Yiddish, after all, was the mother-tongue of the majority of the victims and, as I have already observed, incorporated into its historical lexicon the vocabulary of the camps as it had assimilated attacks on corporate Jewish existence throughout history. But the destruction was so complete, the decimation of a community of readers and of fellow-writers such a death-blow to the entire culture that the word seemed to retreat before the fact. For Yiddish writers, both survivors and those living in America or Israel who had been spared, the language was now the embodied spirit of a dead people, and any form of manipulation in the name of art appeared almost as a travesty of the spirit—even as the imperative for collective commemoration grew. And when they did write, as the Yiddish critic S. Niger observed in 1947, "they no longer [wanted] to be reckoned with as artists or 'mere' artists. It is as if they [felt] guilty that their people's and their own tragedy [had] become no more than a 'theme' for their poems and stories."[4]

We have discussed elsewhere the reticence of survivors during the decade or so following the war; for the Hebraic writers especially, the struggle between the impulse to write and the impulse to remain silent became a haunting dilemma. They raised not only questions of aesthetic boundaries and appropriate forms of memorial, but also doubts about the nature of the world that would inherit their elegy. Elie Wiesel, who began as a Yiddish writer[5] but has since published in French, devotes an entire novel to the struggle against the vow of silence that one survivor assumed—the struggle, of course, ends in the defeat which is the novel itself. At one point, he explains the need for silence after the Holocaust:

> It has been going on for centuries. They kill us and we tell how; they humiliate and oppress us, they expel us from society . . . and we say how. They forbid us a place in the sun, the right to laugh and sing or even cry, and we turn it into a story, a legend . . . . The enemy can do with us as he pleases, but never will he silence us—that has been our motto. Words have been our weapon, our shield, the tale our lifeboat . . . . Since, in the end, someone would be left to describe our death, then death would be defeated . . .[6]

Silence seems to be the unique and most appropriate expression of what André Neher calls the "scenic" context, the only possible sign of the presence of six million dead.[7] This approach, which pays such homage to silence, is perilous insofar as it assigns meaning to the inarticulate and consequence to the unexpressed. Yet it indicates the fundamental anguish which is at the heart of all Holocaust literature: the challenge of generating words that can measure up to the enormity of the devastation while the very voices which violate the silence after the destruction are signs of its antithesis—of remaining life and of possible bridges to the future. Ultimately, it seems, the writer who has witnessed so much is terrified by silence. As the Hebrew poet H. N. Bialik wrote in the early years of this century, "man arrives at speech out of the magnitude of his fear of remaining even one moment in the abyss, face to face with unmediated nothingness..." Yet the poet's language still leaves gaps between the words, gaps which allow for a "glimpse of the abyss"; his words are, at their best, like ice floes with the great sea churning beneath and between them. In this the poet differs from the writer of prose, and the poetry of understatement and intimation from the more declamatory poetry which delineates a specific reality and which provides, like "solid ice," a secure verbal cover over the abyss.[8]

The Yiddish word was, in time, rescued for what may prove to be its final public task. Abraham Sutzkever, who has reconciled the aesthetic and the commemorative impulses in Yiddish poems of great beauty and power, regards words as a kind of link between the living and the dead, between organic and inorganic matter; like Orpheus, he gains his passage to the underworld through his music. In a poem written in 1943, at the height of the terror, he wrote that "death itself recoils from beauty."[9] Years later he described his own sense of mission as a poet collecting and resurrecting the "once-used words":

> Are there birds twittering under the earth,
> choking back
> their holy tears in their thin necks,
> or is that throbbing under the earth
> once-used words that seem invisible birds?
>
> Wherever my feet have the wisdom to walk,
> over snow, over hay, over drunken fire,
> they feel words,
> the souls of words,
> it's a pity my feet can't hold a pencil...
>
> Like a snakecharmer
> I stop my feet in their going:
> here and here and here
> here they are, here.
> Once-used silence.
> Once-used places.
> And I dig with my hands—bony spades,
> down to where the black
> palaces burst,
> where words throb
> hidden in violins.[10]

Hebrew Literature and the Lamentation Tradition

Hebrew shares with Yiddish the status of a medium of collective Jewish expression; if Yiddish was the common language spoken by the

Jews of Europe, Hebrew was the language of their texts. The contemporary Hebrew writer is heir to a continuous tradition of lamentational poetry and prose which commemorated Jewish martyrdom over two millennia. The massacres, forced conversions, crusades, expulsions, and pogroms that punctuate Jewish history from the time of the destruction of the First Temple till modern times were the subject of an unbroken chain of liturgical elegies (*seliḥot* and *kinot*)[11] and folktales (*midrashim*).[12] When we consider the paucity of historical records of most of this period, the mnemonic function of such poems and stories becomes even more apparent: from the time of Josephus until the nineteenth century there are hardly any reliable factual accounts of the persecutions of the Jews. Simon Dubnow, in his *History of the Jewish People,* observes that "the Middle Ages have bequeathed us no systematic chronography, our horrifying tragedies have found no competent annalist."[13] Such annalists have no place in a society in which the principles governing the vicissitudes of human fortunes are not validated by precise factual accounts but by the study of Torah as revelation of eternal and recurrent truths.[14]

Lamentation literature helped to preserve sacred communal memory in a number of ways. In a community in which a mythic view of history prevailed, the *kinot* provided the footnotes to update the biblical revelation of divine purpose. The poems take not only their historical analogues but also their form and idiom from biblical elegy, especially from the Books of Jeremiah and Lamentations. One important purpose of the poems is to commemorate the martyrs; the names of important persons and of whole communities are woven into the verses, as well as other details, such as the date and even the means of torture and the various forms of desecration of the Scriptures.[15] On the whole the *paytanim* (liturgical poets) demonstrated more passion than poetic talent; many of these poems have simple, almost ludicrous, rhyme schemes governed by a greater commitment to commemorative facts than to form. The community did not always inquire into the poetic quality of the *kinot;* an occasional elegist, most notably among the medieval Spanish poets, did, however, produce verses of lasting power and beauty which were incorporated into the liturgy. It is of course an ancient bardic method of preserving communal memory to recite names and historical events in verse—but in the medieval and post-medieval Jewish communities the *kinot* and *seliḥot* often served the additional and more immediate purpose of providing the information that could enable survivors to recite the Kaddish (memorial prayer) for their dead on the proper day. And specific poems were sometimes integrated into the prayer service of local communities—for instance, one *seliḥah* which commemorated the local victims of the Chmielnicki

massacre was incorporated into the Lithuanian *seliḥot* liturgy and contributed over the generations to a unique sense of continuity of place.[16]

Occasionally a single act of bravery took on mythic proportions in
midrashim or poetry, and in its variations one can trace the growth and
uses of legend. Such, for example, is the story of the woman (variously
called Miriam or Hannah) whose seven sons refused to eat swine (or, in
another version, to bow down to idols) and were tortured and killed.
The story is related, with different details and emphases, in the apoc-
ryphal Second Book of Maccabees, in Lamentations Rabbah, and in
other contexts.[17] Through the literature such stories were transformed
into paradigms of the agony and heroic faith of the entire community
and were meant to provide instructional models for the victims of
future persecutions. Writing within such a well defined normative
framework, the *paytan* or author of *midrash* was careful to avoid
mention of acts of betrayal or cowardice on the part of the martyrs.[18]

Although the *paytan* often wrote in the first person and described
particular events, his poems, as specific or autobiographical as they
might be, usually illuminated one of two fundamental axioms: Israel
was suffering because it had erred;[19] or certain innocent persons or
communities had been singled out to sanctify God's name through
martyrdom. There were, also, frequent and impassioned petitions to
God for vengeance and numerous instances of desperate and even
defiant indictments of divine silence or indifference.[20] Nevertheless,
the poet spoke with a prophetic or collective voice and concluded his
lament with an affirmation of faith. The *kinah* was, then, both a poetic
reflection of and a constitutive response to history. As a sustained
literary genre it is, according to A. M. Habermann, unique in world
literature: "the community of Israel, who had forgotten what celebra-
tory poetry was, raised up its voice in one terrible kinah—a long and
bitter shout which incorporated the sorrow and the tears of the
generations."[21]

Even the diffusion of the Enlightenment ideology and the erosion of
monolithic religious beliefs did not significantly alter the image of the
poet in the eyes of the people. Struggle as he might against the summons to a public, prophetic voice, a poet like Ḥayyim Naḥman Bialik
could not escape into an exploration of his private soul so long as his
people needed him as comforter, chastiser, and national poet. His
agony is reflected in numerous poems such as the following: "My soul
bowed down to the dust / Under the burden of your love: / Not a poet,
nor a prophet, / But a hewer of wood am I."[22] Yet even as he responds
to the summons, Bialik represents the lamentation tradition in transition. Straddling the nineteenth and twentieth centuries, open to influences both from within and from without, he was no longer strictly

bound by the religious authority of the tradition or by the formulas with which it had confronted historic crises. His God is elusive and many-faceted: in some poems God has turned a deaf ear to man;[23] in others it is man who has lost the way to Him.[24] Bialik's elegies are far more complex than the traditional *kinot* not only in their theodicy but also in their exploration of the responses of the victims. In the long poem "In the City of the Slaughter," written in 1905 as a response to the Kishinev pogrom, the speaker displays neither pure piety nor un-mitigated compassion; he is repelled as much by the cowardice of the victims as by the brutality of the victimizers. In this poem it is human behavior, as well as divine providence, which is being tested.[25] Yet Bialik registered his protest not by a retreat from but by subtle inversions of the traditional responses to catastrophe; by retaining the familiar symbols and constructs yet altering their context and significance, he succeeded in conveying the ambiguities and complexities of a new spiritual reality while satisfying the community's need for an elegist.[26]

Thirty-five years later, whatever ambiguities or rifts may have been introduced into the tradition were disregarded by those Jews who, in the midst of their suffering in Nazi ghettos and camps, called for a jeremiad that would survive and immortalize them. On November 30, 1939, Chaim Kaplan, whose Hebrew diary is the most complete and methodical record of the life and death of the Warsaw Ghetto, wrote an impassioned plea for poetic testimony:

> Our forefathers, who were experienced in adversity, immortalized their sufferings in lamentations . . . .
> Who will immortalize our troubles? The national splendor inherent in religious poetry is not expressed in newspaper reports . . . . A catastrophe that becomes part of poetry, even non-religious poetry such as Bialik's "The City of Slaughter," which commemorated the Kishinev pogrom, spreads among the people and is transmitted to future generations. A poet who clothes adversity in poetic form immortalizes it in an everlasting monument. And this monument provides historic material from which future generations are nourished.
> Who will write of our troubles and who will immortalize them?
> Poet of the people, where art thou?[27]

With respect to the questions we have raised concerning alternative modes of integrating experience into national culture and memory, Kaplan's plea is especially significant in coming from a historian who regarded his own task as of the utmost consequence. Clearly he felt that historical record alone could not provide the kind of commemoration that a dying people wanted to leave behind. If we consider the social dimensions of elegiac literature, even in a secularizing community, the poem which is invested with mythical or ritualistic functions can also constitute a living historical memory that historiography, in its remoteness, cannot.

Reverberations in Palestine

The Jews of Palestine, sharing the same heritage and the same regard for the evocative power of poetry under critical circumstances, removed from the continent on which the annihilating hosts were gathering though not from the global conflict which threatened to engulf Palestine as well, responded variously to the condition of their European brothers. In the years preceding the war, a surprising number of Hebrew writers had warned of impending disaster in a series of poems and stories which can be read as almost clairvoyant. Some of the major poets, including Zalman Shneur before World War I and Shaul Tchernichowsky in the thirties, invoked grotesque images of medieval torture and mass murder to suggest through an analogous and cyclical reading of history the imminent encroachment of the forces of destruction upon the world in general and the Jews in particular. Among the novelists there were a few who dwelled more directly on the external and internal factors contributing to the erosion of the Eastern European Jewish community as ominous signals of a larger and far more sinister process. In the novel by S. Y. Agnon, *A Guest for the Night,* written in 1939, a visit to the narrator's hometown in Galicia reveals the signs of dissolution that marked a period darkened by the shadows of the past war and the gathering clouds of the coming one. (The autobiographical Yiddish novel *Homeward Bound,* by Jacob Glatstein, who had been living in the United States for some twenty years when he revisited his hometown on the eve of the war, has the same motif and suggests the widespread conviction among Jewish writers outside of Europe that the Jewish community there was doomed.) Even Uri Zvi Greenberg, who later became European Jewry's chief Hebrew elegist, was one of the most prominent prophets of its destruction in the thirties, referring to himself as a creature not quite dog and not quite jackal, "who sniffs out disaster and barks in time."[28]

During the war itself a fairly large number of poems appeared which expressed the sense of helplessness and horror that the Jews in Palestine were experiencing. Much of this poetry was strident and declamatory in tone, uneven in quality, and nourished by both unfounded hopes and the trickles of real news that filtered slowly into public

consciousness. Attentive not necessarily to aesthetic standards, but to
a tradition of public poetry in times of national crisis, a large segment of
the community reproached its poets for not sufficiently fulfilling their
role as spokesmen, and a heated controversy arose in the Hebrew
press. The issue is a complex one which has haunted Hebrew literature
ever since the war, and certainly cannot be dismissed by the kind of
apologetics which equates prophecy with elegy such as Simon Halkin
demonstrates when he writes that "the Hebrew reader's sensibilities,
like the literature itself, had in a way foretasted the catastrophe long
before its arrival and . . . the written word during the war years only
echoed voices that long before the war sounded the same despair."[29]
Surely one truth to which the struggle for form among all Holocaust
writers and the refractions and inversions in the symbolic language of
the Hebraic writers attest is that there were no precedents, even within
the long Jewish memory of persecution, for what took place during the
Holocaust. The clairvoyance of those writers who seem to have anticipated the war can also be seen as serving the ideological struggle of a
community disengaging itself from the ways and the fate of the Diaspora. But as the harassment of the Jews of Europe took on the
dimensions of widespread persecution and then genocide, the pride of
the Yishuv (Palestinian Jewish community) in its separatism yielded to
fear and anguish, and the disparity between the relative security en-
joyed by Palestinian Jewry and the nightmare which raged in Europe
gave rise to an enduring sense of guilt:

> If only our sainted ones could have drawn back our curtains
> And peeked with the blood of their eyes through our windows
> And seen how we lived our lives:
> An inferno engulfed them while Paradise surrounded us

wrote Uri Zvi Greenberg in a major *kinah* in *Streets of the River,* which
appeared a few years after the war.[30]

The post-Holocaust generation of Hebrew writers continued to
struggle with the elegiac mission against constraints that they shared
with other Jewish writers as well as circumstances peculiar to their
own historical situation. A number of writers who had survived the war
immigrated to Israel, but their influence, and the impact of the events
themselves, began to be felt among the younger writers only in the
early sixties; the Eichmann trial proved to be a watershed in Israeli
perceptions of the Holocaust, much as it would prove to be in America,
for reasons we shall consider later. In the years between the war and
the trial, the impact of secularization, the preoccupation with nation-
building and the identification of the Holocaust with the remote condition of "exile," as well as what Robert Alter has called the increasing
"concentration on private and quotidian experience,"[31] may account,

in part at least, for the initial resistance of Israeli writers to the summons to become the vessels of collective Jewish commemoration. Nevertheless, the subject has engaged an increasing number of writers; the voice they adopt is frequently that of the spokesman, and the themes and symbols derive from the motifs and imagery that prevail in lamentation literature. Still, the personal voice is not lost even here, as the speaker or narrator usually strains to find the meeting ground—or the point of divergence—between his present and the past he is seeking to recover.

In fiction, this dialectic is sharply delineated in the novels of such writers as Yehuda Amichai and Hanoch Bartov, and suggests what one critic has defined as a renewal of the encounter between fathers and sons which had characterized Israeli writing in the early years of the separation from its European parent.[32] Yet the conflict now is internal and sorrowful and nostalgic, resembling the agony of an errant son standing over his father's grave. Almost invariably, the speaker or narrator reclaims his patrimony through language that resonates with collective memory even as he may rail against its grasp upon his imagination. In poetry this process, which is long and torturous in the fiction, is encoded in the symbolic inversions which we come to recognize, since Bialik, as modern manifestations of the tension that catastrophe engenders in the traditional constructs of behavior and belief. In poems on the patriarch Abraham by two Hebrew poets, Amir Gilboa and Natan Alterman, the *father* becomes the sacrificial victim and the son survives, alone. In Alterman's poem "On the Boy Avram," Avram is portrayed as the orphaned son (bereft also of his Heavenly Father, as suggested by the use of the prebenedictal version of the name) who returns to his family home in Poland at the end of the war to confront the devastation of the town and the horrible deaths of father, mother, and sister. Finally, however, he must leave to fulfill his mission, "for the command that thundered upon Avram the father/ Thunders on Avram the boy."[33] Gilboa's poem "Isaac" is less nationalistic and more lyrical but in its imagery evokes the same set of biblical associations, transvalued by the actual death of the father in Europe that haunts the son in Israel:

Early in the morning the sun took a walk in the forest
Together with me and with Father
And my right hand in his left.

Like lightning a knife flamed between the trees.
And I fear so the terror of my eyes facing the blood on the leaves.

Father, Father hurry and save Isaac
And no one will be missing at lunchtime.

It is I who am being slaughtered, my son,
And my blood is already on the leaves.
And Father's voice was stifled.
And his face pale.

And I wanted to cry out, writhing not to believe
And tearing open the eyes.
And I woke up.

And bloodless was the right hand.[34]

The dream motif here is a form of acknowledging the speaker's distance from the event, resembling other conventions in Israeli literature such as the dream sequences in Greenberg's poems and an imagined return to postwar Germany in Yehuda Amichai's novel, *Not of This Time, Not of This Place*.

It can be said, then, that even though both internal and external forces had eroded the links between contemporary Yiddish and Hebrew literature and the literary and religious traditions which had reflected and shaped collective responses to catastrophe over the centuries, most of the writers who have appropriated the subject have also appropriated the classical forms, as if these provided access to an otherwise unintelligible and inarticulable experience. Even when a poem is intensely personal, the very formulaic quality of the language usually reverberates with national memories and attitudes. Abba Kovner, a Hebrew poet who, along with Sutzkever, was among the organizers of the underground in the Vilna Ghetto and then fought as a partisan in the neighboring forests, wrote an elegy ("My Little Sister") which traces the sister's fate after being left by her family in the protection of a convent. The Hebrew resonates with biblical allusions and is patterned in part after medieval liturgical poetry, so that the sister is linked both to a historical continuum and to the shared fate of the six million.[35] Kovner himself explains the dovetailing of personal and communal fate and the power of poetry to maintain the connection:

> When I write I am like a man praying. I inherited many things from my ancestors. One is the teaching that a man should not say his own prayer before the prayer of all the people. In the Talmud it was stated that a man should always participate with the community . . . to teach us that poetry does not uplift unless it draws from the mood of the community. And the word of a community cannot be expressed except in the poetry of the individual.
>
> But the community in which I pray and say my poems is half alive and half dead. . . . [Yet] I believe there is one place in the world without cemeteries. This is the world of poetry.[36]

Of course, no literature which is so vast and generated by such radical upheavals will be totally homogeneous; it is not simply that, as Stephen Spender has written, "the end of the world is the beginning of poetry in the biblical tradition," while the "bases of Renaissance individualist art which survived right up until 1939" were shattered by the concentration camps.[37] There are other strains, more individualistic, which can be heard beside the communal voice that echoes through the *ḥurbn* literature. Most of Aharon Appelfeld's Hebrew stories, like Ḥaim Gouri's Hebrew novel *The Chocolate Deal,* concentrate on the struggle of the individual survivor to reconstruct his private world in postwar Europe or Israel. Yet it may come as no surprise that some of the most notable expressions of the private ordeal are found in the work of the victims or survivors writing close to the events themselves; the poetry which was composed in the camps and ghettos and forests during the war tends to be more self-focused, as this was the time when the struggle for survival was uppermost and there could be no distance between the suffering man and the creating mind. David Vogel, whose tracks disappeared into one of the death camps, is a Hebrew poet whose last poem, written during the war, expands apocalyptically to encompass all of humanity poised for total extinction and then contracts to the naked, hungry voice of the speaker awaiting— almost remembering—his own death: "The winds of devastation will blow through the world / And I was here for one more moment."[38]

One poet who wrote simultaneously from a personal and communal perspective while interned in the camps was Itzḥak Katzenelson. By the time he perished in Auschwitz, he had already written his monumental "Song of the Murdered Jewish People." The long Yiddish poem is really a series of short poems of uneven quality. His tone is stark and strident, but attention to literary structures and religious formulas gives relentless pain its form and its link to lamentation tradition and accords it the status of national elegy. In the camps he was regarded, even by resistance fighters such as Mordecai Tenenbaum, as the one who could immortalize their agony and their struggle: "All that we thought, felt, or imagined, he wrote about," Tenenbaum wrote from Bialystok to his sister in Palestine after Katzenelson's death. "We furnished him with the debris of our misery, and he made it eternal, sang of it, it was our common property."[39]

Writing for a Lost Community

Even in the camps, then, there was an audience who not only commissioned its poets to compose its memorial, but read and criticized what was being written. We have already had occasion to mention the manifold artistic activity that took place in the ghettos and camps. Abraham

Sutzkever was awarded, in 1942, the Vilna Ghetto's literary prize for one of his poems, "The Grave Child." Now, from the perspective of the intervening decades since what Mendel Mann has called the "assassination" of the Yiddish language,[40] which was coterminous with the assassination of the Yiddish folk, and given the rather insulated context of Hebrew literature, the Jewish poet or novelist no longer has a cohesive audience to whom he can address himself. Yet, even with such limitations as we have enumerated with respect to the internal Jewish forums of communication and literary continuity, it seems even less likely that a modern Jewish elegy could be written in English or in any of the European languages. Kafka was one writer who acknowledged that his use of the German language dictated, or reflected, his main concerns and perspectives. He once said that he considered himself to be a "guest of the German language,"[41] and showed interest in Yiddish literature because it represented "an uninterrupted tradition of national struggle that determines every work," in contrast with the agonizing isolation out of which he wrote.[42] Many writers have argued that a Jewish literature without a specific language is inconceivable. Yet there are a number of European writers who will be considered at length in the next chapter and who, despite the use of foreign languages, share the collectivist, Hebraic perspective and represent, within the context of European letters, the most manifestly Jewish responses to the Holocaust as a collective tragedy. The fact that they are, nevertheless, writing in French or German renders them immediately accessible to a wider and more diversified readership than that of the Yiddish and Hebrew writers, even as they relate to the concentrationary experience as a common, Jewish heritage and not only as personal biography and their works seek resonance within an identifiable constituency of readers. Yet since in fact such a "constituency" hardly exists, at least outside of Israel, since the Diaspora can no longer be regarded as constituting a coherent cultural unit capable of absorbing, judging, and preserving the oeuvre of its artists, what has replaced the "Jewish public" is the mass media; as W. Rabi has written, "The work in question must be commented upon, discussed, approved or condemned . . . by the . . . press, radio or television so that, finally, Jewish readers will become interested in the work and make it their own."[43] What is important to emphasize here is that for many writers acclaim or censure is no longer an internal, but a derivative, process by which Jewish readers are guided largely by the standards of a non-Jewish audience. André Schwarz-Bart and Nelly Sachs reached Jewish readers in large numbers only after they had received the Prix Goncourt and the Nobel Prize, respectively. The vicissitudes of erratic public attention in a gentile society have conferred laurels on one Yiddish writer, such as Nobel laureate I. B. Singer, and relative anonymity on another, such as Jacob Glatstein or Chaim Grade. In general, however, one can say that the Hebraic literature written in European languages, such as that of Elie Wiesel, Manès Sperber, André Schwarz-Bart, Nelly Sachs, and Paul Celan, has been widely disseminated and enthusiastically received in both gentile and Jewish circles, while the Yiddish and Hebrew literature has remained largely unknown outside of the small pockets of native readers, for reasons that may be only partly the inaccessibility and intractability of an idiom that is rooted in ancient literary tradition. Yet all of these writers draw upon a common heritage and may be regarded—or at least regard themselves—as performing specific cultural tasks as witnesses to the slaughter not of six million individuals but of one-third of the Jewish people.

The writer, as executor of the estate of so many dead, is left to assess how much the people took with them to the grave and how much they left behind. Wherever communal ethics and beliefs survived, wherever a sense of solidarity persisted, they preserved not only the integrity of the individuals who retained them, but also the commitment to a larger order within which this carnage would ultimately have to be subsumed. A primary task that the Nazis had set for themselves was to fracture the Jewish community from within, to undermine—or simply destroy—its moral and spiritual fabric and make the death of one Jew the price of the survival of another. Louis Martin-Chauffier, in his memoir, *L'Homme et la bête,* writes of the "sentiment d'une durée extérieure" which kept the devout Christian, as well as the Communist, prisoners going in the camps.[44] But the Jewish prisoner, whose sense of belonging in the world was mediated through the community which now faced collective extinction and whose God was traditionally called to account for the operations of history, could not view the camps as somehow unrelated to or insulated from a *durée extérieure,* a sphere in which life would ultimately be set to rights again. On the contrary, the camps had somehow to be integrated into that very *durée*—or else they were the sign of its collapse.

It is in this context that the questions of theodicy and cultural continuity are raised in much of the literature we are considering. What is at stake is not only the belief in divine justice but the entire fabric of society and culture which upheld that faith. Many of these writers draw upon the history and the social values embodied in the community, and they struggle not only with the past—the destruction—of the Jewish people, but with its future. Most of them are even more concerned with how Jews lived their lives before the Holocaust and with how they can live after than with how they met their deaths. Here again it is important to remember that we are studying constructs of literary response which are derivative from but not necessarily mimetic of the reactions of the actual victims to the actual persecutions, responses which are meant to be in some way instructive in a post-Holocaust future. There came a moment in the life of nearly every inmate of the ghettos and camps when all supports collapsed and life came to mean nothing but a crust of bread—it was this moment which was encapsulated in the fiction of the concentrationary realists. In the struggle between body and soul, as Elie Wiesel writes in an autobiographical fragment, "a miserable crust of moldy bread came to contain more truth, more eternity than all the pages of all the books put together.... Just as our bodies came to look alike, so our hearts harbored one single wish: bread and soup, thicker, if possible, than yesterday's. We were hungry for nothing else."[45] In light of this, the ultimate confession of ultimate nakedness, it is significant that few of the Hebraic writers focus on the struggle for bread and soup. Their work represents, rather, an attempt to put the pages of the books back together.

A synoptic illustration of the literary process in which, retrospective to the event at least, demands of the spirit prove to be even more pressing than the needs of the body, can be found in the work of the Yiddish novelist and poet Chaim Grade, who escaped from Vilna to the Soviet Union during the war carrying the scars of his own physical deprivation. His story "My Quarrel with Hersh Rasseyner" concerns two former Yeshiva classmates—one, the narrator Chaim Vilner, who has become an "enlightened" Jew and a writer, and the other, Hersh Rasseyner, who has remained a fervent *Mussarnik,* clinging to strict principles of moral and religious purity and Jewish particularity. The two friends meet again as refugees in Paris after the war, and their impassioned discussion, which would seem to bear the most ominous consequence, revolves not around the personal arrangements that each has made with his own pain and loss but around the questions of theodicy and the perception of human conduct as either commanded or autonomous. For Hersh the iniquity of the outside world, which he experienced on his own flesh, only strengthens his faith in a higher order: "When I hear people quibbling about politics and calculating the position of the powers, I know that there is another set of books, kept in fire and blood.... I have never thought for one moment that anyone in the world besides the jealous and vengeful God would avenge the helpless little ones that the Gestapo stuffed into the trains for Treblinka..."[46] His friend, Reb Chaim, would have him "demand an accounting of heaven," and derives his own faith and resources from the collective inheritance that resides in the people, in the surviving remnant. "Don't think it is easy for us Jewish writers," he warns his friend, revealing the simultaneous sense of impoverishment and solidarity that Hebraic writers experienced after the *ḥurbn*. "It's very, very hard. The same misfortune befell us all, but you have a ready answer, while we have not silenced our doubts . . . . The only joy that's left to us is the joy of creation, and in all the travail of creation we try to draw near to our people" (p. 605).

This polarization of attitudes, however trenchantly represented, still resides within one closed universe in which God and the Jewish people are the two poles of reference. Holocaust writing as a whole presents a variety of possible imaginative interpretations of historical events which also suggest alternative ways of being in a world that has countenanced Auschwitz. For a writer like Borowski, or for his protagonists, to whom the concentrationary universe becomes the sole reality, there can be no post-Holocaust existence; the only logical "solution" to survival beyond liberation is suicide—and, in 1951, at the age of twenty-nine, having outlived the Nazi gas chambers, Borowski chose to gas himself. For the survivalists, as for their characters, survival is a slow and often futile rediscovery of relations between persons. For the Hebraic writer, it is both an act of commemoration of what was lost and an attempt to somehow absorb the challenge and the agony into the collective consciousness of the surviving remnant. And that is achieved not only by a dramatic, realistic portrayal of events, but also by presenting a kaleidoscope of history, a contemporaneity or simultaneity of events which places Auschwitz within the context of centuries of martyrdom, and by drawing upon and adding to a literature of "all the Jewish tears gathered together and transformed into a song deeper than any abyss."[47] "The new persecutions, dangers, and hopes were a novelty in name only," the narrator of Manès Sperber's novel *. . . Than a Tear in the Sea* writes: "Even the children knew that the history of the Diaspora was nothing save a continual repetition of Joseph's story. They read it in the second book of Moses at least once a year . . . . Then there arose in Germany a man . . . called Hitler [who] was none other than Haman whom they knew so well from the book of Esther."[48]

The epic events that shaped Israel's legendary beginnings and tested its incipient faith—the fratricide between the first sons of man, the sacrifice of Isaac, and the genocidal threats of Haman—as well as the persecutions launched against Israel through the centuries by emperors and crusaders and inquisitors, become paradigms in the cyclical reenactment of history. Dan Pagis, a Hebrew poet who spent most of his adolescence in a concentration camp, pares history down to its barest,

most primal elements in the short poem "Written in Pencil in a Sealed
Boxcar":

> Here in this transport
> I am Eve
> with my son Abel
> if you see my elder son
> Cain son of Adam
> tell him that I[49]

The poem ends here. As in other poems by Pagis, there is no need for
closure; abruptly, the words slide back into the abyss.

And just as the biblical characters and historical situations reemerge,
transformed utterly, so even the literary artifacts of culture engage in
the historical dialogue: in a poem entitled "A Letter from Menahem-
Mendel," the Hebrew poet Natan Alterman invokes characters from
Sholom Aleichem's stories and assigns them a common fate with their
readers; the narrator, himself a fictional character, writes to his wife:

> My Sheineh Sheindel, white snow is falling.
> There is no one. Everyone is gone. Understand.
> Tevye is dead
> And dead is Mottel the Cantor's son.
> Dead is dear uncle Pinye.
>
> And on the snow rests Stempenyu, small and barefoot,
> And, as always, still full of grace.
> But the violin is mute. It has no more music.
> For it has no one left to play for.[50]

The writers, then, still conceive of themselves and are received as
the elegists of an entire culture, writing the bloodiest and most implacable chapter in the history of what Nelly Sachs calls "das Leiden
Israels."[51] The major themes through which Israel's martyrdom has
been traditionally perceived—the accountability of a God whose presence in history is axiomatic in Judaism, and the ethical and existential
imperatives which are the inheritance that dispossessed Jews of every
generation leave their heirs—become the prisms through which we
approach this literature, and the deviations or discontinuities are a
measure of each writer's struggle between normative values and contemporary reality.

Ironically, the only other body of literature which one would expect to
reflect a collective concern with questions of historical and moral continuity after the Holocaust is German literature. In 1945, Ernst
Wiechert—one of the few antifascist German writers who chose im-

prisonment in a concentration camp over exile—bewailed, in an impassioned postwar speech, the poverty of poetic reponse to the mutations that Nazism had implanted in the German body politic: "The others, where were they in the years of shame and destruction? Where were they who bring into being the imperishable, the poets and thinkers, called by God to be a light in the deadliest night?"[52] In conclusion, Wiechert called upon his fellow writers to finally take the measure of their guilt: "Let us understand that we are guilty and that it may take a whole century to wash the guilt from our hands. Let us realize that our guilt demands atonement from us, a long and hard atonement; that happiness and homes and peace are not for us, because the others became unhappy and homeless and without peace through us."[53]

German writers have responded to Wiechert's challenge in various ways which cannot be explored here except to suggest that only a few have attempted to confront the guilt of genocide directly. While not representing a widespread trend, these do constitute a form of reflection on collective responsibility and destiny; the assumption of guilt by a German can be seen as a way of linking past and present or of testing the continuities. Two of the most common ranges of response stretch from light sentimentalism[54] to maudlin or melodramatic remorse[55] and from light irony or cynicism[56] to biting satire.[57] The ironic mode which prevails in varying degrees in the fiction of Heinrich Böll and Günter Grass represents, as it does in Jewish literature, the most radical expression of the ruptures with tradition that can still abide within a collective framework. A third form of response, which we have observed in a number of documentary writers, including Weiss and Sylvanus, insists on a kind of interchangeability between the roles of victim and victimizer—which, in a sense, serves to exonerate the historical actors of unique responsibility. We will see, in the work of both Schwarz-Bart and Sachs, that the premise of inexorability in the relationship between Jew and gentile has a similar effect. Yet although the Nazi appears occasionally in other Hebraic writing as a demonic species and the Jew appears frequently in German literature as a romantic silhouette, the confrontation between the self and the "other" tends to be tangential to the introspective process taking place in both literatures, and those exceptions which establish a fixed dialectic between the two seem to do so by reaching beyond the internal system to some universal, suprahistorical source of meaning.

In the work of most of the writers we are now considering, the search for a philosophical, as well as pragmatic, stance for the Jew in the world and for a literary manner capable of expressing it is dominant. Many have made the Holocaust the central theme of their postwar writing; this is particularly true of Yiddish writers, such as Glatstein

and Sutzkever, but it is also true of the generation of Hebrew writers
who grew up in Europe, including a number of survivors, such as Abba
Kovner and Aharon Appelfeld. Among the European writers whom we
will consider in the next chapter, only the work of Elie Wiesel and
Nelly Sachs constitutes a continuous, evolving response to the
Holocaust. Other writers, including European novelists such as André
Schwarz-Bart and Manès Sperber and some of the younger Israelis,
seem to incorporate the Holocaust as a station in their personal orientation toward contemporary history. Sperber and Schwarz-Bart have
treated the subject of the Holocaust as part of a larger exploration of
ways of being—and of suffering—in a war-torn world. For Hebrew
writers like Yehuda Amichai or Hanoch Bartov (here the distinction
between the generations is not strictly chronological but more orienta-
tional; Amichai was born in Germany in 1924 but has lived in Israel since
adolescence and bridges between European memories and *Sabra* attitudes), the Holocaust is a prism or catalyst of their own search for
location as Jews and as human beings in the modern world. Amichai's
double narrative in the novel *Not of This Time, Not of This Place*
follows the protagonist, Joel, through two simultaneous and mutually
exclusive courses of action. In the one version, narrated in the third
person, Joel, the young archaeologist, remains in Jerusalem and carries
on a love affair with a gentile American doctor, Patricia, while in the
other, narrated in the first person, he leaves Jerusalem to revisit his
hometown of Weinburg, Germany—from which he had emigrated just
before the outbreak of hostilities—in order to enact revenge on the
Nazis for the murder of his childhood sweetheart, Ruth. This narrative
process explores the schizophrenia of Joel's personality and presents a
resolution in terms of his psychological confrontation with the world of
his childhood, against the background of his adult life; the Holocaust
is, then, a reality which hovers at the periphery of vision but which
must somehow be explored before any self-clarity can be reached.
The narrator of Bartov's novel *The Brigade* is a soldier in the British
Army's Palestinian Regiment whose encounter with refugees in D. P.
camps in Europe acts in similar fashion as a catalyst for integrating the
disparate strands of his own identity. The partial engagement which is
manifested here, the ability to distance and remove himself psychologically from the reality he is confronting in his travels through Italy
and Germany, is a symptom of the empathetic relationship predicated
on historical detachment that we have already observed and that the
younger generation of Israeli writers share with their American-Jewish
contemporaries.

But if the conventional preoccupation of the novel with the individual in his struggle for self-definition vis-á-vis society or history serves

the need for containment and detachment in Bartov's or Amichai's exploration of the concentrationary universe, for other writers the challenge is to establish the contours within which the modern novel can accommodate inquiry into collective fate and theodicy which is usually confined to the domain of religious literature. The same challenge is met by the poets who evoke the collective odyssey in a secular idiom. Yet even among those writers who consciously attempt to write from within an inherited tradition, there are significant differences between those whose search for reconciliation leads them beyond the covenantal dialogue and those who stay within its confines at the price of being trapped and weakened by its inescapable antinomies. A close reading of such writers as Elie Wiesel, I. B. Singer, Manès Sperber, André Schwarz-Bart, Nelly Sachs, and Paul Celan can illustrate these variations.

SIX

The Holocaust as a Jewish Tragedy 2: The Covenantal Context

Elie Wiesel and Isaac Bashevis Singer: From Reality to Legend
The major tensions which the Holocaust activated in Jewish beliefs and ethics as well as the engagement of traditional elements in the search for appropriate forms of expression are discernible in a body of European literature encompassing diverse languages and audiences. The novels of Elie Wiesel are perhaps the most widely read fictional representations of the clashes between inherited religious and moral values and the enormity and inscrutability of contemporary reality.

With the exception of his first book, *Night,* an autobiographical chronology of deportation and of existence and survival in the camps, and a few stories in *Legends of Our Time,* Wiesel's narratives are located on the periphery of or retrospective to the concentrationary universe. *Dawn, The Accident,* and *The Town beyond the Wall* are set in the aftermath of the war, yet treat as morally compelling even in the post-Holocaust world those issues and relationships which arose in the concentrationary context: the roles and responsibilities of victim, victimizer, and spectator, the guilt and death-wish of the survivor. *A Beggar in Jerusalem* is located at the Wailing Wall just after the Six-Day War, yet is haunted by memories and spirits from the Holocaust. Even *The Oath,* the story of a pogrom which took place in the 1920s, can be read as a kind of microcosm of or a prelude to the Holocaust. *Gates of the Forest* explores three possibilities for Jewish survival during the Holocaust on the periphery of the ghettos and camps: alone in caves, with the partisans in the forests, and among the gentiles in disguise. In every one of these books, then, the narrative is haunted by echoes or premonitions of the cataclysm even though the center of dramatic action may be far removed from the actual scenes of massacre.

Wiesel is one of a number of Holocaust writers for whom survival seems to have dictated their choice of profession; when he was deported to Auschwitz from his Transylvanian hometown of Sighet, he was a fifteen-year-old heir to a world view in which, as he says, secular creations had no place:

> If someone had told me when I was a child that one day I would become a novelist, I would have turned away, convinced he was confusing me with someone else . . . . Novels I thought childish, reading them a waste of time . . . .
> As for France—whose language I chose for my tales—its name evoked visions of a mythical country, real only because mentioned in Rashi and other commentaries on the Bible and Talmud.[1]

This statement suggests a kind of pre-*Haskalah* ("Enlightenment") polarization of art and religion. It must, nevertheless, be remembered that it was in the innocence and single-minded piety of youth that Wiesel was suddenly severed from an insulated religious ambience and, overnight as it were ("night" lasted one year), thrust into a secular post-Holocaust universe. The contradictions between the attitudes and the literary conventions that were his heritage, and the medium of the modern French novel in which he chose to write are the main source of both the unique power and the weaknesses in his writing. The tension and its various resolutions can be demonstrated by identifying the elements of religious literature which have been introduced into the novel and the ways they have affected the nature and direction of the narrative. Wiesel has drawn primarily on the midrashic narratives which provide a prototype for the fusion of reality and legend.

The Canadian philosopher Emil Fackenheim has suggested a reading of Wiesel's fiction in terms which oversimplify the complexities of religious-oriented responses in the modern era; his definition of *midrash,* while partial, nevertheless illuminates some of the operations of that literary genre in the collective process whereby the past is rendered continually present. Auschwitz, by assimilation into latter-day *midrash,* becomes, potentially, a "root experience" which is incorporated into the dialectics of Jewish history.[2] While the lofty historical purposes which have been conferred by Fackenheim and others weigh perhaps too heavily on the work of Wiesel, I would isolate two elements which seem to characterize most of the classical midrashic narratives that undertake to interpret cataclysmic historical events and which inform the best of Wiesel's fiction: first, the quality of storytelling which is grounded in historical reality but which serves parabolical purposes ("when facts or texts become unacceptable, fiction or legend weaves the garland of nobler fancy," writes one midrashic commentator);[3] and, second, the mystery which lies at the heart of the Midrash and which is deliberately left unresolved. The principal mystery or contradiction which the *midrash* of catastrophe grapples with is the manifestation of divine providence in human affairs, and parallels have been drawn between the *midrashim* that were written at the time of the destruction of the Second Temple as both a witness and challenge to divine purposes, and the fragments of a violated theodicy that recur in Wiesel's narratives.[4] The antinomies and paradoxes which are countenanced within what remains a normative metaphysical framework constitute the essence of this literature and predominate in Wiesel's early novels particularly, where the bond between God and man, so often activated in classical *midrash,* is sorely tested. It is, therefore, a misdirected enterprise to read his novels either as theological tracts or as psychologically cogent character-studies (although at times, as we shall see presently, Wiesel himself seems to invite such readings and it is in such places that the creative tension between *midrash,* fiction, and philosophy dissolves).

The other literary component that Wiesel has adopted which originates in the pious literature is Ḥasidic legend—which in certain respects is a modern derivative of *midrash,* focusing more on human relations than on celestial drama. As experiments in the incorporation of legend into modern fiction, Wiesel's novels assimilate and adapt elements of structure as well as themes and perspectives from Ḥasidic lore. Yet, given what Buber calls the "formlessness" of most Ḥasidic tales, which are generally corrupted by oral transmission, Wiesel's narratives are more synthetic and contrived than their models, and his dramatic techniques are those of a modern novelist; nevertheless, some of the basic components of the legend—easily identified because they are so decidedly unmodern—are preserved: the relationship of master and disciple which reappears in many different guises in all of Wiesel's books; the master or mysterious stranger as wonder-worker; the repeated accounts of the attempts of holy men to hasten the advent of the messiah. The authority of the saint or master, who usually plays a central role in this fiction, is validated in most cases by the teller of the tale, who is clearly identified (frequently he is the narrator of the story); in that sense the latter becomes the master's disciple and scribe. In most original Ḥasidic legends, the name of the rebbe as well as the name of the Ḥasid who transmitted the tale is mentioned; as one Lubavitcher Ḥasid explained, "the only way to know if a story is true is if it has testimony from witnesses—that is, true witnesses."[5]

It is this, the personal validation of events, which also accounts, in large measure, for the magnetism of Wiesel's presence in America as a "genuine" survivor, as one considered to be qualified to write about and interpret the Holocaust. Yet here, as in the case of the Ḥasidic rebbe, the question of credibility does not revolve around strict adherence to "reality." In addition to the numerous memoirists, other writers we have considered, such as Ilona Karmel, have presented a much more convincing realistic interpretation than Wiesel's of the possibilities of life under the sign of the Swastika. David Daiches offers Wiesel's novels as "important evidence, great documents" of World War II;[6] like traditional Ḥasidic legend, however, which is a record of specific events and often cites places and dates, this fiction is grounded in reality yet is sustained more by the spiritual authority of authentic testimony than by accurate documentary. Even in the autobiographical *Night* and the short sketches located in the camps in *Legends of Our Time,* there seems to be a saturation point beyond which the author refuses to dwell on sordid facts, on the struggle for "bread and soup." It seems as if the aesthetic forms and religious categories that are to constitute the shape and substance of Wiesel's fiction cannot be cultivated on a substructure of atrocity.[7] The novels that follow *Night* still contain aspects of Wiesel's own biography—of what actually happened, and of what might have happened: they are explorations of the various paths a fifteen-year-old religious Jew from Transylvania might have taken. But what emerges as significant is not these events *per se,* but their representational aspect in legends which transform private experience into public legacy.

Nevertheless, the balance between reality and legend is a very delicate one in this genre, and Wiesel's narratives are constantly in danger of being subverted by either too much or too little realism. On stylistic grounds, his occasional lapses into a kind of staccato, journalistic realism are startlingly intrusive; these are most evident in passages meant to provide a *mise-en-scène* in the postwar European metropolis such as one finds in *The Oath* or in *The Town beyond the Wall* ("That year Paris was in the throes of what seemed to be a philosophico-political struggle with its conscience.... Everybody talked existentialism, everybody discussed Communism..."),[8] or in passages meant to establish the simultaneity of past and present history by interspersing contemporary idiom with legendary memories of the past ("Occupy the cities," Israeli officer Gad tells his men in a scene from the Six-Day War in *A Beggar in Jerusalem.* "Surround all pockets of resistance and proceed with the attack. Leave the mopping up for later. Undertake no action which would risk breaking the initial thrust" [p. 170]. In this case the attempt to present a Hemingwayesque battle scene is disruptive to both the tenor and the pace of the narrative and subverts the very claim to a realm of experience which transcends the one-dimensional, reality-oriented view of human history). Where Wiesel's stories are compelling, a generation or so after the war, it is in part because of the legendary quality which that period in history and that geographical location (the shtetl as well as the ghetto and the camp) already possess. Beyond that, Wiesel's almost unique position in the history of Holocaust literature in European languages lies in his attempt to convey in secular fiction the manner of thought and the literary modes practiced by believing Jews who perished; to apply, that is, to the most cataclysmic event of all, the internal methods by which the Jews of Eastern Europe traditionally grappled with and assimilated collective events and tragedies. Memory in this literature is collective, a partner in the unique interaction between past, present, and future which is the key to the Jewish perception of history. Wiesel acknowledges this when his narrator in *A Beggar in Jerusalem* rejects the imperialism of present reality by invoking the contemporaneity of Jewish history: the authentic legends, he says, are those told by people who are the "contemporaries of their ancestors," who are "unwilling to limit themselves to dates and locations. For them, chronological truth or nominal truth is only accidentally related to truth" (p. 45).

Yet, unlike myth, the midrashic manner commands a certain authenticity, and communal experience must be transmitted with a measure of realism as well as miracle. "God bent the heavens, moved the earth, and shook the bounds of the world, so that the depths trembled, and the heavens grew frightened," reports an ancient *midrash* on the revelation at Mt. Sinai; but, "although [such] phenomena were perceptible on Mt. Sinai in the morning, still God did not reveal Himself to the people until noon. For *owing to the brevity of the summer nights, and the pleasantness of the morning sleep in summer, the people were still asleep when God had descended upon Mt. Sinai . . .*" (emphasis mine).[9] It is the role of the witness or transmitter, then, to establish at least a degree of verisimilitude, and then to interpret and explore the event and to assign it a place in Jewish history. The quality of Hebraic legend, which is anchored in historical reality without purging it of the "contradictory multiplicity of events [and] psychological and factual cross-purposes," was identified by Erich Auerbach as characteristic even of early biblical narratives.[10]

Wiesel has defined his writing as an act of commemoration: "for me writing is a *matzeva,* an invisible tombstone, erected to the memory of the dead unburied" (*Legends of Our Time,* p. 25). It is also an act of resurrection—of return to that little town in the Carpathian Mountains just before the doors to the gas chambers were opened, at the moment when reprieve still seemed somehow possible. This is the moment captured graphically in the photographs that were taken in the camps, as Wiesel describes them in *One Generation After:*

> And from Treblinka—or is it Birkenau, Ponar, Majdanek?—this image which one day will burst inside me like a sharp call to madness: Jewish mothers, naked, leading their children, also naked, to the sacrifice.... Look at the women, some still young and beautiful, their frightened children well-behaved.... And you, what are you doing? Go ahead, go on, snatch a flower, offer it to the mothers in exchange for their children—what are you waiting for? Hurry up, quickly, grab a child and run, run as fast as your legs will carry you, faster than the wind, run while there's still time, before you are blinded by smoke... [P. 50]

Deceptively like the "still unravish'd bride of quietness" on Keats's Grecian urn—always about to be kissed—these innocent, naked Jewish mothers will always, inexorably, be leading their naked children to the sacrifice; but, frozen in that moment by the "artist" (in this case a German officer collecting "exotic souvenirs" for his photo album), they will never quite reach the "altar," and the writer is faced with the moral imperative to somehow still save them from the execution.

All of Wiesel's writing can be seen as an attempt to free these victims from their fate, to suspend history, if only for the moment. This is a theme which also appears elsewhere, especially in the poetic literature in which cameos of living memories stand out in temporary relief against the background of the inevitable. In numerous verses, Uri Zvi Greenberg graphically invokes the aborted lives of his family: "Here are mother and father / they have not yet been killed by their murderers."[11] Again, in a dream, he is transported to a snowy forest to cover the nakedness and feed the hunger of his young martyred nephew, "while he is still alive."[12] But since, unlike the urn or the photograph, the history-bound dream and the narrative are not arrested before the consummation of the death sentence, but must conclude by handing the victims back to the executioner, the story is repeated again and again. As Azriel, the only survivor of the town of Kolvillàg, tells his young interlocutor in Wiesel's *The Oath,* "all I can call my own is a forbidden city I must rebuild each day, only to watch it end in horror each night" (p. 9). Yet it is in the very repetition that the reality of character and situation is undermined. The same characters reappear with almost tedious predictability in Wiesel's fiction and eventually lose the husks of peculiarity; at this point, the commemorative impulse to embrace the entire spectrum of attitudes, modes of living, and personalities is transformed into a set of generalized codes which stand like a monument over a common grave, subsuming the richness and diversity of infinite particulars. And in the process, the imperative of

history, to which the elegist must, after all, conform—that the testimony have its story, its *histoire*—is sometimes sacrificed to the
legend. Just as we saw that, in a genre in which history is a springboard
to eternity, an overdose of realism can dispel the aura and mystery of
legend, so an attenuation of realism can betray the *ground* of legend;
this is evident in the extreme in the confrontation of disembodied
spirits in a passage entitled "Dialogues I" in *One Generation After:*
"Tell me: do you know who you are?" one asks the other. "No. Do
you?" "I don't." "Are you at least sure that you exist?" "I'm not. Are
you?" "No. Neither am I" (pp. 31–32).

Often compressing reality until nothing remains but the shadows,
Wiesel nevertheless persists in his efforts to establish the coordinates
by which the individual can orient himself to the memories and the
norms of a destroyed universe. Ironically, perhaps, Hebraic writing
furnishes one of the few instances in the literature we are studying
where a survivor of the Holocaust does not have to invent the cultural
frames within which the events can be transmitted. In the contemporary rabbinic literature we find evidence of the process whereby the
Nazi onslaught was met with the weapon that Jews have always used in
self-defense, that of barricading themselves behind a wall of Torah and
fighting the next round with God. The two-volume *Responsa from the
Depths* is the record of the questions concerning ritual observance that
were addressed to Rabbi Avraham Shapiro by inmates of the Kovno
Ghetto, and his answers. As conditions in the ghetto worsened, the
rabbi suspended more and more of the laws pertaining to ritual obser-
vances (though not the ethical imperatives) until very little remained of
the commandments *but the framework of commandment itself.*[13]
Similarly, in Wiesel's fiction the forms are preserved even if the con-
tent has been inverted. Wiesel retains the form of prayer in *Night*,
though it comes out sounding like a curse; when the *Kapos* come into
the barracks at Auschwitz to collect any new shoes that the inmates
may have brought with them, Eliezer's own pair of new shoes are so
coated with mud that they are not noticed: "I thanked God, in an
improvised prayer, for having created mud in His infinite and wonderful
universe."[14] And when Pinhas, the former director of a rabbinical
school, who appears in Auschwitz in *Legends of Our Time,* fasts on
Yom Kippur, or asks that the Kaddish be recited after his cremation, it
is as an act of defiance: "here and now, the only way to accuse [God] is
by praising him," he explains to his fellow inmates.[15] In the biblical
tradition, euphemism is sometimes used to avoid explicit blasphemy:
"bless God and die," Job's wife counsels her husband in a phrase
generally translated as "*curse* God and die" (2:9). What is crucial is
that the dialogue between man and God—even man's persistent in-

vocation of a God who refuses to answer—is maintained. The evidence of either the indifference or the vengeance of God (it is hard to say which is worse) is in the fate that awaits Pinḥas soon after his defiant act: "he left me a few weeks later," the narrator says, "victim of the first selection" (p. 61).

The inversion of the blessing and the dire fate of the blasphemer are also found in a Yiddish story by Isaac Bashevis Singer, "The Slaughterer." For over two decades Singer, who had emigrated from Poland to the United States in 1935, seemed to be deliberately avoiding the Holocaust in writing about the shtetl as if it still existed. In an interview with Irving Howe in 1966, he admitted that "at the heart of [his] attitude there is an illusion which is consciously sustained."[16] But some of the later stories in *The Seance* and the novel *Enemies, A Love Story* mark a clear turning toward a more direct confrontation with the effects of the Holocaust and an attempt to incorporate the challenges of the destruction into his own mythology and cosmology. In the powerful story "The Slaughterer," the growing abhorrence of the town *shoḥet* ("slaughterer"), Yoineh Meir, for the brutality of the ritual act of slaughter which he must perform leads him to challenge the divine authority that has sanctified it. The ancient ceremony of *sheḥitah* is suddenly transvalued into an act of savage murder. Yoineh Meir addresses God with the blasphemous "Thou art a slaughterer!... The whole world is a slaughter-house!"[17] This indictment of divine indifference to animal (and, by the extention that the post-Holocaust reader makes, to human) slaughter is reminiscent of Bialik's challenge of God after the Kishinev pogroms (the title of Bialik's poem is "On the Sláughter"). And, like the defiant Pinḥas in Wiesel's story but unlike the "pious blasphemers" of Singer's own earlier stories (such as Gimpel or Rabbi Bainish of Komarov, who are invariably saved from their impious words and deeds by a supernatural vision), Yoineh Meir is not rescued from his blasphemous declarations and desecrating acts; he is allowed to commit suicide—and his challenge, like that of Pinḥas, remains, terrifyingly, without answer. If no more miracles are forthcoming, it is, ultimately, the "crust of bread" that emerges victorious—the crust of bread for which the hungry struggle, for which even "saints become criminal." "So that crust could change the natural order, could reverse the structure of creation!" concludes the narrator of Wiesel's *Town beyond the Wall* (p. 59).

It is, then, not only the death of the Jews but their degradation which must be redeemed after the Holocaust. Salvation in Wiesel as in Singer can no longer come through divine intervention. "Do you believe in God?" the narrator of *The Accident* asks the doctor who has just operated on him. "Yes, he answered. "But not in the operating room. There I only count on myself."[18] In the course of Wiesel's fiction, that "operating room"—the human arena—has become his central concern: as Robert Alter observed, "the theological center has shifted to the human spirit; it is pathetically finite man who is the source of miraculous aspiration, of regeneration, in a world where all life is inevitably transient."[19]

It is not a theodicy, then, which evolves out of a reading of this fiction, but an affirmation of the metaphysics of human potential and vision. For these writers the Holocaust seems to have left vast empty spaces that only human compassion can fill. The shift from the cosmic to the human plane appears also to have taken place abruptly, if belatedly, in Singer's writing, triggered not by the chronology of events but by a shift in the writer's perspective. Unlike the earlier fiction, most of the stories since *Short Friday* (*The Seance, Enemies, A Love Story, Friends of Kafka, Passions,* and so on) are located in the United States rather than in the shtetl, and most of the protagonists are survivors. Even in those later stories which are set in Europe, the concentration camp, while never dramatized directly, forms a kind of palimpsest with the shtetl which erases much of the former innocence and exuberance. The main focus in most of Singer's earlier fiction was on the battle between supernatural forces for hegemony over the soul of man, and Singer was frequently berated by the more sentimental guardians of Yiddish culture for overlooking the ethical dimension of Jewish community life. In this respect the stories in *The Seance* especially seem to represent a significant change in focus; there is greater concentration on the earthly plight of suffering humanity, on the problems of physical existence and coexistence. The drama in such stories as "The Seance" lies not in the battle between forces of good and evil in supernal regions, but in the psychological, moral struggle among men or between one man and his conscience. Human feelings have largely replaced cosmic forces as the prime movers in this drama. There is, particularly in the stories in *The Seance,* less of the purely erotic that dominated many of Singer's earlier stories, and more of simple affection and kinship. In "The Seance" and "The Letter Writer," the two stories in which these qualities are most manifest, something of the vitality that was part of the turbulent sexuality of the earlier work has been sacrificed. The characters are old and tired; they have seen much and suffered much, and their energies are exhausted. They are attracted to each other not out of strong passion but out of the very depth of their weakness.

And the ghosts and demons, it seems, have shared the fate of the community that believed in them. In the story "The Last Demon," from *Short Friday,* the narrator makes a rather astonishing confession that can perhaps be read as a sign of a change of direction in Singer's writing: "I, a demon, bear witness that there are no demons left.... I've seen it all, the destruction of Tishevitz, the destruction of Poland. There are no more Jews, no more demons.... There is no longer an Angel of Good nor an Angel of Evil. No more sins, no more temptations!... There is no further need for demons. We have also been annihilated. I am the last, a refugee."[20] Wallace Stevens, surveying another corner of the same destroyed universe, wrote, "How cold the vacancy / When the phantoms are gone and the shaken realist / First sees reality."[21]

The supernatural has not been entirely banished from Singer's cosmos, however, but has been transfigured. Unlike the grotesque and often malevolent role they played in the earlier tales, the ghosts in the later stories are universally benevolent. They may even be reincarnations of the dead martyrs, come to console the survivors:

> Yes, the dead were still with us. They came to advise their relatives on business, debts, the healing of the sick: they comforted the discouraged, made suggestions concerning trips, jobs, love, marriage. Some left bouquets of flowers on bedspreads, and apported articles from distant places.... If this were all true, Herman thought, then his relatives, too, were surely living. He sat praying for them to appear to him. The spirit cannot be burned, gassed, hanged, shot. Six million souls must exist somewhere.[22]

The "annihilation" of the demons, like the "demise" of Sholom Aleichem's fictional characters in Alterman's poem, suggests the link between the death of the Jews and the collapse of their cultural universe; in Singer's story the new phantoms represent both a different cultural framework (America) and different communal concerns: no longer the agents of temptation, sin, or redemption in a religious community, the spirits function more as social advisers or personal counselors in a vision permeated by both anguish and irony.

Writing from within Jewish literary and cultural traditions, Wiesel's, like Singer's, indictments of God or demotion of the supernatural places an even greater onus on man, on the surviving remnant of Israel. More than most writers, who peek but do not linger in the concentrationary universe, Wiesel has been unswerving in his attention to the dead and their legacy; led by repetition into frequent overstatement and redundance, he has nevertheless persisted in the attempt to transmute destruction and death into legend that can abide both within the canon of lamentational literature and within the province of the modern novel. Singer, on the other hand, who celebrated the teeming life of pre-Holocaust civilization, traces its shadows in a post-Holocaust diaspora. Both writers reveal the agonies inherent in the confrontation between a religious universe committed to continuity and salvation through and beyond the vicissitudes of human affairs, and the compelling reality of the discontinuities induced by catastrophe.

While Wiesel and Singer explore certain classical religious positions which were challenged by secular patterns of thought and finally violated if not altogether shattered by the Nazi cataclysm, they avoid positing any historiosophical overview which could provide an accounting for or a logically coherent response to the Holocaust. "Without God," Wiesel writes in an essay, "the attempted annihilation of European Jewry would be relevant only on the level of history . . . and would not require a total revision of seemingly axiomatic values and concepts. Remove its Jewish aspects, and Auschwitz appears devoid of mystery."[23] Yet he resists any suggestion that design or purpose can be extracted from the events, whether in traditional religious terms according to which individuals or communities are singled out for the glorification of God's name, or in terms of a process of Jewish history by which reconstruction follows destruction. He goes so far to avoid any intimation of a causal relationship between the devastation of Diaspora Jewry and the restoration of Zion as to alter the conclusion of a Talmudic *midrash*. In the original, Rachel intercedes on behalf of the bereaved remnant of Israel who survived the destruction of the Temple and were driven into exile, and she is assured by God that for her sake He will "lead the children of Israel back to their land"; in Wiesel's version of this *midrash,* a compassionate but impotent God can only descend from heaven, weeping, to join the Jews in their martyrdom.[24]

Other writers have drawn on the schema of return that is rooted in midrashic and biblical tradition (Jeremiah assured the survivors of his generation that God would "take you one of a city, and two of a family, and . . . bring you to Zion" [3:14]) as well as in contemporary political events. The most completely constructed philosophy of return predicated on the rebirth of the State of Israel and on legendary sources can be found in the poetry of U. Z. Greenberg: "By their merit [the martyrs'] we have the Land," he writes at the conclusion of his "Crown of Lamentation for the Whole House of Israel."[25] More fragmented responses can be seen in the writings of the younger Israeli writers we have mentioned, for whom Israel offers the pragmatic answer of self-defense and a capacity for revenge to the meek submissiveness of Europe's Jews. Ḥanoch Bartov's *The Brigade* reconstructs the brazen, self-confident attitude of a generation of Israeli soldiers who regarded the victims with disdain mingled with a determination to avenge their death. The soldiers in the "Jewish Brigade" tauntingly paint "Die Juden Kommen" on their armored cars and proceed through enemy territory, but their "attack" comes *after* the Allied victory and the most their avenging arm can achieve is the belated and rather absurd act of pelting a convoy of returning German soldiers with tin cans and stones. And when the Jewish soldiers finally encounter the refugees in the D.P. camps, all confidence in the simple equations of Jewish history vanishes before the otherworldly physiognomy that suffering has carved out of the faces of their kinsmen.

Yehuda Amichai's *Not of This Time, Not of This Place* is a more probing and sensitive exploration of the personal need for vindication which can yield no historic results. In his imagined return to a reconstructed Germany and his belated attempt to uncover and retaliate against the Nazis who were responsible for the deportation and death of his childhood friend, Joel assembles an "army" which includes an Indian tourist, an American film producer, and an Israeli figure skater. Action reduced to gesture and inflated rhetoric masking small deeds comprise the irony of diminished heroics of the would-be warrior and redeemer of his people: "I thought, I will blow a shofar to summon my army, as they used to do in the Bible," the narrator boasts. "But I said, 'Let's order beer.' "[26] In the end it is Joel himself, Joshua manqué, who is conquered, petulantly confessing himself to be "like Jericho [with] a terrible army of conquerors [raging] on my ruins" (p.269). Amichai probes the deeper psychological needs for a redress of wounds carried since childhood, but here, as in Bartov's novel, nothing but the rubble of a former existence and the anonymous faces of a suspect generation of Germans, camouflaged by social decorum, confront the narrator's frenzied crusade. These novels reveal the frustration and futility of the attempts made by post-Holocaust Jews to leap over the unyielding gap of time and absorb the Holocaust into the unfolding drama of return and liberation.

In poetry Abba Kovner has delineated the internal struggle over alternative Jewish responses to an opportunity for resistance during the war itself. There have been many documentary and artistic accounts of the revolts in ghettos and camps, but only a few of them focus less on the historical events and more on the ethical and religious implications of conflicting forms of Jewish response to the threat of collective extinction. Kovner is able, both biographically and imaginatively, to link the call to arms with which the partisans confronted Jewish nonviolence during the Holocaust and the armed struggle for liberation which took place in Israel a few years later. The unfolding of the larger process of return, while not conceived as an immanent metahistorical or

theological design as it is in Greenberg's poetry, does vindicate the
blood of the martyrs who died with only the dream of Zion in their
hearts no less than that of the soldiers who later fought and died under
a national banner. Yet the poet's memory, like his poetry, is haunted
by the thought of those whom the partisans left behind in the ghettos as
they fled to the forests—often to suffer terrible retaliation at the hands of
the Nazis for the escape of the few: Kovner's magnificent long poem
"The Key Sank," which traces the prewar life and ghettoization of one
small town in Poland and the escape into the forests of twelve youthful
Resistance fighters, concludes with three short, staccato lines that
compress so much of the anguish that the survivor carries with him into
the future and that undermines any attempt at reading causality into
events: "In the end / We are all vanquished. / The dead. And the
living."[27]

Manès Sperber: From Kiddush ha-Shem to Kiddush ha-Ḥayyim

Like Kovner in his poems, Manès Sperber in one short novel explores
the implications for Jewish tradition of the conflict between mutually
exclusive forms of resistance to the Nazi threat. But unlike Kovner and
other survivors possessed by one subject, Sperber, a Galician Jew who
spent his young adulthood in Vienna as assistant to Alfred Adler and
found asylum during the war years in France, places the Holocaust
within the larger context of modern warfare and the struggle for human
rights. His novel ... *Than a Tear in the Sea* is part of a trilogy that
portrays the lives and diverse activities of members of a Polish Resistance organization. Still, even within this wider purview, Sperber succeeds in insulating the events of the Holocaust and relating them
primarily to the internal history and values of the Jewish people; in an
essay introducing the novel, the author defines the particular historical
challenge to which his narrative responds:

> Throughout the entire history of [the Jewish people], this
> Civitas Dei without a country...the survivors of each
> catastrophe discovered their invincibility anew. It was the
> invincibility of their faith; God was just, for he condemned
> their enemies to be transformed into murderers, while to the
> Jews he accorded the grace of being victims only, who
> thereby died sanctifying the Almighty....
>
> Now, this had ceased to be true: the Hitlerite fury took
> the Jewish people by surprise: they were no longer inclined
> and in no way prepared to die for God. If, for the first time
> on Christian soil, Jews were going to be murdered *en masse*
> without any demands being made upon them in the name of
> Christ, European Jewry itself was *going to perish for noth-
> ing, in the name of nothing.*[P. viii]

The essence of this novel, then, is the challenge to the ultimate significance of martyrdom by such an unprecedented threat to the body as well as the soul of the Jew—and the struggle for the proper Jewish response to an opportunity for resistance.

The setting of . . . *Than a Tear in the Sea* is the Jewish town of Wolyna and its environs. The town is defined by its own inhabitants through its history of suffering—of "wars, uprisings, pogroms, epidemics, great fires" (p. 7). So inured are they to disaster that when a stranger, Edi Rubin, who has escaped from the death camps, appears in their midst in order "to describe those camps in detail, to tell of the unimaginable organization for annihilation against which he must pronounce his warning" (p. 16), he is hardly listened to. Rubin does, however, succeed in convincing twenty-eight men from Wolyna, including Byrnie, the rabbi's son, to take to the woods to fight "so that, if it must be, they might at least die like men and not like sheep" (p. 17). Just as they reach underground headquarters, the roundup of the remaining Jews begins, and soon the town is empty and the mutilated corpse of the old rabbi lies in the village square. The twenty-eight Jews, together with some volunteers from the Armia Krajowa, the local unit of the Polish Resistance, succeed in ensnaring into a nearby ravine and slaughtering a number of Ukrainians in the service of the SS. But anti-Semitism erupts within the ranks of the Polish Underground itself, and most of the fugitive Jews are slaughtered. Byrnie remains alive long enough to confront Edi Rubin's cynicism and despair with his own faith, to invest in him the message of the Jewish people's death, and to pledge him to survival.

The novel opens in those halcyon days when an eternal rhythm of recurrence, and not the contingencies of the present, still regulates the lives of Wolyna's inhabitants. The narrative weaves an aura of legend reminiscent of a Chagall tapestry: the Jews of the town are carpet-makers and violinists, and include the usual quorum of Jewish types—a pious rabbi, his sensitive young son, a few panderers, good housewives, innocent children. Character stereotyping, which we come to recognize as a hallmark of the commemorative enterprise that would sort out the general from the incidental, is particularly striking in Sperber's novel because the characters in his other fiction are much rounder and more individuated and, as André Malraux remarks in his introduction to the novel, when "a story in which psychological analysis plays a negligible role [is] written by a former assistant of Adler, [it] is a fact that gives pause for reflection." And, indeed, it is not psychology but something else which, as Malraux goes on to observe, governs a character like Byrnie, the rabbi's son: "Byrnie has all the ambiguous intensity of the great modern creations; but his language expresses what he has conquered, the presence within him of the eternal" (p. xix).

But whereas Malraux defines the "eternal" which abides in Byrnie as a "universal" quality, "the essential expression of the religious experience," and in this sense insists that "this is no more Jewish literature than Tagore is Vedantist literature" (p. xviii), I would argue that this is, on the contrary, precisely where Sperber exposes the particular agony that lies at the very core of Judaism after the Holocaust. Malraux opposes "history" to the "Eternal," recognizing, on the one hand, that "the townspeople of Wolyna take on the centuries of which Wolyna is composed," but contrasting this to what "Byrnie takes on [of] the Eternal." The "Eternal" as a "universal" force is thus understood to transcend both the parochial and the temporal. "Sperber," Malraux continues, "owes to Hegel his obsession with history as something intelligible; now, his entire narrative is a revolt against history" (p. xx). It is, however, not Hegel who has rendered history "intelligible" for Sperber (*The Phenomenology of Mind* figures in the novel as a lower form of perception of history, Hegel representing what Byrnie calls the "arrogance" of the human spirit who believes he is "his own creator" [p. 19])—but Judaism. And history, in Judaism, is coterminous with the Eternal. Byrnie's own perception of the Eternal (and of eternal values) is integral to his perception of Jewish history; although, in joining the partisans, he seems to have rejected his father's attitude toward martyrdom (the old rabbi dismissed Rubin's plea for armed resistance by adopting the traditional Jewish stance toward the persecutor as a "scourge" that God uses "to chastise us," and was concerned with ensuring that he and his people "die not as murderers but as martyrs" [p. 18]), Byrnie, no less than his father, sees divine providence in events—even in the imperative of action, of armed rebellion. A transcendent history may, then, subsume events, but it does not negate them. The "higher will" acts, mysteriously, *through* the Jewish community, even if that community is reduced to only twenty-eight men—or, eventually, to only one or two. It is, then, in a context in which the Holocaust is presented not only as the crucible of the individual or of the universal human spirit but as the agony of the soul of Israel that stereotyped characters appear in this literature—as representatives not of moral or religious positions such as those embodied by the dramatis personae of the Christian moralities, but of the clash of spiritual attitudes *in history,* under the aspect of eternity.

One of these attitudes legitimates the massacre of the Ukrainian collaborators by Byrnie's "partisans"; while armed resistance cannot begin to redress the evil done to the other Jews of the town, it does provide the men with a catharsis of sorts. Nevertheless, although

Sperber seems to espouse a consistent historical overview, the time-hallowed values continue to clash with the imperatives of the hour within the soul of the protagonist who is still committed to the ancient tradition; it is Byrnie's resistance to setting up barricades on the Sabbath which finally leaves him and his men exposed to the guns of the Polish partisans.

A tentative faith in the transcendent spirit which orders the cosmos and leads Israel through the fires along inscrutable paths emerges from the clash of attitudes in ... *Than a Tear in the Sea*. But in the entire trilogy of which this novel is a part, the faith that survives adversity is in the beneficence of the *human* spirit. Even Byrnie, who is most clearly invested with a kind of saintliness, is equally the personification of "human goodness"; a series of healing miracles that he works as he lies dying are more the function of psychological perception than of divine powers. Even as he dedicates his life to God, he consecrates life itself; in casting his lot with the partisans rather than with the passive victims of Wolyna, he affirms the imperative of survival (*kiddush ha-ḥayyim*) which was articulated by Rabbi Nissenbaum, one of the spiritual leaders of Polish Jewry, as the equivalent of martyrdom (*kiddush ha-Shem*) in other times.[28] Yet even such survival cannot be anarchic, and when he feels that the very structure of the Law is being threatened by a pledge to survival at all costs, Byrnie barricades himself and his men behind the Torah. If they are destined not to survive, as he has anticipated, their deaths will at least have been carved out of the affirmation of life and the pride of self-defense as well as the glorification of God, like the deaths of the fighters in the Warsaw Ghetto. The spiritual magnetism of this young rabbi lends a kind of sanctity to his convictions and acts even over the ascetic saintliness of his elderly father, with which they seem to clash. And here Malraux seems justified in concluding that the "tragic conflict" in this parabolic novel, between martyrdom and armed resistance, "tends neither towards the victory of one or the other of the opposing values in it, nor to their reconciliation; it would seek to reveal the presence of a mystery rather than to achieve the solution of a puzzle" (p. xix). Yet behind this mystery lie the terrible, unremediable lacerations which the Holocaust inflicted in the body of normative Judaism.

André Schwarz-Bart: The Last Passion

Jewish suffering seems to have become a salient literary subject in post-Holocaust France with the award of the Prix Goncourt to three French-Jewish writers within seven years (1955–62) for novels in which the Holocaust figures as a theme. And, like the other two authors (Anna Langfus and Roger Ikor), André Schwarz-Bart reached Jewish circles mostly through the mediation of wider social acclaim. The scope of the public interest may be all the more remarkable as his novel, *The Last of the Just,* is, ostensibly at least, concerned with the internal processes of Jewish history. It is a quasi-factual account of the genealogy of the Levy family of Just Men whose tradition of self-sacrifice originates with the suicide of Yom Tov Levy and the other besieged Jews of York in 1185—whose ashes were "cast to the winds"[29]—and culminates in the martyrdom of Ernie Levy among the Jews in Auschwitz, where *his* ashes are cast to the winds.

In its focus on persecution as the organizing principle of communal memory, *The Last of the Just* is a fictional derivative of the medieval lamentation literature. And, just as the medieval authors of those elegies or elegiac chronicles were held accountable less for the facts than for the transmission of the events within a traditional normative framework, so in the case of Schwarz-Bart, accountability is measured less in terms of fidelity to history than in terms of the traditional codes by which experience is interpreted. Whereas questions of "validity" are hardly germane to an imaginative interpretation of history, the normative premises which such a writer invokes and the habit of a public literature through which, as Maurice Samuel put it, events "establish" [themselves] in the Jewish people," engage Schwarz-Bart in a special kind of dialogue and could account for the controversy which followed the publication of his book. The bond linking the generations of Levys is the spiritual genealogy of the *lamedvovnik,* the Just Man, who constitutes one of the thirty-six pillars of human goodness (*lamedvov* is the equivalent in Hebrew gematria of thirty-six) by which it is believed that the perpetuation öf the world is ensured. In his fictional adaptation, Schwarz-Bart took liberties in molding the cultural meanings of the folk beliefs embodied in the legend. Propelled by the interest in the concept of the Just Men which Schwarz-Bart's book generated, Gershom Scholem wrote an essay explicating the origins and the substance of the legend, illuminating the discrepancies between the two versions but refraining from passing judgment: "As a novelist Schwarz-Bart is not bound by scholarly conventions and can give free reign to his speculative fantasy."[30] "Speculative fantasy" is of interest here as more than a deviation from scholarly conventions, however, as it is in the shifts and transformations of traditional sources that we can identify the orientations of each of these writers toward the Holocaust. Schwarz-Bart's major departure from the sources lies in his eschewal of the principle of the anonymity of the Just Man. By establishing the position as hereditary, he actually alters the concept of righteousness which was traditionally regarded as both self-effacing and socially unrewarded. No homage is paid to or canonization conferred upon the man whose saintliness is matched by his obscurity. Scholem elucidates the "anarchic morality" which underlies the *lamedvov* tradition: if there are no external markings of election, each man remains responsible as potentially just in the sight of God and should regard his neighbor as having the same potential and refrain from passing any moral judgment on him.[31] There are no designated saints whose function it is to relieve others of their troubles or their sins. The legend places emphasis on goodness which can never be hereditary but must involve the effort of a lifetime to acquire.

Schwarz-Bart's emendation of cultural and religious categories proves to be less an exploration of, or even a challenge to, traditional attitudes toward theodicy and Jewish destiny than an interpolation of extrinsic attitudes into the traditional forms. By changing the essence of the legend of the Just Man, Schwarz-Bart has delineated an altogether different way of being and of relating to the community from what has been indigenous to it. The Jews have had their revered leaders and even their "dynasties" of holy men, especially within the Hasidic community—but the idea of a kind of predestined assignation of individual martyrdom in the context of some sort of communal redemption is foreign to normative Judaism.

In spite of appearances, then, the organization of Jewish history around a succession of pogroms in this novel does not either serve or defy the specific purposes of the traditional poems and chronicles of lamentation—namely, commemoration of the martyrs and affirmation of faith in God at the moment of supreme sacrifice—but presents Jewish history as an adjunct to or a whipping boy for Christian history. It has already been observed, by Pierre Aubéry and other critics, that Schwarz-Bart's "vision of Jewish fate comes closer to the Christian punitive concept than the Jewish prophetic vision."[32] The roles of victim and victimizer appear as preordained and the Nazis, who in fact are portrayed in this novel more extensively and realistically than in most of the literature we are considering, become the latest in the inevitable procession of executioners. Their partners in this reiterated passion are the willing victims, the dynasty of Just Men. And the central character, the last of the Just Men, is the one who most clearly embodies this Christological role.

It should be stressed that it is not the subject but Schwarz-Bart's treatment of it that is striking within the Hebraic context. Jewish literature, as insulated as it may often appear to be, has reflected an ongoing dialogue with Christianity—in often subterranean but nonetheless persistent ways which focus variously on Jesus as an ancient model of Jewish martyrdom and on institutionalized Christianity in its historical relation to the Jews. Irving Howe points to the contemporary manifestations of this strange magnetism in the poetry of Yiddish writers such as H. Leivick and Itzik Manger.[33] Some of the most controversial expressions are to be found in the Yiddish writings of Sholem Asch—in his historical novels on the life of Jesus and in the Holocaust stories in his collection *Tales of My People,* in which the victims are portrayed as sacrificial lambs through a veil of gentle lyricism that belies the atrocities much as portraits of the crucifixion elevate physical pain into spiritual passion. Asch explicated his vision in an *Epistle to the Christians,* published in 1945: "Suddenly [at the moment of death in the camps] everything becomes understandable, realizable, clear, and beautiful. Suffering acquires a reason, an explanation—it is the highest price exacted for one's faith . . . . The prophet Elijah leads the way and makes a path for [the victims]. King David is among them as are the patriarchs and the prophets. And so is the Nazarene."[34] Other Hebraic writers reflect the dialectic between Judaism and Christianity through the more ambiguous role the Church has played in Jewish history and, most recently, in the context of the Holocaust. In Kovner's poem "My Little Sister," and in the Hebrew short story by Aharon Appelfeld "Kitty," the convent provides both a temporary refuge to the body and an ultimate lair for the soul of a young Jewish girl.

In Schwarz-Bart's novel, Christianity is represented both in the historical context of the interaction of the Church with the Jews and in the allegorical model presented by the figure of the suffering Christ. Ernie Levy appears as an archetype of the tormented Jew from earliest childhood when he is subjected to torture at the hands of his gentile playmates. As a youth he begins to court martyrdom by bravely facing a cordon of SA soldiers in the synagogue courtyard. "He is the lamb of suffering; he is our sacrificial dove," his grandfather declares (p. 175), and proceeds to initiate him into his otherworldly mission as a Just Man: "A day will come when all by yourself you will begin to glow . . ." (p. 179). From that point on, Ernie inflicts a succession of physical and spiritual stigmata upon his body and soul in anticipation of "offer[ing himself] heroically to the holocaust" (p. 185)—a process that culminates in the final martyrdom enacted when he abandons the asylum he has found in France and voluntarily forces his way into a transport bound from Drancy to Auschwitz.

The story of Ernie's last days, of his short love affair with Golda, consummated the day before her deportation and consecrated in the gas chamber, has the human warmth and gentle, legendary sentimentality of the most idyllic portrait of romance in the valley of the shadow of death. But Ernie's last role is not only that of the Romeo who has chosen to die with his Juliet, but of the martyr who has chosen to die with and for his people, to suffer little children to come unto him; he dies embracing the children whom he has accompanied from Drancy, crying tears of blood, the "blood of pity" (p. 406).

It is here, in the quality of mercy, that Ernie's passion acquires its ultimate significance. The final scene of the novel is one of the very few accounts in the literature of the last moments in the gas chambers—for, since there were no survivors, only an act of imagination can invoke that scene. Yet there is nothing grotesque or horrible about this passage, only an infinite sadness which pervades the conclusion of the novel, like the gas which permeates the cubicle of death. As Ernie encourages "his" children to "breathe deeply, my lambs, and quickly," to shorten the suffering and hasten the end, as the Jews recite together "the old love poem" which, "above the funeral pyres of history, the Jews ... [had] traced in letters of blood on the earth's crust—'SHMA ISRAEL ADONAI ELOHENU ADONAI EH'OTH [*sic*]'" (p. 407)— as one by one they die and Ernie and Golda embrace in one last loving gesture, it is not the horror of dying which emerges but a kind of hagiographic parable of mercy and comfort.

In the end, then, it is not simply the reenactment of the Jewish destiny of martyrdom which remains as Ernie's final legacy; although, as we have suggested, the inevitability of martyrdom is the organizing principle of the novel, what emerges is not an affirmation of metaphysical *purpose*. There are in fact occasional instances of religious doubt and even blasphemy in the novel; when Ernie is at his lowest, after receiving knowledge of his family's murder and before taking the decision to join the other imprisoned Jews, he rails against a Divinity that could have designed such a fate: "If it is the will of the eternal, our God, I damn his name and beg him to gather me up close enough to spit in his face" (p. 308). And the narrator, who introduced himself at the beginning of the novel as a "friend" of Ernie's, mourns Ernie's death in the words of a violated Kaddish which may be compared to the inverted prayers and ceremonies we have encountered in other fiction:

> And praised. Auschwitz. So be it. Maidanek. The Eternal.
> Treblinka. And praised. Buchenwald. So be it. Mauthausen.
> The Eternal. Belzec. And praised. Sobibor. So be it...
> [P. 408]

Yet, while these passages impugn divine beneficence, they do not rend the heavens asunder. There is a lack of real tension and hence of engagement between the fate of the victim and his inherited system of values. The compassion which Ernie embodies in his last moments becomes almost a messianic force which, in the lack of divine comfort, eases the dying multitudes into the next world. Although messianic expectations abound in lamentation literature, this is a vision of consummation which is rare, if not unique, and goes beyond even Asch's sentimental portraits of calvary in the concentration camps. As his life is snuffed out on a twentieth-century crucifix of gas, Ernie Levy becomes the Christ whom he has revered as the model of a Just Man—not the "blond Christ of the cathedrals," whose cross was "turn[ed] around" to make a sword to strike down all the generations of his descendants, but the Christ who, as Ernie tells Golda, was "a simple Jew... a kind of Hasid... a merciful man, and gentle" (pp. 351, 384). And in the last lines of the narrative the compassion of the last of the Just Men is generalized and canonized into a transcendental spirit:

> At times, it is true, one's heart could break in sorrow. But often too, preferably in the evening, I cannot help thinking that Ernie Levy, dead six million times, is still alive, some-where, I don't know where.... Yesterday, as I stood in the street trembling in despair, rooted to the spot, a drop of pity fell from above upon my face; but there was no breeze in the air, no cloud in the sky... there was only a presence.
> [P. 409]

This image resembles the metaphors of phantoms or clouds or other transmigrations of the souls of the martyred Jews which we frequently encounter in Hebraic literature. Yet the lyrical element of reconcili-ation wrought by pity and of transcendental harmony which concludes this tale of genocide is absent among the other writers, who reflect a tradition in which no human being is invested with the power to relieve the sins, or the sufferings, of another, a tradition in which the *Shekhinah* itself, an emanation of the Divine, is believed to have ac-companied Israel into exile and to share in its suffering.[35] The same kind of reconciliation is effected in Schwarz-Bart's second novel, *A Woman Named Solitude,* the story of the massacre of the slaves of West Africa; the narrator of that novel instructs the reader that if he wishes to visit the site of the massacre, he will find mounds of bone and wall, testifying to a former human presence and randomly buried and dug up by the "innocent hoes of [today's] field workers." His concluding passage is an attempt to link this massacre with the Holocaust by the kinship of martyrdom and the author's sense of the written text as monument: "If [the reader] is in the mood to salute a memory, his imagination will people the environing space, and human figures will rise up around him, just as the phantoms that wander about the humiliated ruins of the Warsaw ghetto are said to rise up before the eyes of other travelers."[36]

The ghosts of these and other genocides still hover, then, over the ruins of their former homes—a presence that can be resurrected by the imagination which provides them with a foothold. The two novels are a double testament to the eternal recurrence of human suffering. The black woman Solitude, like Ernie Levy, is destined from birth for martyrdom by an inexorable historical process that ordains that certain groups be lambs and others butchers. And her passion, like that of Ernie Levy, is ultimately redeemed by the harmony and ascendancy of her being—and by the imagination of a compassionate artist who invokes the phantoms and transmutes a bloodbath into a gentle lyrical parable.

As Milton Hindus has written, Schwarz-Bart is "obviously universalistic in his aspirations . . . as an artist [and] . . . conceives of himself as a mediator between several cultures." His novels of suffering may then be read as attempts to travel the "road to the universal . . . through the particular"[37]—without, however, being necessarily constrained by the boundaries of the particular. In this sense, *The Last of the Just*, suffused as it is with a sense of Jewish destiny, with Jewish values and mores, remains, ultimately, outside the internal polemic in which the Jewish artist who is also the scribe struggles with ancient forms of collective perception and modern forms of collective death. Ernie Levy's messianic role is realized in his martyrdom; it is as if the world has been redeemed by the last of the Just, "dead six million times," and there is nothing beyond his death but a kind of *grace*. For most of the writers who are linked to the lamentation tradition, the struggle of man betrayed in Auschwitz by a helpless or indifferent God and a tarrying messiah only intensifies as it is multiplied by six million. And it is not human compassion which is primary in this struggle, but human *responsibility*. *The Last of the Just* is a call for sacrifice and mercy beside the more consistently Hebraic demand for human responsibility and divine justice. It is a message of comfort beside the demand for anguished engagement.

Nelly Sachs: From Mount Moriah to Majdanek

The perception of Jewish suffering as an invariable, eternal component in human history and the cosmic absorption of that suffering also appear as a recurrent theme in the poetry of Nelly Sachs.

Sachs's poems are free from the didacticism, apologetics, and sentimentalism which characterize the poetry of so many lesser Holocaust poets. Some of her most powerful poems are those which are universal lyrics of pain—especially the lullabies and laments to the slaughtered children ("O Night of the Weeping Children," "A Dead Child Speaks")—or those which reflect the poet's own personal angst as a survivor ("If I Only Knew," "We the Rescued"). Nevertheless, Sachs also invites a reading as a "public" poet. Not only has she been accorded the status of the poet who "speaks for the fate of the Jews" by the Germans themselves (the quote is taken from the citation on the Frankfurt Peace Prize which she received in 1965)[38] and by many

Jewish readers, but she has explicitly assumed that role; in a letter acknowledging her use of biblical and Ḥasidic sources in the mystery play *Eli,* she writes: "I just have the deep feeling that Jewish artists must begin to listen to the voice of their lineage, so that the old spring may awaken to new life. With that in mind I have attempted to write a mystery play of the sufferings of Israel."[39]

Biblical and Ḥasidic, even Cabbalistic, themes are woven into Sachs's poetry as into her play—but without the flesh of living transmission. They are *sources* rather than *traditions,* serving the search for an attitude toward death. As in the writing of Schwarz-Bart, it is death—the enormity, the mystery, the place of death—which is at the center of Sachs's poetry. Where other Hebraic writers do concentrate on dying, it is more for the legacy that the manner of dying leaves to the living than for the repulsive—or redemptive—power of death itself.

None of this figures into Sachs's postwar poetry, which is totally informed by the act of slaughter that brought the poet herself back to Judaism (an assimilated young woman living in Berlin and writing neoromantic poetry, she was forced to flee from Nazi Germany in 1940 and found a haven in Sweden). In the one instance where she reconstructs the Jewish town—the play *Eli* which, written in 1943, envisions the return of survivors to their hometown and their attempts to rebuild it—it is to fix the moment of death rather than to convey or recapture the spirit of life. As David Bronsen has said of the characters in the play—of the workers who dig up the rubble before laying new foundations—they are "archaeologists of the immediate past,"[40] discovering a ribbon or a skullcap or a shoe and trying to guess who its owner had been and to reconstruct the manner of his death. They are archaeologists, then, not of the kind who reassemble the shards of their own lost communal past and who try to leap back over death to recapture the pulse of a civilization, but of the kind who excavated Pompeii and were far more intrigued by the death-pose than by the life which was snuffed out by lava.

This point is, I believe, crucial to an understanding of Sachs's poetry, as the death of Israel becomes the essential fact on which attitudes toward mankind and toward the universe are based. The Bible appears here not as the epic of a living people, but as a kind of compendium of the signs of martyrdom which will furnish the references for future sacrifice. There is, in short, no *history* in Sachs's universe: there are archetypes of events and of relationships and functions, but there is no biography or history. It is not simply an absence of "reality," for, although the "facts" have been raised to the level of metaphor in her poetry, the agony and even the details of dying are conveyed here more powerfully than in many other, more graphic, descriptions of death in the camps. A close reading even suggests the specific correlatives of death by gas in the expressionistic lines of one poem, "Landscape of Screams," which appears in the volume of her selected poems, *O the Chimneys:*

> O, O hands with finger vines of fear,
> dug into wildly rearing manes of sacrificial blood—
>
> Screams, shut tight with the shredded mandibles of fish,
> woe tendril of the smallest children
> And the gulping train of breath of the very old...
>
> [P. 127]

But this reality, the things and events of this world, takes on significance not in its peculiarity but in its symbolization of something beyond itself—of the eternal recurrence of the pattern, and even the manner, of death. The characters in *Eli* are nonspecific archetypes of social roles (Washerwoman, Baker Woman, Knife Grinder, Rabbi, and so on). Even those few who have names—such as Michael, the central character—are the embodiments of certain tasks (Michael represents, as Sachs herself explains in the postscript, one of the Thirty-six Just Men). And the ultimate division of roles is into those of murderer, victim, and survivor (weeper); the Knife Grinder, accused by the Old Woman that his grinding "carves up the world in pieces," answers that he grinds because "it's my trade," and the Old Woman acknowledges, "so it's his trade, / as it's mine to weep—/ and another's to die" (p. 335).

This is a recurrent image throughout the poetry as well as the play, the image of the "age-old game of hangman and victim, / Persecutor and persecuted, / Hunter and hunted—" (p. 340). Among the victims there are no persons but the totality of Israel as an abstract quantity of prospective martyrs: children, nursing mothers, old men, bakers, rabbis, and so on; they are not the archetypes that distill a living organism into its most representative members, such as we have encountered in other Hebraic writing. And among the hangmen, not only do the Nazis remain anonymous; they become at times no more than the dismembered instruments of a transcendent will. A recurrent synecdoche in the poetry is the "fingers of the killers"; in *Eli,* each finger represents a different form of death (one finger strangles, another administers injections, and so on), and in the poem "O the Chimneys," the "fingers" are the agents which build the chimneys that are to direct "Israel's body as smoke through the air" (p. 3). And even those devices of concentrationary death, the chimneys, are transfigured into latter-day conveyances for facilitating the flow of dust that is as ancient as the martyrdom of Jeremiah and Job:

O the chimneys
Freedomway for Jeremiah and Job's dust—
Who devised you and laid stone upon stone
The road for refugees of smoke?

[P. 3]

The implication is that there can be more than one answer to the question, "who devised you?" The latest martyrdom of Israel was, then, prefigured and preordained as long ago as in the time of Jeremiah and Job—and even before that, in the time of Abraham; one of the instruments of death has even been passed down from Mount Moriah to Majdanek:

Above Moria, the falling off cliffs to God,
there hovers the flag of the sacrificial knife
Abraham's scream for the son of his heart,
at the great ear of the Bible it lies preserved.

...Job's scream to the four winds
and the scream concealed in Mount Olive
like a crystal-bound insect overwhelmed by impotence.

O knife of evening red, flung into the throats
where trees of sleep rear blood-licking from the ground,
where time is shed
from the skeletons in Hiroshima and Maidanek...

[Pp. 127, 129]

The reference to Hiroshima suggests the unity of suffering; this is rare in the poetry of Sachs, which is explicitly concerned not with the universality of suffering but with the universal and eternal role of Jewish suffering; otherwise, this poem is fairly representative of the theme of recurrence that emerges in most of her Holocaust poems. Jewish history, or the continuum of Jewish existence, becomes a series of reenactments of the pageant of death which take place not in a civilization but in a barren landscape of screams. Death is consecrated by divine will—but not by the God of revelation and covenant, not by the God who is called into dialogue with man. The significance of this becomes sharper if we compare the above stanzas with similar passages that appear in the literature in which Mount Moriah is associated with Majdanek. In a Yiddish poem by H. Leivick, for example, unlike in Sachs's poem, the same imagery of continuity which affirms the cyclical nature of Jewish history also constructs an irony of juxtaposition or inversion that characterizes most of postwar lamentation literature. The speaker in Leivick's poem links the two places, the mountain on which Isaac was nearly sacrificed and the death camp in which thousands of Jews were actually slaughtered, in an effort to force God to honor His covenant with His people as they have honored theirs with Him.[41] A similar image appears in Aaron Zeitlin's Yiddish poem "Ani Ma'amin": "Who is so volcanic as my God? / If he is Sinai to me, / He is Maidanek as well." This poem, like Zeitlin's other poems, is a declaration of faith (one volume of his poetry is entitled *Poems of Hurbn and of Faith*), yet it is faith secured only after struggle and protest. And his God is a God who commands and who lives in history: "I believe / He suffers with me; / if I cry out against Him with me He cries..."[42] In Sachs's poems, God is unreachable and unaccountable, and the recurrence of martyrdom is accepted almost as a law of nature. Sachs herself, in a letter to Walter Berensohn in 1946, attaches a mission of enlightenment through suffering to the destiny of Israel: "When each of the peoples of the earth seeks for meaning, why should not Israel again offer mankind a draught from its own ancient source? I do not think it is enough to win fruit and home from our inherited earth when it is in our power together to fulfill the ancient call of our people—new and purified by suffering."[43]

There is, then, a "meaning" which Israel is meant to extract—and to share—out of its sufferings. But the ultimate resolution is not in the social message, or even in the messianic compassion which redeems the passion in a work like *The Last of the Just,* but in a kind of transcendental synthesis. Without attempting to present an exegesis of the metaphysics which informs Sachs's poetry, at the heart of which lies unfathomable mystery, I would only call attention to the manner in which Israel's latest martyrdom is absorbed into the larger, cosmic design; the speaker, like a seventeeth-century English metaphysical poet, reaches from the particular property which designated the victims—the numbers engraved on their arms in the camps—to a mystical, quasi-Cabbalistic, assimilation of numbers as components of an organic universe:

> When your forms turned to ashes
> into the oceans of night
> where eternity washes
> life and death into the tides—
>
> there rose the numbers—
> (once branded into your arms
> so none would escape the agony)
>
> there rose meteors of numbers
> beckoned into the spaces
> where light-years expand like arrows
> and the planets
> are born
> of the magic substances of pain—

> numbers—root and all
> plucked out of murderers' brains
> and part already
> of the heavenly cycle's
> path of blue veins.
>
> ["Numbers," p. 71]

The unity of the universe is so complete that no part of it can be violated without all the others being affected. The "Star" in *Eli* testifies to its role in accepting the "dust" of Israel as it traveled through the chimneys: "I was the chimney sweep— / my light turned black—"; and the tree testifies: "I am only a tree. / I can no longer stand straight..." (p. 363). There is, then, terrible, cosmic sadness for the loss—"there, always, / where a place has been left / for heartbeats" ("Who knows where the stars stand," p. 103)—but the loss and the sadness are ultimately absorbed into the divine harmony:

> The child murdered in sleep
> Arises; bends down the tree of ages
> And pins the white breathing star
> That was once called Israel
> To its topmost bough.
> Spring upright again, says the child,
> To where tears mean eternity.
>
> ["The Voice of the Holy Land," p. 45]

Of her own verse, Sachs says that it is "always designed to raise the unutterable to a transcendental level, so as to make it bearable and in this night of nights to give a hint of the holy darkness in which quiver and arrow are hidden" (a reference to the prophet Isaiah, who says that "the Lord puts the arrow he had used back in its quiver so that it may remain in darkness").[44]

Just as Sachs's universe is organic and totally interconnected, so all the poems written since 1946 are aspects of a unifying vision. At her death in 1970, this gentle poet left to her people a strange and beautiful volume of consolation which seeks refuge in a Divinity whose ways are inscrutable and in a community which fulfills its tragic mission in death.

Paul Celan: No Consolation

Paul Celan has been regarded by many as the most accomplished German lyric poet of recent decades. He and Sachs are among the few who did not exchange their language when they emigrated from Germany and whose writing remains, in part at least, rooted in German literary traditions. The German of Celan, it has been argued, was significantly influenced by the literary conventions of his adopted home, France;

nevertheless, his language is such a unique construct of deeply rooted idiom and neologism that he can hardly be considered a "displaced" writer. As Alvin Rosenfeld writes: "When all else had been taken from Paul Celan, when his homeland had been occupied by the Nazis and his parents deported to one of the death camps, his language alone remained as a link to the past, and the poet lived in it as permanently and as securely as he ever did again in any physical landscape."[45] Celan was born in Czernowitz, capital of Bukovina (where most of the Jews spoke German), and barely escaped the death by gas that was the lot of his parents; he spent the war years in a work camp and then returned to Romania for a short time before his exile to Paris. His death in 1970 was, apparently, a suicide.

Celan's poetry, which explores vast territories of the human soul, is not concerned exclusively with the Holocaust, and it is not primarily as a poet of the Holocaust that he has been read; in fact, except for his widely acclaimed poem "Todesfuge," the depth of his involvement with the Jewish catastrophe and his extensive use of Jewish sources have often been overlooked. What is needed is a reading of Celan, as one would read other Hebraic writers, with an understanding of his origins so that one can appreciate his deviations. Celan himself described the landscape—internal as well as external—that was his heritage in an acceptance speech in 1958 when he was awarded the Bremen Literary Prize: "The landscape from which I come to you—by way of what detours! but are there even such things as detours?—this landscape may be unknown to most of you. It is the landscape that was the home for a not inconsiderable part of those Hasidic tales that Martin Buber recounted to us all in German."[46] Against this landscape, the question of continuity or discontinuity in the traditional perceptions of martyrdom is crucial to an understanding of the few poems which are clear responses to the Holocaust.

Celan is the artist who is most often invoked in the ongoing debate on the potential of aesthetic forms to capture the horrors of the concentrationary universe. The challenge, it will be recalled, was formulated by Adorno when he discussed the dangers inherent in any "artistic representation of the naked bodily pain of those who have been knocked down by rifle butts"; it contains the potential, he continued—"no matter how remote—to squeeze out pleasure." We saw that Borowski expressly banished "beauty" that would betray the sweat and blood of the victims, and that Hochhuth rejected for the stage, as providing too much distancing, the method used by Paul Celan in "Todesfuge," in which "the gassing of the Jews is entirely translated into metaphors."

Sachs and Celan are the most extreme examples of artists who have transmuted the ugly realities into works of aesthetic perfection without detracting from the horror. In Celan, in fact, the horror of physical defilement and psychological degradation is overshadowed by the spiritual emptiness and desolation experienced by the victim and the survivor in an abandoned universe. Here, ironically, Celan is more firmly rooted in traditional Jewish beliefs than Sachs, and therefore his despair is so much more endemic and shattering than her quiet acceptance. Using many of the same images and invoking many of the same associations as Sachs, he constructs a world as bleak and rudderless as hers is whole and mysterious. Sachs's repeated invocation of the dust of martyred Israel—the dust of ancient sacrifices and the ashes of contemporary incinerations—is echoed repeatedly in poems of Celan's, but whereas for Sachs the dust of today's sacrifice mingles with the sand of Sinai and the wisdom of Solomon and finds its resolution in the eternal process by which "the fingers" (of the murderers) which "emptied the deathly shoes of sand" will tommorrow "be dust / In the shoes of those to come" ("But who emptied your shoes of sand," p. 9), Celan can offer no consolation in the cosmic design, or even in the artistic reconstruction of the event:

> There was earth in them, and
> they dug.
>
> They dug and dug, and thus
> Their day wore on, and their night. And they did not
>   praise God,
> who, they heard, willed all this,
> who, they heard, knew all this.
>
> They dug and heard no more;
> they did not grow wise, nor contrive any song,
> or any kind of language.
> They dug...[47]

The God whom they "did not praise" is the God of the covenant, the God who must be held accountable for the operations of history. In another poem, the victims' silence, their refusal to pray, is transformed into a prayer of defiance which is perhaps the most anguished of the blasphemies to be encountered in the literature:

> No one kneads us again of earth and clay,
> No one incants our dust.
> No one.
>
> Blessed art thou, No-one.
> For thy sake we will bloom.
> Towards
> thee.

> We were, we are, we shall remain
> a Nothing,
> blooming:
> the Nothing-, the
> No-one's Rose...
>   ["Psalm," p. 183]

Jerry Glenn, in his analysis of this poem, notes that the "majority of interpreters . . . feel that the blasphemy is only apparent, and that Celan is here following the old Jewish law that the name of God must not be spoken, but rather a circumlocution must be found." By this interpretation, then, Celan is "actually affirming the God of Judaism."[48] This approach, it seems to me, represents a common attempt at plastering over the cracks that the Nazi earthquake caused in the foundations of Judaism which the artist, in his agony, reveals.

In Celan, as in several of the other writers we have considered, the ghosts of unfulfilled lives still haunt the natural world:

> Whichever stone you lift—
> you lay bare
> those who need the protection of stones:
> naked,
> they now renew the intervolving...
>   ["Whichever Stone You Lift," p. 71]

In Sachs's universe, the stones are the petrified vessels of the generations of human history:

> We stones
> When someone lifts us
> He lifts the Foretime—
> When someone lifts us
> He lifts the Garden of Eden
>
> ...For we are memorial stones
> Embracing all dying.
>
> We are a satchel full of lived life.
> Whoever lifts us lifts the hardened graves of earth.
>   ["Chorus of the Stones," p. 35]

Sachs's poem concludes with the promise of dreams and angels that the stone which served as a pillow for the patriarch Jacob confers on Jacob's ancestors:

> You heads of Jacob,
> For you we hide the roots of dreams
> And let the airy angels' ladders
> Sprout like the tendrils of a bed of bindweed.
>   [P. 35]

But, for Celan, there is no blessing in the stones. His poem concludes
with a curse:

> Whichever word you speak—
> you thank
> perdition.

[P. 71]

Celan directly acknowledges the gap between his compatriot's quiet
faith in an inscrutable Deity and his own angry prosecution of an accountable God, in a poem dedicated to Nelly Sachs:

> ... The talk was of your God, I spoke
> against Him, I
> let the heart that I had,
> hope:
> for His highest, His deathrattled, His
> angry word ...

["Zurich, Zum Storchen," p. 179]

Finally, whatever his brief against God, Celan casts his lot with the
folk of Israel—especially in some of his earliest and some of his latest
poems (in *Mohn und Gedächtnis* and in *Die Niemandsrose*). When he
speaks of the victims he usually speaks in the first person plural, and
his identification with the suffering lot of his people is nowhere more
apparent than in his masterpiece, "Todesfuge": "Coal black milk of
morning we drink it at evening / we drink it at noon and at daybreak we
drink it at night."[49] In this poem, in which life and death in the camps
are translated into surrealist metaphor without in any way betraying
the situation, there is a clear juxtaposition of the people of Israel on the
one hand, represented by the narrator and his fellow victims as well as
by the vision of the biblical "Shulamith," and the Germans on the
other, represented by "the man," clearly an SS officer, as well as by
the vision of Goethe's "Marguerite." The clash here is not simply of
two inexorable forces, but of two civilizations. And Celan's is not a
legacy of consolation or resolution but of confrontation and defiance.

It can be said, then, that it is not a recounting of atrocities which
produces the terror in the elegiac poetry and prose we have been reading, but the reflection of a world which has lost its center, a world
abandoned by God and filled with the corpses of His worshipers. The
echoes of phrases from lamentation literature appear all the more terrible here because the ultimate source of meaning and consolation which
informed the interpretation of catastrophe throughout the generations
has been withdrawn. In the Midrash, as in the Bible, all of nature, all of
the cosmos, participates in the suffering of Israel. One *midrash* recounts that when the Temple was burning and the Jews were being

slaughtered, Moses reprimanded the sun for shining on such devastation. The sun replied, in sorrow and shame, that it was forced by higher powers to shine[50] Compare this with the poems and stories of the *hurbn* in which the outside world—nature, the cosmos, Divinity—appears repeatedly either as a memory or a mockery. Although, as we have learned, a defiance which borders on apostasy accompanies the response to catastrophe in nearly every generation, never, I believe, in the lamentation literature does man's loneliness appear so vast and implacable or the desolation of his world so total. Tradition flounders here like a boat whose course was charted long ago but which has lost its compass and most of its crew.

And yet the classical themes continue to reverberate through Hebraic literature; to whom, to what force can the Jewish writer appeal other than to the God of his fathers, who still belongs to the folk of Israel, even in the hour of His eclipse and their death: "In whom can I believe, / If not in Him, my beloved God of cataclysm?" asks Aaron Zeitlin in his poem "Ani Ma'amin"; "I am a Jew, as He is God."[51] Even if the poet would construct his world anew, *ex nihilo,* his creation is the prisoner of memory, and for all the would-be autonomy of his imagination he resurrects the little town in Europe with its pious men and cradle-rocked children—and its watchful God. Jacob Glatstein writes:

> ...I'll be stubborn,
> plant myself
> in my own intimate night
> which I've entirely invented
> and admired from all sides.
> I'll find my place in space
> as big as a fly,
> and compel to stand there
> for all time
> a cradle, a child,
> into whom I'll sing the voice
> of a father drowsing,
> with a face in the voice,
> with love in the voice,
> with hazy eyes
> that swim in the child's sleepy eyes
> like warm moons.
> And I'll build around this cradle a Jewish city
> with a *shul,* with a God who never sleeps,
> who watches over the poors shops,
> over Jewish fear,
> over the cemetery
> that's lively all night
> with worried corpses.

And I'll buckle myself up with my last days
and, for spite, count them in you, frozen past
who mocked me,
who invented my living, garrulous
Jewish world.
You silenced it
And in Maidanek woods
finished it off with a few shots.[52]

What emerges from a comparative study of these Hebraic writers is a pattern which at first appears surprising but which derives from the immeasurable trauma which the Holocaust wrought not only in the flesh of Israel but in its spirit. For those writers who remain within the parameters of the tradition, the attempt to recreate the Holocaust in terms of its collective legacy is accompanied by the risk of exposing the ruptures, the discontinuities, and the cracks in the most fundamental codes of Jewish faith and conduct. On the other hand, those few writers, such as Schwarz-Bart and Sachs, who would "conquer" the Holocaust by seeking in the abyss the sparks of redemption or consolation have done so by going beyond the tradition, beyond the covenantal relationship between God and Israel, and beyond the internal literary and philosophical dialogue through which Israel has confronted catastrophe throughout the ages.

SEVEN

The Holocaust Mythologized

A Disaster

There came news of a word.
Crow saw it killing men. He ate well.
He saw it bulldozing
Whole cities to rubble. Again he ate well.
He saw its excreta poisoning seas.
He became watchful.
He saw its breath burning whole lands
To dusty char.
He flew clear and peered.

The word oozed its way, all mouth,
Earless, eyeless.
He saw it sucking the cities
Like the nipples of a sow
Drinking out all the people
Till there were none left,
All digested inside the word.

Ravenous, the word tried its great lips
On the earth's bulge, like a giant lamprey—
There it started to suck.

But its effort weakened.
It could digest nothing but people.
So there it shrank, wrinkling weaker,
Puddling
Like a collapsing mushroom.
Finally, a drying salty lake.
Its era was over.
All that remained of it a brittle desert
Dazzling with the bones of earth's people

Where Crow walked and mused.

Ted Hughes, *Crow*

Crow is that creature who has somehow survived all the military and technological assaults which herald the end of the world and embodies all the negative forces that made its destruction inevitable. His creator, the poet Ted Hughes, relinquishes all efforts to salvage the human image from the "pervasive and deep feeling that civilization has now disappeared completely."[1] In all the literature considered up to this point, a respect for the primacy of "historical reality," placed within specific normative contexts, has oriented the imagination's reconstruction of the Holocaust. Whatever else these authors may attempt to do, they are, first of all, witnesses or transmitters of historical events that are fixed in time and space. Even the Hebraic writer who converts reality into legend does not lose a primary sense of accountability to the matter in which his tale is grounded. At the furthest end of the spectrum that measures the imaginative representation of cataclysmic history is the writer who distills reality into the essential symbols or myths of the concentrationary universe, which is thereby transformed from a historical event or social aberration into a human mutation. As in the fiction of the concentrationary realists, the pervasiveness and perniciousness of the mutation are measured in this fiction in degrees of inner submission to the norms of evil or the spirit of desolation, and neither history nor biography can provide escape from events so totally assimilated by the imagination.

Frank Kermode draws a distinction between fiction and myth that is useful in distinguishing between the history-bound, but imaginatively free, reconstructions of concentrationary reality and the historically liberated, but imaginatively imprisoned, visions of a holocaustal universe: "Myth operates within the diagrams of ritual, which presupposes total and adequate explanations of radically unchangeable gestures. Fictions are for finding things out, and they change as the needs of sense-making change. Myths are the agents of stability, fictions the agents of change. *Myths call for absolute, fictions for conditional, assent*" (emphasis mine).[2] With the exception of such writers as Borowski and Hilsenrath, the authors we have encountered so far have invented fictions which, subordinated as they are to an oppressive reality, nevertheless persist in their attempt to "find things out." In those works in which the imaginative appropriation of the symbols of Holocaust presupposes stasis or "a sequence of radically unchangeable gestures," the social and moral norms of the system extend beyond the temporal and spatial dimensions of the concentrationary universe while history, with its promise of possible growth and ultimate reconstruction, is suspended.

There is in some of the writing in this genre an apocalyptic quality which, though perhaps predictable in the literature of any catastrophe, appears only rarely in the general body of literature we are studying. The images, of course, are at hand; the Jews were branded on their arms with numbers which easily recall the decree of the "second beast" in the Book of Revelation: "He compelled everyone—small and great, rich and poor, slave and citizen—to be branded on the right hand or on the forehead" (Rev. 13:16). Certainly the abundance of death and even the manner of death (in a "huge furnace" [Rev. 9:2]) have their analogue in the massive death which precedes redemption in the New Testament version of the Apocalypse. And the religious imagination had already built the bridge between the visionary events and the historical victims by identifying the Jews with the hosts commandeered by the Antichrist, who are destined to battle the army of Christ in the final Armageddon.[3]

But apocalyptic literature is, traditionally, anticipatory, and there is hardly a writer who, *after* World War II, would dare to suggest that the death of six million Jews was somehow instrumental (and therefore necessary) in expediting the final redemption.[4] The writers we are considering are secular apocalyptists for whom neither the status of the Jews as the traditionally unregenerate enemy nor the promise of ultimate redemption is meaningful, but only the pervasiveness and finality of the destruction and its preemption of the possibilities for a normal future. Although like the Hebraic writers they focus on the destruction not of individuals but of entire civilizations, their versions of apocalypse are fundamentally different from the Hebraic visions of a post-Holocaust future. If any group of people might have been expected to regard Holocaust history in terms of the End, certainly it is the Jews, whose lives and civilization were totally dismantled; but, although there are a number of Jews among the writers we are about to discuss, they rather reflect other influences in contemporary, especially contemporary American, literature. Martin Buber was perhaps the first to call attention to the distinction between *prophecy,* which is a traditionally Jewish mode of perceiving history, and *apocalypse,* which is not. Applying this distinction to modern literature, Robert Alter explained that the "fundamental difference between prophecy and apocalypse, as Buber describes it, is between courageous engagement in even the most threatening history, on the one hand, and a total withdrawal, on the other hand, from a history that has become unbearable." The ancient and modern authors of lamentations write within a framework of faith; the secular apocalyptists share with such writers as Ellison, Heller, and Pynchon what Alter calls a "complete failure of faith."[5]

Perhaps the best example of the polarity generated by the temptations of apocalyptic surrender can be found in Saul Bellow's *Mr. Sammler's Planet*. The novel, which was included in our discussion of
survival literature, is the story of a Holocaust survivor who might have
been tempted into believing that he had lived beyond the great cataclysm that should have led either to final salvation or to final dissolution.
But when challenged by the option of a new space-age alternative to
religious apocalypse—Dr. Govinda Lal's proposal for abandoning the
teeming, strife-torn earth in favor of colonizing the moon—Sammler
replies in the weary but engaged manner conditioned by Hebraic,
"prophetic" tradition:

> "When you know what pain is, you agree that not to have
> been born is better. But being born one respects the powers
> of creation, one obeys the will of God—with whatever inner
> reservations truth imposes. As for duty—you are wrong.
> The pain of duty makes the creature upright, and this up-
> rightness is no negligible thing. No, I stand by what I first
> said. There is also an instinct against leaping into Kingdom
> Come." [P. 220]

The myths of surrender delineate a realm that is the very antithesis of
the civilized social order. John Locke, one of the leading architects of
Western liberal democracy, defined the state of law as the guarantor of
"life, liberty [which protects man 'from restraint and violence from
others'], and estate."[6] The concentrationary universe, by contrast,
appears in the mythical literature as the realm of *death*, of *evil* (or
unrestrained violence), and of dispossession or a *ruined estate*. Pierre
Gascar's short story "The Season of the Dead" exposes and explores
the anarchy of death which usurps the dignity and rhythm of the natural
cycle. Jerzy Kosinski's novel *The Painted Bird* and Jakov Lind's early
stories in *Soul of Wood* and his novel *Landscape in Concrete* are
allegories of the diffusion of evil so far beyond the perimeters of the
ghettos and camps that it becomes a prevailing human force. Jorge
Semprun's novel *The Long Voyage* and Adolf Rudnicki's story "The
Crystal Stream" define the Holocaust geography: the ruins of the
ghetto and the confines of the camp which ultimately become the only
and the inalienable property of the survivor.

Jerzy Kosinski and Jakov Lind: "Evil Be Thou My Good"

In some respects Jerzy Kosinski's slim novel *The Painted Bird* is the
most relentless example of the imaginative representation of the
Holocaust, because it universalizes the demonic values of the concentrationary universe and traces the inception and growth of evil in the

soul of a young child—a slow but sure catechism that ensures the propagation of evil as the legacy of concentrationary "civilization."

Kosinski is a Polish Jew who spent his childhood and early adolescence in Hitler's Europe and immigrated to the United States in 1957. He published *The Painted Bird* in English eight years later. On the surface, the novel is a loosely coherent narrative of the struggle for self-preservation which could be classified with surivalist fiction: it is the story of the wartime wanderings of a persecuted young child through peasant villages until he is finally liberated by Russian troops and reunited with his parents. Yet, in spite of the verisimilitude of event and situation established in the first-person narrative, the novel lacks a plausible existential center and takes on the dimensions of a folk or fairy tale. The boy is never named (the author himself, in notes to the German translation of the novel, refers to him as "the Boy";[7] even in a universe in which characters exchange names and forge identities so frequently, such complete anonymity is rare), and he soon relinquishes as useless whatever biography he had. In the early months of his flight he often recalls his parents, who had left him in the care of temporary guardians, but his sense of belonging to them fades with his gradual realization that they are powerless to protect him from the adversities he is facing ("what were parents for if not to be with their children in times of danger?").[8] Hailing from a "large city in Eastern Europe," the Boy takes after his mother, who "was dark," but his features blur into the generic physiognomy of the persecuted: he is "olive-skinned, dark-haired, and black-eyed," and the fact that he had a father with "fair hair and blue eyes" cannot save him from the fate reserved for the dark-haired and black-eyed people of Europe during World War II (pp. 1, 85). He is taken alternately for a Gypsy and a Jew ("what was the difference between a Gypsy and a Jew, since both were dusky and both were destined for the same end?" [p. 85]) and, even more absurdly than the anomic victims we discussed in the fiction of survival, he has no coordinates other than these arbitrary features by which to gauge his fate. He is, as it were, a *tabula rasa*, Everychild, on whom the mark of the victim is imprinted; since he has no substantial memories of life in a sane, ethical society, he internalizes the norms of power as he comes to understand them. He searches for the key to the operations of the world to which he must adjust as his only insurance of survival. At first normal feelings, the residue of an indulged, cultured childhood, guide his responses: fear of torture and death, compassion for the suffering of others, sadness and loneliness. But gradually these give way to the more utilitarian responses of one who is educating his impulses to conform with the laws of his environment as they manifest themselves. The first law he apprehends is that of a kind of primitive, talionic justice by which, eventually, the "victim punished the executioner." "Justice hangs over the world like a great sledgehammer, lifted by a powerful arm," the peasants assure him, "which has to stop for a while before coming down with terrible force on the unsuspecting anvil" (p. 77). But such a principle is too remote from the Boy's own experience of the power of the "executioners" to be incorporated as a strategy in his own struggle for survival. He begins to appreciate the force of the passions that govern the brutality of the peasants: the miller's jealousy which drives him to gouge out the eyes of a plowboy who, he suspects, is cuckolding him; the carpenter's fear that the Boy's "black hair would attract lightning to [his] farm" (p. 49), which leads him to chain the Boy to a heavy harness and abandon him in the fields in the midst of every thunderstorm; farmer Garbos's boundless resentment against this "unbaptized Gypsy bastard" (p. 102) who was allowed to live when his own sons had died young, which impells him to string the Boy up to the rafters every day in hopes that his dog, Judas, will devour him. But even as the Boy succeeds in escaping from the miller's hut, in bringing about the death of the carpenter, and in learning to endure the dog's incessant attacks on his gibbeted body, the principle of power eludes him—until one day he overhears the local priest explaining to an old man that in exchange for certain prayers God grants a specific number of indulgences, and that this has the immediate effect of alleviating one's present suffering:

> Suddenly the ruling pattern of the world was revealed to me with beautiful clarity. I understood why some people were strong and others weak, some free and others enslaved, some rich and others poor, some well and others sick. The former had simply been the first to see the need for prayer and for collecting the maximum number of days of indulgence. Somewhere, far above, all these prayers coming from earth were properly classified, so that every person had his bin where his days of indulgence were stored. [P. 111]

Such faith, which generates an endless recitation of prayers, only lands the Boy in a manure pit after he has failed to hold the missal in church properly. He emerges from the pit mute—and stumbles forward in terror, convinced that "there must have been some cause for the loss of my speech. Some greater force, with which I had not managed to communicate, commanded my destiny. I began to doubt that it could be God or one of his Saints" (p. 126). Not long after this, the sight of a young woman who had made love to him now coupling with a goat causes something to "collapse" inside the Boy. In a flash "all these events [become] suddenly clear and obvious" and the governing powers of the universe are revealed to him as the "Powers of Evil":

I tried to visualize the manner in which the evil spirits operated. The minds and souls of the people were as open to these forces as a plowed field, and it was on this field that the Evil Ones incessantly scattered their malignant seed.... From the moment of signing a pact with the Devil, the more harm, misery, injury, and bitterness a man could inflict on those around him, the more help he could expect. If he shrank from inflicting harm on others, if he succumbed to emotions of love, friendship, and compassion, he would immediately become weaker and his own life would have to absorb the suffering and defeats that he spared others.... What mattered was that a man should consciously promote evil, find pleasure in harming others, nurturing and using the diabolical powers granted him by the Evil Ones in a manner calculated to cause as much misery and suffering around him as possible.... I felt annoyed with myself for not having understood sooner the real rules of this world.

A man who had sold out to the Evil Ones would remain in their power all his life. From time to time he would have to demonstrate an increasing number of misdeeds. But they were not rated equally by his superiors.... An action harming one person was obviously worth less than one affecting many.... Hatreds of large groups of people must have been the most valuable of all. I could barely imagine the prize earned by the person who managed to inculcate in all blond, blue-eyed people a long-lasting hatred of dark ones.

I also began to understand the extraordinary success of the Germans.... Every German must have sold his soul to the Devil at birth. This was the source of their power and strength. [Pp. 135–37]

The Germans become, then, simply the most highly placed disciples of the Devil in a hierarchy of universal evil. This conviction is to become the guiding principle in the Boy's life as he evolves from victim into victimizer. There is a brief, and not altogether convincing, interval in the narrative when the Boy is befriended by a group of Communist liberators and is taught that "in this world there were realistic ways of promoting goodness, and there were people who had dedicated their whole lives to it. These were the Communist Party members" (p. 172). But after he is consigned by these soldiers to an orphange, at which his parents eventually locate him, he reaffirms his pledge to the Evil Ones through acts of vengeance that include collaboration in the derailment of an entire train and the murder of a theater attendant. In the end, after a skiing accident in the mountains, the Boy's speech is suddenly restored—but there is no indication of moral or spiritual regeneration, and his childhood leads, unredeemed, into adolescence.

Most of the other children in Holocaust fiction emerge from their ordeal morally unscathed—or, where there is no survival, at least preserve their purity in tragedy. The author who chooses his protagonists from among the millions of young victims of Nazism may have to allow his innocents to die—but refuses to allow innocence to die. Arnošt Lustig is an example of such a writer; in a series of short stories, he carves islands of adolescent love, loyalty, and moral sanity in the midst of the squalor and misery of the ghetto.[9] The concentrationary universe is the given reality in Lustig's fiction; as in the writing of the concentrationary realists, the boundaries of the ghetto or the camp are the boundaries of existence in his narratives. Very few of these stories tell of the before-time or the after-time; the genre of the short story in a sense frees the writer from the chronological demands of the survival novel which must carry the protagonist to the end of the line. Yet, sharing the survivalist perspective, Lustig's characters struggle to preserve moral and emotional freedom in defiance of the pressures of the system. And the children, in their vitality, their ability to dream, and their refusal to relinquish their toehold on life, are the most successful—and therefore the most tragic—of the freedom fighters. Lustig's children are individuals with specific identities that resist the reduction to Manichean principles which prevail in *The Painted Bird*.

In a different way, Ilse Aichinger's German novel *Herod's Children* preserves the insulation of childhood. The narrative, which is a string of tenuously connected vignettes, is a highly poetic—at times overly contrived—attempt to present, through a variety of literary devices, the fantasy world of a group of persecuted children. True, the fantasies of these children often turn into nightmares, and reality intrudes rudely at times to shatter the dreamers with their dreams, but until the end the surviving children retain their solidarity and their ability to love: "It was," the narrator says of these children, "their shame to have been born, their fear to be killed and their hope to be loved."[10]

Precisely, then, because the tainted hero of Kosinski's novel is a child, he taps the most primary sources of fear and terror that have been out of bounds in most of the literature of the Holocaust. In the notes to the German edition of *The Painted Bird*, Kosinski acknowledges that the "essence" of his novel is "hate" and that the world of the Painted Bird is the world of elementary symbols, "simple keys to the European culture of the mid-twentieth century."[11] The child, who in Jungian terms represents the "collective unconscious" of mankind, dramatizes in the crudest, most penetrating way the bestiality of the age.

Kosinski shares this perspective with a number of contemporary writers who offer as a legacy of two world wars a profound distrust in the beneficence of human nature—which traditionally reposed in its purest form in the image of the child. Jean Cocteau's *Les Enfants terribles,* written during and perhaps influenced by the gathering storm of fascism, and William Golding's *Lord of the Flies,* written in the wake of the storm, unmask the grown-up passions behind childhood's innocent façade, revealing among the pygmies a microcosm of adult sadism and victimization. Georg Kaiser's *The Raft of the Medusa,* a German postwar play which in many ways anticipates Golding's novel, is a more specific allegory of Nazi-Jewish relations. It traces the precarious voyage of a group of English children on a raft that is the target of torpedoes from Nazi planes. The drama, which contains elements of Old Testament as well as New Testament legend and which concludes with the hero's (Allan's) self-sacrifice in a watery calvary, revolves around the decision of another member of the group (Ann) to throw a small, mute boy—presumably the only non-Christian among them—overboard in order to save the lives of the rest. When, at the end, the children are saved—all, that is, except for "Little Fox," the poor drowned victim, and Allan, the suicide and "savior,"—the pilot of the rescuing plane calls down to Allan, trying to convince him to abandon the raft and be saved: "People will be better someday—they'll be just like children again." "No," Allan answers; "children will be like grownups—because they're like them already!"[12] There is, then, by these sights, no age-group or ethnic group which is immune to the prevailing forces of evil, and even the passion which concludes Kaiser's play is but a religious version of the same apocalyptic surrender which we encounter in the secular writers.

Most of these fictions of corrupted childhood have about them the unreal quality of myth or folktale. Kosinksi likens his own story to a fairytale—as experienced by, rather than told to, the child.[13] And even where there are rescuers in these myths, the tainted soul of the child remains unremediable, and the poison that has been planted there grows to maturity with him. The Boy's hatred is far more pernicious than that of the peasants from whom he learns; like the animals with whom these unlettered people live (and, at times, copulate), they are driven by blind, instinctual forces, whereas the Boy, as Kosinski himself says, is the only character who "hates consciously and most deeply; he desires and thirsts to hate others for all that had happened to him in this world."[14]

Hatred becomes, then, the instrument by which the victim manages to stay alive—but it is an instrument which ultimately signals the total victory of the "executioners" over his soul if not over his body, because it is the instrument that transforms him into a victimizer of others. The symbol of this transformation involves the only instance in

Kosinski's novel in which the fate of the Jews is specifically portrayed. During the mushroom harvest, in which the Boy participates with the other villagers, a succession of camp-bound trains passes over the railroad tracks, leaving behind packets of letters, pictures and, occasionally, children who are thrown between the slats of the cattle cars. The Boy, whose looks mark him for the same destination as that of the Jews, watches silently and a few times even presses himself between the rails and allows the trains to go over him, symbolizing his own narrow escape. And he learns the lesson well and efficiently. Determined never to find himself in a train with the victims, he becomes an accomplice to the derailment of a train filled with other victims—innocent, market-bound peasants—and this incident closes the cycle by which, as Kosinski says, the oppressed becomes oppressor.[15]

It is significant that, although the Jews appear, quite literally, on the periphery of the world through which the Boy wanders, the manner of their appearance provides the missing link in his education. The trains themselves represent the technology of death which is the hallmark of the Nazi system, and the machines of torture and murder that have been perfected by "civilized" humanity in concentration camps are far more efficient than the crude instruments of torture improvised by the unlettered peasants a few miles away. Ultimately, then, although the Boy has served his apprenticeship among the peasants, it is the demonic control, the premeditated savagery and sadism of the Nazis which appear as the superior method, and when the Boy collaborates in his act of revenge, it is by mass murder, and it is effected through the use of technology.

Jakov Lind was born in Vienna in 1927 and survived the war as a laborer under an assumed identity in Germany. After the liberation he immigrated to England where he wrote first in German and then in English.[16] The essence of Lind's as of Kosinski's fiction is not the tragedy, but the evil and the madness, of the Holocaust. The Nazi character who is conspicuously absent in the realistic fiction, perhaps because the enormity of his deeds defies the psychological analysis which in modern literature is predicated on understanding, empathy, and compassion, finds a home in these myths of absolute, unfathomable evil. Although the surrealism of situation and action is offset in Lind's early stories (collected in *Soul of Wood*) by the presence of a sane touchstone—in most cases, the narrator—and by a warm stream of humanity and humor that mildly subverts the forces of cold, ruthless cruelty, Lind's first novel, *Landscape in Concrete,* has neither the sanity nor the humanity, and very little of the humor, of the earlier stories. It is an apocalyptic vision of postwar man transmuted into a heartless, violent creature. The specific relationship of Nazi to Jew has been generalized into a universal dialectic of victimizer and victim not unlike that which appears in *The Painted Bird*. The landscape of Lind's novel, however, is far more bleak than that of Kosinski's, and the characters hardly have a real presence. In general, Lind's stories tend to be utterly improbable; to borrow a formulation of Kermode's, the End is "no longer imminent; [it is] immanent."[17] Its "immanence" is manifested in the suspension of causality and history, the inversion of values, the defeat of normal expectations, and the relentless threat of violent death.

The central protagonist in the title story in *Soul of Wood* is Anton Barth, a twenty-year-old Jewish quadriplegic who has been left on a mountaintop to die by Wohlbrecht, the Barths' one-legged servant, in whose care the parents had entrusted their son when they were deported. Wohlbrecht is himself detained in an "insane asylum" and forced to help give air injections to the Jews who are sent to the asylum and to measure their reactions. At the war's end, somewhat guilt-stricken—Wohlbrecht is not really an evil man, just a coward—he goes up to the mountaintop to retrieve the corpse of his young master, only to find Anton fully recovered and functioning as a member of a deer herd. In a scuffle with two of his hospital superiors who are looking for his Jew, whom *they* would claim to have "saved" at war's end, Wohlbrecht is shot and left to die on the mountaintop, his wooden leg propped up against a tree, "waiting patiently for the resurrection of its master, which will surely happen some day. Any day."[18]

This half-earnest, half-cynical declaration of redemptive faith is another manifestation of the "immanence" of apocalypse in Lind—the human, messianic aspect of apocalypse. A similar message of ironic consolation binds the wounds in the final story in this collection, "Ressurection." Another unlikely tale of Jewish destiny, it tells of two men hiding from the Nazis within the walls of a Dutchman's house: one (Goldschmied) is a Protestant minister who converted from Judaism and the other (Weintraub) a young, tubercular Zionist. The two eventually become fast friends, Goldschmied's dialogue providing the humor of outrageous paradox (I am, he explains to Weintraub, "a Christian, see, a goy, not one of us, one of them" [p. 171]) and Weintraub's incessant cough eventually giving them away. They are reunited in the transit camp and, reassuring each other that those "stories about Poland" are nonsense, vow to meet again:

> A week after this conversation the two did indeed meet.
> Weintraub was climbing the steep stairs to his holy

Jerusalem and Goldschmied to his Jesus on the Cross. For
to tell the truth, the city of Jerusalem is not so very big. [P.
190]

The rhetoric of redemption can, of course, be read as the cynical
euphemism for concentrationary death attended by religious or
ideological illusions. It is less the protestations of faith and more the
warm, human friendship between the two men which redeems this
story.

Other stories in this collection, grotesque allegories of sadism in the
technological age, are alleviated only by the sanity and innocent be-
wilderment of the narrators. In *Landscape in Concrete,* even that small
degree of orientation toward sanity and civilized morality is absent.
The central figure in this novel is Sergeant Gauthier Bachmann, a
goldsmith serving in the Nazi army, whose infantry regiment, it seems,
sank into the mud—after which he (a kind of survivor who emerged
from the slime by spontaneous generation) was treated for insanity and
released from the army. The disjointed narrative traces Bachmann's
pursuit of his "duty"—his search for another unit to join—and the
succession of brutal assaults which he commits on various unwitting,
but not particularly innocent, victims along the way.

This novel, which captures the essence of victimization under the
Third Reich, portrays the victor as a composite of all the inhumanity of
the system. He represents the principles of Darwinian survival and
natural selection in a postapocalyptic age; he is defined as "*Homo
bachmannus,*" a member of the species that "survived the deluge
[and] will never be extinct" (p. 110). As Lawrence Langer writes in his
analysis of this book, Bachmann's "behavior is not the exception but
the norm for measuring humanity."[19] Like Crow, and like the Boy who
at first resembles a "painted bird," a marked target, but who soon
learns to be a beast of prey, Bachmann is indestructible—he is what is
left over after everything vulnerably human has been destroyed.

And just as the nature of man has been transformed, so has his
environment. Bachmann inhabits a world of concrete, of stones which
cover over the flesh of the human massacre ("when it is all put under
the concrete and the sun shines fiercely on it, nobody'll know any more
what's underneath. The *corpus delicti* will be gone" [p. 183]). As in any
true apocalypse, all of nature participates in the cataclysm, in the cosmic alchemy of de-creation which Bachmann—the *gold*smith—has
helped to bring about: "gold has turned to dirt, man to animal, animal
to stone, and from stone gunpowder and dust are made" (p. 160).

The final scene is one of total desolation, and Bachmann and a girl
friend, Helga, emerge from their bomb shelter the sole survivors. And
since, as Kinglsey Widmer put it, "Paradise lies on the other side of

Armageddon,''[20] they are, as it were, resurrected into the primordial idyll: "they rose from the grave to the surface of the earth and looked around"—"We're in paradise, Helga," Bachmann says (p. 188). The difference, of course, is that the hero is not *Homo sapiens* but *Homo bachmannus;* true to his nature, he proceeds to kill Helga and then goes off again, the eternal remainder, reactivating history: "Then he stood up and marched off toward the East, toward the war, to search for his regiment once more" (p. 190).

The irony which generates such an unlikely and unlikeable victim as Bachmann is a grotesque extension of that narrative mode which Northrop Frye defined as emphasizing "the sense of arbitrariness, of the victim's having been unlucky, selected at random or by lot, and no more deserving of what happens to him than anyone else would be." He is the victim as "*pharmakos* or scapegoat," neither innocent nor guilty but partaking of a "guilty society, or living in a world where such injustices are an inescapable part of existence."[21]

Lind and Kosinski reach what may be the boundary between the symbolic representation of the Holocaust through the apocalyptic images of evil and violence, and a kind of "pornography of death" which provides an orgy of scatology and cruelty and dwells on the grotesque details of sexual perversion and death largely in order to exploit the shocking, sensational effects which no other historical experience so easily affords.

Adolf Rudnicki and Jorge Semprun: The Ruined Estate

> The great city was split into three parts and the cities of the world collapsed.... Every island vanished and mountains disappeared.
>
> Rev. 16:19–20

Adolf Rudnicki's short story "The Crystal Stream" is located in the same concrete anti-Eden as that in which Lind's novel concludes. However, whereas the Holocaust signifies for Kosinski and Lind primarily an assault on and victory over man's moral self, for Rudnicki it signifies primarily an assault on his emotions and on the affects that make life meaningful. "The Crystal Stream" is one story in a collection of narratives about Poland's Jewish victims, *Ascent to Heaven*. Rudnicki, one of the few surviving Jewish writers to have remained in Poland after the war, set himself the task of commemorating the death throes of Polish Jewry out of the conviction that no one else could do it: the victims are all either dead or exiled, and most of the other Polish writers who write about the concentrationary universe—such as Borowski—write from their own perspective as political prisoners. In 1943, Czeslaw Miłosz express the helplessness of the

Polish writer who would elegize Polish Jewry but feels he can hardly
claim that right:

> Bees build around red liver,
> Ants build around black bone.
> It has begun: the tearing, the trampling on silks,
> It has begun: the breaking of glass, wood, copper, nickel,
>   silver, foam
> Of gypsum, iron sheets, violin strings, trumpets, leaves,
>   balls, crystals.
> Poof! Phosphorescent fire from yellow walls
> Engulfs animal and human hair.
>
> Bees build around the honeycomb of lungs,
> Ants build around white bone.
> Torn is paper, rubber, linen, leather, flax,
> Fiber, fabrics, cellulose, snakeskin, wire.
> The roof and the wall collapse in flame and heat seizes the
>   foundations.
> Now there is only the earth, sandy, trodden down,
> With one leafless tree.
>
> Slowly, boring a tunnel, a guardian mole makes his way,
> With a small red lamp fastened to his forehead.
> He touches buried bodies, counts them, pushes on,
> He distinguishes human ashes by their luminous vapor,
> The ashes of each man by a different part of the spectrum.
> Bees build around a red trace.
> Ants build around the place left by my body.
>
> I am afraid, so afraid of the guardian mole.
> He has swollen eyelids, like a Patriarch
> Who has sat much in the light of candles
> Reading the great book of the species.
> What will I tell him, I, a Jew of the New Testament,
> Waiting two thousand years for the second coming of Jesus?
> My broken body will deliver me to his sight
> And he will count me among the helpers of death:
> The uncircumcised.[22]

It is, then, a nearly impossible task for a non-Jewish writer to assume
the burden of creating a literary monument to Polish Jewry. Piotr
Rawicz, an expatriated Eastern European Jew who survived the war
and has also attempted to find the right literary medium for the commemoration of his exterminated people, considers Rudnicki to be the
"grand bard of [the Jews'] vanished world." Rudnicki, he continues,

has dedicated to the extermination of Polish Jewry . . . a cycle of narratives which is unparalleled in all the "martyrological" literature of the world. Working in a métier which is still warm, recounting the destiny of others, of those close to him but not his own (in constrast to the great majority of "concentrationary" and ghetto narratives, the work of Rudnicki contains practically no autobiographical elements, *stricto sensu*), he has attained the summits of art with a series of small *chefs-d'oeuvre* which the survivors of the deluge, the Polish Jews dispersed all over the world, have perceived as the incarnation of the collective memory of the assassinated people.[23]

Rawicz may be too quick to acclaim Rudnicki as the "grand bard"—later he even hails him as the "last of the prophets of Israel,"[24] a title which should perhaps be reserved for the writer who explores the inner soul of the people and its dialogue with Jewish history and theodicy. Rudnicki's province is, rather, that mysterious relationship between the Jews and *Poland*, between the people and the land which hosted them for a thousand years. The land itself, which was at once the site of most of the Nazi death camps and the target of some of the most devastating military attacks, approximates the terrible landscape envisioned in the Book of Revelation. Rudnicki, in an essay based on a trip he made to the West in 1956, refers to himself as "l'homme des ruines," and evinces surprise at the absence of a sense of apocalypse with which Westerners reconstruct their postwar lives: for us, he says, "the Eschaton descends on our everyday lives; there [in the West] it does not . . . ." The high suicide rate in Poland is alone a testimony to the desperate sense that the Poles have of having lived beyond the End, he says.[25]

In "The Crystal Stream," it is the physical ruins of the once-thriving Jewish community of Warsaw which form the ambience and reflect the inner devastation of the lives of a couple who meet after the war at the site of their former home. This brief story, narrated in simple, realistic prose, is a legend or myth of the "immanence" of the apocalypse and its victory over the memory—and the promise—of Paradise. It is one of the most powerful narratives of the postwar struggle and, at the same time, an allegory of what Rudnicki has referred to as "l'époque des fours."[26]

Abel, a Jew who managed to survive the war in a prisoner-of-war camp, returns with the liberation to his former home in the Jewish section of Warsaw. The journey takes him first through Polish Warsaw, and he is overwhelmed by the destruction of a city "which had been struck by a cosmic anger . . . . The empty shells, the empty windows, the mounds of foul earth inside the shells, breathed horror and filth, the dreary dreariness of corpses.''[27] And yet there are, at least, shells and mounds here, to mark the location of former habitations; "a former resident returning to this district would still be able, after a moment's thought, to say, 'my house stood here'" (p. 78). How great, then, is the shock of discovering that not even such minimal traces exist of the former Jewish district:

> He refused to believe his own eyes. He had expected to see destruction, but on the same scale as in the other districts; he had expected to see some traces which would enable him to recreate what had formerly existed here. There were no traces whatever. There were no buildings, not even gutted shells.... No walls—no chimneys—which clung so tenaciously to life—no outlines of streets, no sidewalks, no tramlines, no roads or squares; on no floor had anything survived, to give the eye a moment's rest. Here there was not one of the elements created by organized human effort, nothing to establish that this spot had been inhabited by man. Over an area which the eye could encompass only with difficulty, where formerly the greatest concentration of Jews in Europe had been housed, there was nothing but rubble and broken brick, with here and there yellow and grey sheet-iron... [P. 79]

And here, as elsewhere, we encounter the violation of the decorum of death as symbol of the ultimate violation of life: "In other districts there were dead bodies; here there was not even a dead body.... And though beneath these fields of rubble rested more dead than in a hundred cemeteries, there was nothing to suggest a cemetery" (p. 79).

Into this utter desolation comes Amelia, Abel's wife, to whom six years of separation and incarceration had lent in his imagination the image of the perfect woman. Their meeting, among the rubble of the neighborhood in which they used to live, is described in great detail but takes on mythological dimensions as the couple comes to represent not only the personal but also the *human* options that their past—or at least Amelia's past, which is no longer personal biography but the Jewish experience as paradigmatic of the extreme in human suffering—affords them. It takes some time for Abel to comprehend the distinction between his own trials as a prisoner of war and those of Amelia as an inhabitant of the besieged ghetto of Warsaw, as one who was smuggled out under heaps of garbage in the municipal dustcart and survived under an alias on the "Aryan side" till the end of the war. At first his joy at being reunited with her is so great that it banishes the desolation around him, as well as his own memories of deprivation, and invokes the original Edenic myth: "Over this soil of the most terrible of all human suffering, Abel walked, clinging to Amelia's arm, as though it were a rose-garden" (p. 91).

Slowly, however, Amelia makes Abel see how totally violated, how utterly ruined is the soul of the woman he loved; the ghetto ruins through which they walk become emblematic of a far greater desolation of spirit which the Holocaust survivor must bear forever. Patiently but relentlessly Amelia explains to Abel the transformation of the inner life which the ghetto years have wrought:

> "After all, you see what is left of our life . . ." said Amelia. "This is not the result of a half-hour raid by the Royal Air Force. At night we did not go to bed, and in the morning those left alive did not see what we now see. The death agony of the ghetto, the death agony of our community went on over years. Before the Jewish nation was sent up in smoke it was changed into mud and dung." [P. 94]

And for those who remained, "death dwelt among us and changed much in our ideas of life," Amelia continues. "The only joy we had in those years . . . was to kill a German" (pp. 95, 97). Fidelity, marital vows, and above all love ceased to have any meaning:

> "Love—that's a word I haven't heard for a long time. A word quite forgotten. A fiction . . .; when a man went away he went into the darkness, and usually did not return. We did not dare to let our feelings accumulate, they had to be spent at once. Women gave themselves to men just as though they were doing them a justice, as though they were righting a wrong." [Pp. 92, 95]

Somewhere in this process of sexual abandon and emotional barren-ness, Amelia gave herself to other men, stayed with one of them and had a child by him. But it is not the bond to this other man which makes reunion with Abel impossible; rather, it is the total destruction of the past which the six years of Holocaust have accomplished in her: "Abel, my dear, what can I bring you back?" she asks. "This body, this body which is like a conquered land . . ." (p. 101). And although Abel desires her more than anything else in the world, he realizes finally that return is impossible.

This little domestic scene, painted in gentle, compassionate tones, is an inexorable myth of the End. If human history begins with Adam, it ends with Abel—the eternal victim. All about him the life-sustaining waters recede; love, which was to Amelia a "crystal stream" that she tried hard to keep pure, has dried up. And Abel, left finally alone, is surrounded by a "dead sea" (pp. 99, 100, 102). In an act of cosmic empathy, the sky turns the "colour of soapsuds" (p. 98). What remains is nostalgia: "If anyone were to ask me if I regret . . . all that period when my body...whimpered for the fiction of a crystal stream, I would answer: 'No,'" says Amelia before her departure. "For in the face of this end of the world which we now see, what deserves to be called a fiction, and what does not deserve to be called it?" (p. 100).

The protagonist of Jorge Semprun's French novel *The Long Voyage* carries the concentration camp within him into the future as inexorably as Amelia carries the ghetto, and, as in her case, it imposes itself upon his past as well. Where Rudnicki captures the desolation in spatial symbols, Semprun captures it both spatially and temporally. The physical context in which his novel unfolds—a boxcar transporting one hundred and twenty political prisoners to Buchenwald—is as indigenous to the landscape of the Holocaust universe as the rubble of the Warsaw Ghetto. And, again like the ghetto, it becomes the inalienable possession of the survivor who is condemned to live in it long after the trains have been stilled and the tracks dismantled. The fiction ostensibly traces only the five-day journey to the camp, but this journey also informs all the events that preceded and succeeded it, transforming historical incident into myth. Buchenwald becomes the central reality and the new measure of human value. Still, the values remain the same; it is the unit of measure which changes. Where the concentrationary universe imposed its inner logic on the minds and hearts of the characters in the novels of Kosinski and Lind, it is only external reality which is imperative in Semprun's novel. And, unlike the torment and desolation and loss of hope which penetrate the soul in Rudnicki's story, the concentrationary experience becomes in Semprun's novel the crucible by which all human endeavor is tested.

The first part of *The Long Voyage* is narrated in the first person by "Gérard," which is the *nom de guerre* of one Manuel, a non-Jew who (like the author himself) was born in Spain, fought in the Spanish Civil War, and was arrested for underground activities with the *maquis* in France. As I have pointed out before, it is this existential premise— that he was arrested for something he had *done* and not for the color of his eyes or the traces of ritual circumcision—which enables the political prisoner to maintain standards of conventional morality even under the most inhuman conditions. As Gérard says, "the historical essence common to all of us who are being arrested in this year 1943 is freedom.... I'm in prison because I'm a free man, because I found it necessary to exercise my freedom, because I accepted this necessity" (pp. 44, 45). The Jew, especially the assimilated and atheistic Jew, is in an essentially *absurd* position; as Gérard says of a fellow comrade-in-arms, "Hans didn't want to die, insofar as he had to die, merely because he was Jewish... he refused to have his destiny inscribed in his body" (p. 178).

Like the Jew, the German guard is viewed as someone who inhabits the concentrationary universe out of necessity; the German is here, Gérard speculates, "because he is not free" (p. 45). The inquiry, the philosophical quest for an understanding of the behavior of oneself and others in extremity becomes the essence of this narrative. This is "myth," by Kermode's definition, only insofar as it is a myth of *place*, of inexorable, external reality which can never be altered. But the self-probing, the challenge which constantly snags on the barbed wire of reality, persists in "finding things out" and in finding out how things have changed on this voyage through time and space. "Why am I here guarding you?" the narrator imagines the German guard as asking. "Why have I been ordered to open fire on you if you should try to escape? In short, who am I?" (p. 43).

> In the camps [Gérard acknowledges], man becomes that animal capable of stealing a mate's bread, of propelling him toward death. But in the camps man also becomes that invincible being capable of sharing his last cigarette butt, his last piece of bread, his last breath, to sustain his fellow man... [P. 60]

But even as he judges the entire world, including those who never entered the gates of the camp, by the measure of ultimate nakedness, Gérard becomes gradually aware that he has inhabited a universe whose boundaries, with the liberation, have shrunk to the limits of his own memory. Unlike most of the other apocalyptic fiction we have just considered, *The Long Voyage* does not insist on the universal diffusion of the concentrationary paradigm; on the contrary, the cosmos is indifferent to, and the surrounding countryside untouched by, the existence of the concentration camp. As the train carrying prisoners to the camp passes through the Moselle valley, the narrator notices the serene indifference of nature: "Even if all of us in this boxcar were dead, stacked in dead standing up, a hundred and twenty in this boxcar, the Moselle valley would still be there before our dead eyes" (p. 15).

Nature is beneficently blind; the villagers of the surrounding areas are not but, with rare exceptions, they shield their eyes and, presumably, hold their noses against the sweet smell of burning flesh. "Jesus Christ!" one of Gérard's comrades says, as they pass through one of these villages after their liberation, "they had front-row seats!" (p. 152).[28]

Only the survivors, then, can testify to the reality of Buchenwald. A

short concluding chapter is, unlike the others, narrated in the third
person, as if to confirm the likelihood of the victim's extinction or his
loss of memory; but sixteen subsequent years of attempted amnesia are
vanquished in the inevitable act of recall and reiteration. The concentrationary experience is filtered through the memory of the narrator by
a complex Proustian juxtaposition of temporal states which has been
studied by Péter Egri. Semprun not only employs the Proustian techniques of kaleidoscoping time, incorporating dreams into reality, and
using memory as an integrating mechanism, but also makes direct reference to *Swann's Way* as a catalyst for the narrator's own rec-
ollections of childhood. These early memories are invoked here initially, as Egri says, in the same manner as they are invoked in Proust,
for the purpose of overcoming the misery of the present,[29] although in
the case of Gérard, this becomes a positive strategy for survival:

> It must have been during these hours that there oc-
> currred . . . the dream or memory of that calm place with the
> smell of wax (the books, rows and rows of books) where I
> sought refuge, to which I fled from the fetid dampness of the
> boxcar . . . the ever increasing commotion of the car . . . . It
> was Martinus Nijhoff's bookshop . . . . This quiet, closed-in
> place was only one of the points around which was con-
> structed my childhood universe . . . [Pp. 200–201]

But, by the same token, such activity also seals present misery like a
time capsule for future memory.[30] I have already called attention to the
contrast between the chronology of the survival novel, which structures a way out of as well as the way into the concentrationary universe
(and which renders past time a hedge against the present and a promise
for the future), and the simultaneity of past, present, and future in
Semprun's narrative which, from the very first sentence, fixes the
Holocaust in the eternal present: "There is the cramming of the bodies
into the boxcar, the throbbing pain in the right knee" (p. 9). The collapse of a chronological time-scheme allows the concentrationary universe to pass through the narrator, rather than he through it: "But is it
we who are advancing?" he asks himself during this interminable journey; "we're motionless . . . it's the night that is advancing . . . toward
the motionless corpses we are destined to be" (p. 9).

Egri points out that, unlike Proust's narrator, whose experience is
personal, self-referential, and isolated, whose dreams are the visions of
the hypersensitive individual, Gérard's experience comprises the
"common historical experience of a socially determined group," and
his nightmares "capture absolutely normal people in an abnormal situation, in a form of collective historical experience . . . . Semprun never
ceases to emphasize, by every possible means, that the nightmare . . . is

reality itself.''[31] This is the crucial distinction between *Remembrance of Things Past* and *The Long Voyage*, and even if the basically sanguine Marxism which underlies Gérard's—and Semprun's—faith occasionally suggests the possibilities of the amelioration of the human condition (''all of us, together, that ridiculously small percentage of us who are going to survive ... are the possible negation of that society, of that historical entity, that system which the German nation is today'' [p. 46]), the concentrationary reality which has invaded the psyche remains there inexorably. The narrator, standing outside the camp after the liberation, celebrates his freedom: ''We have tenaciously survived for this unique moment when we could look at the camp from the outside'' (pp. 115–116). And yet the lesson that it takes him sixteen ''liberated'' years to learn is that just as he can never forget, so he can never look at the camp from the outside—that, having survived Buchenwald, it has become his inalienable possession: ''maybe you can never erase this voyage'' (p. 24). Years after he has traveled the road that leads away from Buchenwald, the memory comes unbidden, as with Proust's *madeleine;* he bites into a piece of black bread while conversing with some friends before a crackling fire, and ''the slightly acid taste of the black bread, the slow mastication of this gritty black bread, brought back, with shocking suddenness, the marvelous moments when, at camp, we used to eat our ration of bread, when ... we used to stretch it out, so that the tiny squares of wet, sandy bread which we cut out of our daily ration would last as long as possible ...'' A friend notices his reverie, but he is unable to satisfy her query: ''Obviously, I couldn't tell her that I was in the throes of dying, dying of hunger, far far from them, far from the wood fire and the words we were saying, in the snow in Thuringia amid the tall beeches through which the gusts of winter were blowing'' (p. 111).

Gérard is that Orpheus who has managed, somehow, to visit Hades and come back; but if the fires which rage over the earth in the apocalyptic literature remain below ground here, the shades still come to haunt the soul of this survivor. He is the only one who carries within him the ''guy from Semur'' with whom he made the five-day voyage that ended, just before the arrival at camp, in the other's death. And only he who has ''experienced their death'' can, and must, bestow a ''pure, fraternal expression'' on the hideous pile of corpses stacked up in the liberated camp, the corpses of his ''comrades'' (p. 75).

For Semprun as for Rudnicki, for whom there can be no Holocaust-free memories, the arrival at the camp is, as it were, the first day of a new calendar. As a group of Jewish children enter the camp, they are murdered; sixteen years later, the narrator says, ''that death is already adolescent'' (p. 162).

Pierre Gascar: The Anarchy of Death

EXAMINATION AT THE WOMB-DOOR

Who owns these scrawny little feet? *Death.*
Who owns this bristly scorched-looking face? *Death.*
Who owns these still-working lungs? *Death.*
Who owns this utility coat of muscles? *Death.*
Who owns these unspeakable guts? *Death.*
Who owns these questionable brains? *Death.*
All this messy blood? *Death.*
These minimum-efficiency eyes? *Death.*
This wicked little tongue? *Death.*
This occasional wakefulness? *Death.*

Given, stolen, or held pending trial?
Held.

Who owns the whole rainy, stony earth? *Death.*
Who owns all of space? *Death.*

Who is stronger than hope? *Death.*
Who is stronger than the will? *Death.*
Stronger than love? *Death.*
Stronger than life? *Death.*

But who is stronger than death?

                                                            Me, evidently.

Pass, Crow.

                                                            Ted Hughes, *Crow*

The dominion of death is the territory of Pierre Gascar's short story
"The Season of the Dead." In its gradual and utterly realistic descent
into the very bowels of the concentrationary universe—the catacombs
which form the substratum of the entire system—this narrative distills
the horror into its most essential components.

   "The Season of the Dead" is one of several realistic or sur-real
allegories of the sadism and bestiality of war in Gascar's collection
Beasts and Men. These narratives are, like Lind's, Kafkaesque in style,
but unlike them they are, at least ostensibly, predicated on specific
historical realities. In "The Season of the Dead," the first-person narrator, a French prisoner, takes great pains to establish verisimilitude:
the setting is a detention camp for political prisoners at Brodno, which
"consisted of calvary barracks built by the Red Army shortly after the
occupation of Eastern Poland at the end of 1939" and was renovated by
"a certain number of Jews" who live in the area and are awaiting their
turn to be deported.[32]

   The narrator and his companion, Cordonat, have the task of tending
the small graveyard in which those who have died and are dying in the
detention camp are buried. Ostensibly a gruesome task, it nevertheless

affirms the harmony of a natural cycle in which death has a fixed, even decorous role. Tending the flower beds, pruning the weeds, and watering the shrubs, the two graveyard attendants "led that orderly existence depicted in old paintings and, even more, in old tapestries and mosaics" (p. 167). Death here, even under the unusual circumstances of incarceration, is both natural and civilized; even the social amenities are meticulously observed as the narrator and his companion decide "to bury the dead facing towards France" (p. 181). These two believe, as Frederick Hoffman writes in his brief analysis of the story, "that they are assisting in a ritual which will preserve the continuity of life and death."[33] The conditions of the work are so pleasant and the location so idyllic that they evoke the most pastoral memories; "only the lady-bird's carapace and the red umbrella of the toadstool were lacking to link up the springtime of the world with one's own childhood," the narrator admits (p. 168).

Into this idyll the first cold winds penetrate from the nearby town where the Jews live. These Jews, the condemned ones, awaiting their own appointment with destiny, watch the French prisoners "with eyes that revealed neither curiosity nor envy nor dread; . . . they had not left fear behind, but they had been married to it for so long that it had lost its original power" (p. 171). The Jews are the narrator's unwitting guides into the real horror of the concentrationary world. He gradually becomes aware that their death has neither the ceremony nor the identity that attends the death of anyone else; this is not sacrificial death—"hunger, cold, humiliation and fear leave corpses without stigmata" (p. 172). It is uncelebrated, unadorned, anonymous death, first encountered as a corpse by the roadside, unidentified except for the star on his armband.

Some time after the discovery of that emaciated body, Ernst, the German guard in charge of the graveyard detail (a pastor who had himself been a political prisoner) takes the narrator on a walk into the forest, where he reveals to him an ancient Jewish cemetery. It is here, in this quiet forest burial ground, that the dying begin to crowd out the living, that death begins to preempt life. The narrator is overwhelmed by the "symbolism of these graves"—a "breaking branch" carved onto most of the headstones: "On the stone, the branch was endlessly breaking, it would never break," he considers (p. 179). He argues with Ernst, who of course affirms his belief in "Heaven and in the communities of Heaven" to which the dead are instantly admitted; the narrator refuses such consolation, especially for those whose lives have been cut short: "I cannot and will not believe that those who are murdered here cease their cries the moment after . . ." (p. 180).

Yet even he, the digger of graves, has not yet touched the depths of the truth that he has glimpsed. The dead Jews in this ancient cemetery have, at least, their graves and their gravestones. It is only some time later that the real dimensions of concentrationary death are revealed. As the two graveyard attendants are digging a trench to drain off the rainwater that has been pouring down on their French graves, the narrator's pickaxe strikes the arm of a man, a Jew by the appearance of his clothes, who has been murdered and hastily buried. Then Cordonat uncovers another corpse and then another, until they realize that they "had struck the middle of a charnel, a heap of corpses lying side by side in all directions..." (p. 201). Suddenly the narrator understands the anarchic nature of Jewish death under the sign of the Swastika; as the Jews were outcasts from the society of the living, so they had become "irregular troops on the fringe of the army of the dead...'partisans' of another sort." Night starts to fall, and the two men work frantically to cover these bodies with earth, to grant them even the most hasty burial; they become "grave diggers possessed by a feverish delirium...we should never have finished burying them" (p. 201). Even if the Jews were pariahs, their murder is a major event in Western civilization. As Lawrence Langer writes, the death of the Jews which the gravediggers uncover is "a kind of parable of the Holocaust for all humanity." Their unshrouded, unmarked, and decaying bodies demonstrate that "the possibility of death as a personal tragedy has been eliminated from the universe, and that this in turn has altered the meaning of living, of survival itself."[34]

We have already encountered the unsparingly realistic accounts of brutal, unmourned, anonymous death in the writing of the concentrationary realists and others; sometimes, even in a story which stops short of the camps, the anarchy of death intrudes rudely into the tranquil narrative to give the reader just a glimpse of what awaits those who are still quick. In the foreword to his story, the narrator of Giorgio Bassani's Italian novel *The Garden of the Finzi-Continis* explains that it was a visit to the Etruscan tombs near Rome that motivated him, after so many years, to write about the pre-Holocaust lives of his friends the Finzi-Continis. He imagines the effect on the Etruscans themselves of the proximity and resemblance of their tombs to their dwelling-places:

> Once inside the cemetery where each of them owned a second home, and in it the bed on which he would soon be laid to rest with his fathers, eternity must no longer have seemed an illusion, a fairy-tale, a priests' promise. Let the future overturn the world, if it cared to; but there, whatever happened, in that small space sacred to the family dead; in the heart of those tombs where they had the foresight to take,

not only their dead, but everything that made life beautiful and desirable, there at least nothing would change, and their thoughts . . . still hovered around the conical mounds covered in coarse grass after twenty-five centuries.

The narrator's mind then wanders to the Jewish cemetery in Ferrara, and to the "monumental tomb of the Finzi-Continis," which had been set up, like the Etruscan tombs, "to guarantee the everlasting repose of its first customer—his, and that of his descendants," but which now housed only one member of the family whom the narrator had known—Alberto, who had had the good fortune to die before the deportation. Where the others, "all deported to Germany in the autumn of '43, found their burial place is anyone's guess."[35]

Gascar's story stakes out the territory of the "burial place" of such as the Finzi-Continis. It is a "bog full of bones" (p. 200), and standing in the midst of this bog like a latter-day Ezekiel, deprived even of the promise of resurrection, the narrator and his companion have become, as Hoffman writes, "a part of an insane world, from which all propriety and decorum have fled."[36] Like the visitors to the Etruscan tombs who could, perhaps, deduce the system of social values from the shape and contents of the sarcophagi and the arrangements of the catacombs, they learn the nature of concentrationary life from the disposition of the dead. Death is, after all, the *raison d'être* of this universe; the rest—the tooth-gold, the hair for mattresses, the fat for soap—are mere by-products of the system. In effect, all of the characters who appear in Gascar's story, with the exception of the narrator, his companion, their guards, and one or two others, are either dead or dying. The Jewish dead are differentiated by seniority, the oldest lying in decorum in the ancient Jewish cemetery, the most recent in chaotic abandon at the foot of the French cemetery. And even dying has its stages: the stage of frozen fear, in which the Jews of the town live in anticipation of deportation, and the stage of "the death-agony of fear" in the trains, which the narrator views from his little burial ground: "They [the Jews in the train] watched the interminable unrolling of that luminous landscape which they were seeing for the last time, where there was a man standing free and motionless in the middle of a field, and trees, and a harvester, and the impartial summer sun, while your child was suffocating, pressed between your legs in the overcrowded van and weeping with thirst and fright" (p. 203).

Here too, as in Semprun's novel, the serene landscape mocks the agonies of the Jews in cattle cars. Many of them will die on the trip, the rest will die in the camps and, like the other unmarked, unmourned Jews, they will be tossed anonymously into mass ditches or incinerated in huge crematoria. Here, however, the outside world is not totally indifferent; the narrator, by his act of witness, has appropriated their death—through a leap of the imagination marked by a change in the narrative person from third to second, he has even managed to enter the cattle car and stand beside the dying victims. Nevertheless, because they will find no graves, no tombstones to commemorate their lives, their can be no end to the suffering of these Jews and no season to the grief of the witness who would try to mourn them: "Death can never appease this pain," he thinks as the trains speed by; "this stream of black grief will flow forever" (p. 205). The souls of the unburied dead can find no peace even in death.

The crying is forever, the dying is forever, the grieving is forever. Death stalks wantonly through this allegory of Holocaust, ultimately displacing even the ancient dead from their subterranean addresses: eventually the Jewish cemetery in the forest is raided, at German command, and its tombstones used for paving roads. Boris, the narrator of Rawicz's *Blood from the Sky,* records a similar scene; he wanders through the Jewish cemetery in his hometown and comes upon a group of Jewish *Häftlinge* demolishing old tombstones:

> After gazing at the death of human beings, I was confronted, on my way out, by the death of stones.
> The blind, deafening hammer blows were scattering the sacred characters from inscriptions half a millennium old.... An *aleph* would go flying off to the left, while a *he* carved on another piece of stone dropped to the right. A *gimel* would bite the dust and a *nun* follow in its wake.... Several examples of *shin,* a letter symbolizing the miraculous intervention of God, had just been smashed and trampled on by the hammers and feet of these moribund workmen.[37]

Like some sinister realization of the vision of Rabbi Ḥananiah ben Teradyon, who in his last moments of martyrdom under the Roman emperor Hadrian is reported to have cried out that the Torah scroll in which he was wrapped was burning, while the "letters soared upwards,"[38] Boris sees the letters of the alphabet flying about and wonders whether, "once the dissolute army of letters had broken free of its ordained contexts, it [was] going to invade the world of the living.... Was it going to deal blind and deadly blows like a whole band of Golems run riot?" As he escapes from this scene, Boris vows to "rescue the old cemetery" just as he had been appointed to carry the town itself with him into lonely survival. But, he asks, "shall I ever be able to take it upon my shoulders, like a black cloak?"[39]

For the narrator of "The Season of the Dead," who discovers the death, but unlike Boris has had no acquaintance with the life, of these people, death is the final message. "Nothing makes you feel so impoverished as the death of strangers; dying, they testify to death without yielding anything of their lives that might compensate for the enhanced importance of darkness" (p. 225).

For these writers, these mythmakers, the Holocaust can never be integrated into a preexistent world view which could provide a link between the past and the future. In the fiction of Kosinski, Lind, Rudnicki, Semprun, and Gascar, the Holocaust becomes the primary and the only given, an event whose essential reality is evil, or ruin, or death—a voyage from which there is no return, an invincible enemy which has conquered the imagination as well as the battlegrounds of civilized mankind.

EIGHT

History Imagined: The Holocaust in American Literature

> When six millions are slaughtered, in effect twice or thrice that number are [killed]. For the Jews [on all the other continents] die with them. All those that have not yet [perished] are not dead simply because they do not know what has happened . . . . A cold shiver passes over me when I think of their remorse when they do get to know, after the War . . . . Oh, merciful and gracious God! If the circumstances had been reversed, we the Jews of the great European religious academies would have known what was taking place! We would have shrieked to the high heavens and shaken the whole world to its very foundations.
>
> Itzhak Katzenelson, *Vittel Diary*

The European writer—Jew or gentile, survivor or observer—could hardly escape the visions of a Holocaust which was enacted on his native soil. The Poles, as Rudnicki demonstrates, inhabit a land which was physically devastated by military attack and spiritually violated by the presence of the death camps. The Germans were at best observers—as, in fact, were most of the peoples of Europe, whose "undesired" neighbors were rounded up under their very eyes. François Mauriac recalls "the trainloads of Jewish children standing at Austerlitz station,"[1] a spectacle which was reenacted time and again for the non-Jew during the war years.

On the other side of the ocean, the American writer, unless he actually participated in the military liberation of the concentration camps, had no direct contact with the life and death struggles of the victims of Nazism. Nevertheless, an event of such enormity, which clearly carried far-reaching implications for the future of the Jewish people in particular and of mankind in general, could not be passed over in silence, even by Jewish writers in America who only a few years before were endorsing universalistic causes and may have been indifferent to or even contemptuous of their Jewish origins. Yet few if any of these writers possessed the resources from which an immediate response could be shaped. In retrospect, many years later, Saul Bellow articulated the challenge they had faced while at the same time acknowledging the empirical constraints inherent in their creative engagement with the subject:

> Just what the reduction of millions of human beings into heaps of bone and mounds of rag and hair or clouds of smoke betokened, there is no one who can plainly tell us, but it is at least plain that something was being done to put in question the meaning of survival, the meaning of pity, the meaning of justice and of the importance of being oneself, the individual's consciousness of his own existence. It would be odd, indeed, if these historical events had made no impression on American writers, even if they are not on the whole given to taking the historical or theoretical view. They characteristically depend on their own observations and appear at times obstinately empirical.[2]

When he referred to the "reduction of millions of human beings into heaps of bone . . . or clouds of smoke," Bellow could have been alluding to the atomic blasts as well as the Nazi Holocaust; Hiroshima weighs almost as heavily on the American conscience of the American-Jewish writer as Auschwitz preys on his Jewish sensibilities. And he is calling attention to a basic characteristic of the American temper, its fact-minded attachment to empirical criteria of validity. Finally, he is deploring the threat to the self, the loss of identity, which both the Nazi and the nuclear forms of mass extermination represented, perhaps even more than the threat to the entire corpus of Judaism which the destruction of European Jewry signified.

No single work expresses the historical insulation of the American-Jewish writer of the 1940s and his regard for the primacy of the self as effectively as Bellow's own first novel, *Dangling Man*. Published in 1944, before the war had ended, yet not before news of the destruction of European Jewry had received wide publicity, it concerns a young American (incidentally Jewish) who, in the end, resolves his own problems of alienation by enlisting in the army. Except for one dream-sequence filled with physical torture and murder which are associated with unspecified atrocities being committed in Europe, there is no sense of connectedness to the larger events in which he will, by his act of enlistment, be forced to take part. The novel concludes with a tenuous entry into history—but it is not until *Mr. Sammler's Planet*, published twenty-five years later, that there appears in Bellow's fiction a Jew who has lived through and absorbed the major cataclysms of Jewish history in the twentieth century. That quarter-century measures a gradual shift in the engagement as well as the familiarity of the American-Jewish writer with the fate of the Jews of Europe.

Even the writer whose sense of community was stronger in the forties than Bellow's could hardly have broken through the empirical barriers and assimilated into his writing the reports of horrors that were broadcast to him over the radio or glared at him from the newspapers; while they may have dwarfed and mocked his own "mercifully more humdrum" existence,[3] they could not, in their terrible strangeness, furnish new subjects for his art. As early as 1940, Shlomo Katz reported, with probing candor, a conversation which had taken place among a group of young Jewish writers. The writers remain anonymous in his essay, but the condition they describe may be considered as fairly representative. When the "news from Europe" started coming in, Katz reports, these writers, most of whom were American-born and had not written on Jewish subjects for some time—if ever—were nonetheless shaken: "The awareness of their Jewishness transformed the news from Europe into a personal injury and tended to replace other subjects in importance." One writer expressed the dilemma in which they all found themselves:

> How can I write of loneliness in New York, or poverty, or the despair felt by one of the economic outcasts, after I had just read some particularly gruesome piece of news from Germany or Poland? . . . True, one does not rule out the other, objectively. But keenly as I may feel the situation I wish to write about, I cannot help repeating to myself the particular piece of news I read about, and the loneliness of the great city as well as the tragedy of poverty recede in importance; for I visualize the victim in Poland or Germany and I know that he would be happy to exchange positions with the lonely soul, and be thankful for it. I am then confronted with a new theme which in artistic intensity overshadows the one I originally conceived. You will admit that the prospect of one so crushed as to be humbly thankful for that against which we protest, and mind you, honestly and sincerely thankful, is certainly a more moving subject. My first hero who tears his hair in the loneliness of his room while listening to the monotonous ticking of the clock (but after a fair meal), and my heroine who is about to jump off the George Washington Bridge because she cannot practice her art as freely as she would like to while she remains on a W.P.A. project, become shadowy in outline. Again, I repeat, these subjects are still powerful and justify treatment, but I lose my approach; I fall out of the mood and can no longer do these subjects that justice which I feel is their due.

And yet, Katz explains, such a writer cannot incorporate into his art the themes which have come to haunt him, for "only the slimmest of cultural and psychic ties bind him to the Jews of Poland . . . Germany or Russia." Nearly every American-Jewish writer, son or grandson of immigrant parents, felt some personal bond, it is true, to an ancestral home or family in war-torn Europe. Yet the process of acculturation in America had been swift, and "between him and the European scene there lie years" of cultural estrangement.[4] The emotional bond, then, could prove not only insufficient as a creative resource for the writer, but positively detrimental to his art, and the paralysis of creativity which Katz diagnosed in 1940 was to worsen in the ensuing years.

On the most fundamental level, then, it is clear that the absence of direct experience or at least of a cultural ambience that could render the unlived experience familiar, as well as a paralyzing sense of the enormity of the unexplored event, impeded—and eventually shaped—the assimilation of the Holocaust into American, and particularly into American-Jewish, literature. Several stages can be identified in the slow process by which the remote event eventually entered the literature, a few of which correspond to specific historical developments and others to the gradual evolution of a literary milieu. The focus here is not, then, on a specific genre or genres of the literature of displaced and culturally unconnected persons, but on a phase in the literary history of a distinct community of writers. Like the Hebraic, the American literary response to the Holocaust can be examined within a specific and preexistent cultural context, although in the first case it is the proximity to and in the second the distance from the events that maintains the boundaries and the inner coherence of a distinct literary universe.

The war literature, which began to appear in America shortly after the demobilization, established the camps somewhere on the outer boundaries of human geography. During the next several years, which were marked by introspection and a sense of diffidence or vulnerability on the part of American Jews, the magnitude of the fascist threat was probed, but not the historical events of the Holocaust, by a number of serious as well as more popular novelists of the period; the novels by Saul Bellow, Arthur Miller, and Laura Z. Hobson which appeared in the mid-forties reflect a kind of transference of the patterns and fears of anti-Semitism into the American context. Some writers regarded themselves during this same period as spokesmen for the victims and combed the ruins of Europe for their testimonies. During the fifties, the growing documentation by survivors and historians lent greater visibility and familiarity to historical events, although a certain resistance to confronting the American "complicity of silence" or to dwelling on the particularity of Jewish suffering could also be detected during those years. The Eichmann trial proved to be a watershed in the American perception of the Holocaust, as it provided near-personal contact with survivors and an unprecedented immersion in the facts for those who followed it through the public media. The trial itself generated a number of poetic and fictional explorations into the concentrationary universe by writers such as Denise Levertov and Norma Rosen. And the heightened interest which the Eichmann trial precipitated may have been one of the factors behind the proliferation of translations into English of European literature of the Holocaust, which appeared in America in the 1960s. At the same time a number of survivor-writers, including Ilona Karmel, Zdena Berger, Elżbieta Ettinger, and Jerzy Kosinski published their novels in English, adding to an evolving literature that was to provide the outsider with a map of the landscape and possible avenues of approach to it. The realistic fiction written by American-Jewish writers in the sixties and seventies tries to make up for the lack of empirical resources by a thoroughly researched representation of events which were still unknown and by literary models which had not yet been established in the 1940s.

Yet the historical remove remains the basic existential premise on which any American writer confronts the Holocaust, and in the work of certain writers such as Irving Feldman and Arthur Cohen, it is this fact which constitutes the boundary and the resource as well as the ultimate challenge for the imagination. These writers represent two of the most radical attempts to possess the universe of camps and ghettos by a kind of literary fiat.

Parallel with the development of a realistic historical fiction on the one hand, which presupposes an acquired familiarity with the subject, and of a literature that engages history imaginatively on the other hand, have been attempts to distill the experience into its basic symbols and its moral or social legacies. A partial, though intriguing, early example of this is to be found in the parables of Isaac Rosenfeld, which explore the terror of the closed society. For a number of other writers, Jews and non-Jews, the Holocaust is a symbol of the ultimate in human suffering; in Arthur Koestler's words, Jewish suffering represents "man's condition carried to the extreme."[5] These writers range from the proletarian writers of the thirties and beyond, who incorporated the Holocaust into their litany of the class struggle against oppression, to Arthur Miller and Sylvia Plath, for whom personal agony finds its "objective correlative" in Auschwitz.

Where the imagination is not bound by imperatives of personal experience, the symbolic transmutations of historical events disengage more easily from the compulsion to "represent." As such, while nearly every European novel, poem, or play is a form of witness, for American literature the stark realities constitute a stimulus for a process essentially more introspective, self-referential, and autonomous with respect to the haunting memories and less charged with the moral responsibilities and dilemmas of survival and testimony.

The Holocaust and the Literature of World War II

Even as the war literature began to appear, the fate of the Jews and the existence of the concentration camps remained as much on the periphery of consciousness as they had during the war itself.[6] In an occasional novel a soldier does stumble across a death camp or a D.P. camp or the ruins of a ghetto. Yet such a discovery is in most cases as abrupt and unintegrable as the discovery of a Martian spaceship would have been. It was an event which the Americans, British, and Russians experienced as liberators, and the condition of the prisoners they liberated was so unlike anything they had ever witnessed, even on the battlefield, that the event had to be isolated, circumscribed, in order to be communicated at all. In Stefan Heym's novel *The Crusaders*, the decision to liberate a camp near Neustadt is a "bootleg affair"[7] embarked on by one General Farrish; the camp itself is not even on the map—of either the Americans or the Germans. The description of the actual operation of the camp is stiff and reads rather like a textbook account of the system which the author must have come to understand only much later. But what this passage does dramatize with the force of authentic witness is the horror of the first sight of the camps for anybody outside the system. Perhaps the most telling sign of the fact that the very existence of the camps is extraneous to civilized concepts of social order is the wild, enraged reaction of the American soldiers who join the camp inmates in massacring the SS men who are found in the camp; as one of the Americans says, in reply to the officer who wants to capture these men alive so they can be brought to trial, we've "got to do this job before our civilized inhibitions catch up with us" (vol. 2, p. 704). Finally, as they evacuate the camp the dejected, disoriented soldiers look forward only to doing "some fighting, some clean fighting" (vol. 2, p. 706).[8]

Another American war novel, *The Trumpet Unblown*, by William Hoffman, illustrates even more forcefully the remoteness of the concentrationary universe from the experience or imagination of even the most war-weary soldier. In this novel, as in *The Crusaders*, American troops stationed in Germany on a mop-up operation discover traces of concentrationary existence. At one point they come across a barn piled high with charred corpses and force the German townspeople from nearby to dig some graves; in the course of this work, "they found a little life in some of the flesh. It was nothing much, just some stinking organisms, weighing a few pounds at the most, that had managed to

live at least a week under ten feet of decomposing flesh. But there was
life. The organisms responded to light and touch and sipped water.
Sometimes lashless eyelids would flicker a few times before the
organisms died.''[9] The anonymity and dehumanization to which the
victims were subjected even before their deaths is never more apparent
in the literature of the Holocaust than in this passage in which the word
"man," "woman," or "child" is never used.

Frederick Hoffman, in analyzing this novel, draws no distinction in
kind between the horrors of modern warfare and of the concentration
camp. Shelby, a soldier who is one of the main protagonists in *The
Trumpet Unblown,* is described as "as much a victim of the war as if he
had spent the years in a concentration camp." Hoffman calls this book
the *"terminus ad quem* of the literature of violence."[10] But even
though some of the imagery of decomposing bodies and severed limbs
is common to both situations, there is an important distinction between
the above passage and even the most lurid descriptions of combat in
this novel and in most of the other novels which cover the same terrain;
the distinction derives from the perception that the horrors of the concentration camp are the deliberate product of a social organization in
which the victims and the victimizers are clearly and demonically
defined and are not the blind casualties in a declared war between two
parties who share the status of soldiers and enemies. Nor, for all the
anonymity and routine of mechanized mass death in the concentration
camps, were the victimizers insulated from the instant connection between their sadistic acts and the deadly results.

The soldiers who stumble upon the dying victims do not, of course,
understand the operation of the system and its clear-cut distinctions;
but they do perceive that there was a system behind this hideousness,
whose sole purpose was the manufacture of pain and death. The existence of the camps as an incomprehensible social order located at the
extreme borders of the imaginable is dramatized in the scene in *The
Trumpet Unblown* in which a group of D.P.'s in striped pajamas, with
"bald heads and lustreless eyes" (p. 200), comes out of the woods:
"One of the D.P.s had somewhere gotten hold of an old trumpet. The
other D.P.s collected around him and began to chant. It was not a song.
It was a melodic wail. Then the trumpet came in. It was a straight,
unwavering tone upheld by the voices. The music was barbaric and like
no music ever written..." (p. 201). Even when the camps appear in
the pages of a war novel, then, they are unassimilable, mysterious and,
necessarily, tangential to the business at hand.[11]

Among the American novelists and poets of the war, Randall Jarrell
is one of the few who attempted to explore the concentration camp
beyond the barbed wire delineation between the human beings on the
outside and the skeletons on the inside. In his few Holocaust poems, as

well as in his other war poems, Jarrell—the gentile from the American South—attempted to remake himself, according to M. L. Rosenthal, into "a sort of German-Austrian Jewish refugee of the spirit."[12] But unlike Sylvia Plath, whom we will consider later and whom A. Alvarez described in nearly identical language when analyzing her homeopathic appropriation of Holocaust symbols (for Plath the adult is a survivor, "an imaginary Jew from the concentration camps of the mind"), Jarrell does not adopt these symbols as metaphors for his own personal suffering, but assumes the burden of the witness who inherits the dying victim's portion of pain. And yet, like Rudnicki and Gascar, he can not get beyond the death and the dying, for that is the sum total of the reality that greeted him and the other liberators of the camps. The closest he comes to a "life portrait" is in his imaginative evocation of the survivor in a "concentration camp burned by its guards, deserted by its prisoners, and not yet occupied by the Allies," in the poem "In the Camp There Was One Alive."[13] Yet this survivor, abandoned in a "charred cave" in the burning camp, is himself only a heartbeat away from his own death, and his comforters are the already-dead who "come" to him in his last lonely moments. The poetic imagination still cannot take the solider-explorer beyond the terminus of the camp system.

Another of Jarrell's poems, "A Camp in the Prussian Forest," which is one of the most powerful of the Holocaust poems written in America, is concerned directly with death in the camp and with the ritual of burial and elegy that the observer would grant the corpses, both as a tribute to the victims and a defiance of the anarchy of death. Yet as in Gascar's story, the hideous facts of death resist the decorous finale that the poet would accord them, and the camp and its inmates remain inexorably outside the amenities that would civilize them. The speaker, who participates in the mass burial of "load on puffed load" of "corpses, stacked like sodden wood," saws a star from the pine tree which graces the grave (the tree, in a gentle pathetic fallacy, will "pine if it is able"), paints it, and plants it, along with a wreath of pine needles, in the soil that covers the bodies. But his gesture is mocked by the other form of death—the Zyklon B death and the crematory interment from which the dead emerge again as "smoke" to "foul" the memorial star and "chalk with ash" the needles of the pine wreath:

> The needles of the wreath are chalked with ash,
> A filmy trash
> Litters the black woods with the death
> Of men; and one last breadth
>
> Curls from the monstrous chimney . . .
> ["A Camp in the Prussian Forest," pp. 167, 168]

Yet, the most forceful representation of the remoteness and mystery of the concentrationary universe lies not in the symbols but in the syntax of Jarrell's poem. The first line of the fifth verse begins innocently—almost jocularly—by invoking images of mass inebriation ("Here men were drunk"), but the reversal lies in the radical use of "drunk" not as an adjective but as a passive verb: "Here men were drunk *like water,* burnt *like wood*" (p. 167, emphases mine).[14] By an act of grammatical transformation which excludes them from the rules of social discourse, the victims are reduced from agents to objects of normal human functions. This process continues in the next lines, in which the levels of communication are violated by an undifferentiated yoking of literal and metaphorical language:

> The fat of good
> And evil, the breast's star of hope
> Were rendered into soap.
>
> [P. 167]

Yet the speaker, nearly trapped in the uncharted regions of violated syntax and reified metaphor, is carried out of the concentration camp by the familiarity and continuity of a meter and rhyme scheme which threaten to break down in a few places but regain their regularity, and by the latent Christian imagery which is both mocked and affirmed in the final apostrophe:

> ... and one last breath
>
> Curls from the monstrous chimney ... I laugh aloud
> Again and again;
> The star laughs from its rotting shroud
> Of flesh. O star of men!
>
> [P. 168][15]

Because the perspective of the American soldier-poet or soldier-novelist must inevitably be from the outside, and must encompass a vast panorama of destruction with few if any *points d'appui* to facilitate identification with specific individuals, a whole range of empathetic emotions seems to be inaccessible to him. There is sympathy in Jarrell's poetry, but it is undifferentiated and must give way to horror and shock and to an ultimate despair at the inability to rescue character and personal destiny from the piles of ruined humanity. Those writers, survivors or expatriates from Eastern Europe, who were intimately acquainted with the way of life as well as the mutilated death mask of the victims, were able to reconstruct their world and to reassemble random bones into persons. But the first encounter of the outsider with concentrationary death defied all the literary conventions by which tragedy has been conveyed through character, martyrdom through spiritual authority, and agony through personality.

A small group of soldier-writers did, however, attempt to integrate the camps into a larger scheme of meaning which also had a personal, existential referent; they include Jewish novelists such as Irwin Shaw and Louis Falstein, in whose novels the discovery of the camps forms an important link in the protagonist's pursuit of his own identity, a process shared by some of the Jewish soldier-writers from Palestine for whom the European manoeuvres in which they participated served primarily as a catalyst for expeditions into their own souls.

Shaw's *The Young Lions* gained instant popularity and is in certain respects a good representative of the middlebrow war literature of the period and of the earliest perceptions of the Holocaust in the American imagination. The private mission of the American Jew in Europe dovetails neatly in this novel with the ideological commitment that had incubated under the American left wing during the thirties. It is in this regard that such fiction differs markedly from other American novels of the Second World War; both Paul Fussell and Stanley Cooperman, in their studies of the literature of World War I in England and America respectively, demonstrate how the brutality of the Great War destroyed for the postwar writers both the sense of moral seriousness and the expectation of personal valor and glory that soldiers had carried with them into battle since time immemorial and that had shaped the aesthetic conventions of a long tradition of war literature. Although fascism was considered to be a valid and even compelling *causus belli*, war was no longer regarded by the combatants of the Second World War either as a pledge to social amelioration or as a "proving ground of combat"; "almost all of them agreed that Hitler and the Japanese had to be stopped, but they couldn't understand why somebody else than they, individually, shouldn't have done the stopping."[16] For the American-Jewish soldier-novelists, however, the war against Hitler was regarded as a mission in which they had a sanctified role to play, and something of the sense of personal valor and purpose was rescued by these writers from the lost chivalric tradition.

Aesthetically, however, these novels add little to the serious experiments which characterized much of the literature after World War II. Despite the epic sweep of events and plethora of characters, *The Young Lions* is so schematic that there is no room in all its six hundred and eighty-nine pages for coincidence. The two major themes, or convictions, which underlie the narrative may be summed up in what Frederick Hoffman calls the " 'crusading spirit' (that is, that this is a 'must war' against a clearly seen, an obvious enemy)" and the "fear of an indwelling Nazism, a self-analytic devil search." Three wooden characters spar in this Manichean drama until both these convictions are vindicated: Noah Ackerman, the American Jew who "is going into the war to fight both the Nazi evil and its native American examples," Michael Whitacre, the American gentile who is Noah's disciple in moral education, and Christian Diestl, "the finest product of Nazi demonology."[17]

It is significant that the final scene, in which the extremes meet and are resolved, takes place in the woods adjacent to the concentration camp which has just been liberated and occupied by the American forces. The camp itself is not much more than a stage prop into which Christian Diestl wanders and from which, finding himself trapped by the masses of insurgent inmates who have been abandoned by the SS, he manages to escape in the striped prison clothes of a *katzetnik*. It is a stage prop for Noah Ackerman too who, having fought his private war in the army against American anti-Semitism, discovers the ultimate products of the same venom in the concentrationary universe—but at the same time discovers the potential for future regeneration in the person of his commanding officer, Captain Green, who has shown compassion as well as efficiency in his operation of the camp. "When the war is over," Noah shouts in the forest, only seconds before he is shot down by Diestl, "Green is going to run the world . . . . The human beings are going to run the world! . . . There's a lot of Captain Greens! . . . There're millions of them!"[18] Christian kills Ackerman as a German soldier killing an American soldier, while the Nazi in Diestl kills the Jew in Ackerman. Finally Diestl's nemesis materializes in the form of Whitacre, who has served his apprenticeship at Ackerman's side and must now try to live up to the legacy of the "human beings" with which Ackerman charged him.

Due reverence, mingled with a measure of disgust, is granted the camp inmates; the approach of the American soldiers to the camp is described in terms of an encounter with impenetrable horror that are characteristic of the war literature:

> The men in the trucks fell quiet as they drove up to the open gates. The smell, by itself, would have been enough to make them silent, but there was also the sight of the dead bodies sprawled at the gate and behind the wire, and the *slowly moving mass of scarecrows* in tattered striped suits who engulfed the trucks . . . .
>
> They did not make much noise. Many of them wept, many of them tried to smile, although the cavernous eyes did not alter very much, either in weeping or smiling. *It was as though these creatures were too far sunk in a tragedy which had moved off the plane of human reaction onto an animal*

> *level of despair—and the comparatively sophisticated*
> *grimaces of welcome, sorrow and happiness were, for the*
> *time being, beyond their primitive reach.* [P. 672, emphases
> mine]

Here, again, there can be no further penetration of the "mystery" of the death camp, of the system that prevailed there and that brought the victims to their present state, and no empathy for the separate individuals who now constitute a mass of skeletons differentiated only as the "dead," the "dying," the "critical," and the "out of danger" (p. 674). The scénario in the camp serves rather to establish Green's humanity—in his calm and just dispensing of rations and medical supplies and his dry-eyed but compassionate assent to one prisoner-rabbi's request to hold a mass Kaddish for all the dead. It is, ultimately, the American Green who comes to liberate the Jews in the camps—and it is the American in Noah Ackerman who liberates the Jew in him. Ackerman's earlier response to the crude anti-Semitic remarks directed against him by men in his own company is a microcosm of the American response to fascism; he becomes a powerful avenger, learning to fight even the most formidable bullies and brandishing a knife against any further threats. "As he walked toward the barracks, he realized suddenly that he had discovered the technique of survival" (p. 352). And even though he must ultimately die at the hands of Diestl, his death is avenged by his American buddy. Implicit in this is the lesson that the Jews of Eastern Europe were deprived of on any large scale: the lesson of the strength of arms that can secure justice.

This route is pursued even more doggedly in another minor novel of the period, Louis Falstein's *Face of a Hero*. A first-person narrative concerned primarily with the terrors and triumphs of airborne combat (the narrator, Ben Isaacs, like the author, was an aerial gunner in the Air Force), the novel incorporates a visit to an Italian D.P. camp for Jews who had escaped from camps and ghettos in Eastern Europe. The narrator's initial response, predictably, is one of strangeness, even alienation, of recognition that as an American he can never fathom the suffering of these people: "At that moment I was sorry I had come; I felt like an intruder from another world that did not know the smell of the crematoria and the yellow Star of David. And if they resented me I did not blame them. *They* were the survivors of the six million slaughtered Jews, not we American Jews."[19]

And yet if it is as an American that he has been spared the Holocaust that Hitler arranged for the Jews, it is also as an American that he has come to liberate the survivors. Again, like Noah Ackerman, it is the American soldier in Ben Isaacs who liberates the persecuted Jew in him; "were it not for the fact that I was a 'bombadier,'" he muses, the inmates "would have resented my intrusion." As it is, they practically worship him; they crowd around him, staring at him, touching him, asking him questions. An old woman begins to weep and scream: "A Jewish bombadier who has been bombing *him* [Hitler] has come to visit us!... There he is! May he live to one hundred and twenty, Riboinoy shel Oilom. Come, Jews, behold him!" (p. 190).

Like so many other Jewish soldiers who fought in the European theater, both Ben Isaacs and Noah Ackerman rediscover their Jewish origins by association—both voluntary and involuntary—with the victims of Nazism. Their Jewish consciousness is, then, activated and shaped in World War II by a reversion to European perspectives which the immigrant had abandoned when he reached American shores. The dying words of Ackerman's father, who at the beginning of the novel lies destitute in a damp hotel in Santa Monica, concern the brother whom he had left behind in Europe when he emigrated: Your uncle, Jacob Ackerman says to his son, "is not a stranger to you. He is a Jew and the world is hunting him, and you are a Jew and the world is hunting you" (p. 46). Months later, after the anti-Semitism at home and abroad has kindled in him a new sense of kinship with his people, Noah is identified in his own mind as "Ackerman, out of Odessa..." (p. 548).

Ben Isaacs is also made aware by Hitler that his destiny is inexorably linked to that of the Jews behind the barbed wire. Himself an emigré who had arrived in America at the age of fifteen, he returns to Europe "because Hitler made me conscious, again, that as a Jew I must assume the role of scapegoat" (p. 42). He is advised by his buddies to remove his dog tags before flying over Germany; as he does so he realizes that he "hadn't the slightest idea what they did to captured American soldiers of Jewish extraction" (p. 70)—but he is fearful that they accorded them the same treatment they accorded Jews of any other nationality.

Heroism, then, is the answer that Shaw and Falstein would give to the real or potential threat of fascism. Just as in other popular novels of the Holocaust, such as those of J.-F. Steiner and Leon Uris, and much of the Hebrew war literature, heroism is exalted above martyrdom, so in *Face of a Hero* and *The Young Lions* the hero, the Jew as American, finally supersedes and redeems the victim, the Jew as European.

Any American-Jewish writer who, after the war, would attempt to penetrate the concentrationary universe armed only by the imagination would risk being regarded—or regarding himself—as an "intruder." The soldier was in the unique position not only of liberating the few surviving victims but of avenging them and their dead. Nevertheless, most of the literature which reconstructs the engagement of the Jewish soldier with the Jewish victims is so schematic, ultimately serving primarily the patriotic and ideological purposes for which so much war literature is written, that it does not survive as art but as an attitude—as one of the first encounters, authenticated by direct experience, with the Holocaust in American literature.

American Projections of the Holocaust

For many of the civilian American-Jewish authors writing in the years immediately following the war, the Holocaust prompted introverted responses similar to but even more insular than those we have just encountered in the war literature: in some cases it confirmed the faith in the strength of American ideals which, having proved triumphant in the war against evil in Europe, should ultimately prevail in the internal war against social injustice, while in other cases it served to highlight the anti-Semitism inherent in American society. What is common to this literature is a primary concern for the status of the Jews of America, for which the Holocaust serves as a point of reference, not as the focus of attention.

The belief in a dialectical process of moral ascent, which tried to embrace even the Holocaust as part of the great confrontation between the forces of good and evil, justice and injustice, socialism and fascism—the last flickering of the proletarian faith of the thirties—underwent a short revival in the postwar period. Clifford Odets's anti-Nazi play, *Till the Day I Die*, written in 1935, had focused on the clash between ideologies and glorified the sacrificial heroism of those dedicated to overthrowing the "animal kingdom" and establishing "a world of security for all mankind";[20] such a play could hardly be written in 1945. Alfred Kazin, in his autobiography *Starting Out in the Thirties*, writes of the optimism generated in his contemporaries by Odets and the ideals which his art embodied; he recalls that as he had watched Odets's plays he too had been convinced that

> history was going our way, and in our need was the very lifeblood of history . . . . It was as if the planet had locked in combat. . . . There seemed to be no division between my effort at personal liberation and the apparent effort of humanity to deliver itself. Reading Silone and Malraux, discovering Beethoven string quartets and having love affairs were part of the great pattern in Spain, in Nazi concentration camps. . . . Wherever I went now, I felt the moral contagion of a single idea.

Ten years later, Kazin and his compatriots learned what pattern life had in fact taken in the concentration camps:

> One day in the spring of 1945, when the war against Hitler
> was almost won, I sat in a newsreel theatre in Picadilly
> looking at the first films of the newly-liberated Belsen. On
> the screen, sticks in black and white prison garb leaned on a
> wire, staring dreamily at the camera; other sticks shuffled
> about [while bulldozers worked] . . . . Then the sticks would
> come back on the screen, hanging on the wire, looking at
> us.[21]

It is difficult to hang the old ideologies on such sticks. Occasionally a
writer like Albert Halper went so far as to attach the fate of the Jews to
the sense of a general sellout of the old ideologies: "I do not pester my
gentile friends about the plight of these five million expiring Jews, nor
do I allow the cries of these Jews to interfere with my appetite," he
said in a symposium, "American Literature and the Younger Generation of American Jews," sponsored by the *Contemporary Jewish Record* in 1944; "Hell, my gentile friends are as intelligent as I am. They
know that the betrayal of the Jews is part of the whole stinking betrayal
of the world. In time, a man learns to eat his dinner sitting on a garbage
dump."[22] And yet, even if the conviction of a "single idea" of social
justice had not proved as "contagious" as Kazin and others had envisioned, many writers clung to the promise of American democracy as
the last haven for the Jew from international fascism. Even Budd
Schulberg, who gained notoriety in Jewish circles in 1941 with his
unsympathetic portrait of a ruthless, scheming Hollywood Jew
(though, ironically, the novel, *What Makes Sammy Run?* which traces
the unscrupulous rise of Sammy Glick in the movie industry, is also a
testimony to the opportunities which America affords anyone ambitious enough to grab them), wrote a story as early as 1938 about a
persecuted Polish Jew, Nathan, who meets an American Jew and is
overwhelmed by the promise of security which he represents:

> There was something about Democracy, Nathan thought, as
> he listened to Mr. Brownstein . . . . The confidence: being
> able to lift up your head and look the moon in the face. Even
> when Mr. Brownstein bitterly denied there was Democracy
> in the States, where the Yids couldn't work for Universal
> Electric or get to be President, he leaned over the table and
> spoke at Nathan and waved his arms, and puffed his
> cigar . . . and grandly produced his business card like an
> American, a Walt Whitman Democrat, something whole, a
> man with a vote, a man to stare you down, no Polish Jew.[23]

Another writer who represents the same spectrum of cultural attitudes in popular literature is Ben Hecht, whose novel *A Jew in Love*,
published in 1931, had exalted as primary the opportunity which

America afforded the Jew of *disappearing as a Jew.* In a post-Holocaust story, "God Is Good to a Jew," the refugee from Hitler, far from seeking to emancipate himself from his racial origins, discovers, as he dies on a street in New York, that America is the one place where he is not persecuted as a Jew. Having barely escaped death in Poland, Aaron Sholomas dies finally not from being a Jew but from heart failure. Witnessing a neighborhood fire and assuming it to be a pogrom which will soon engulf him, he faints; as he gains consciousness he realizes that the crowd around him is a solicitous, not a murderous, group. "In these last moments of his life, the torn soul of Sholomas filled with love.... After many years and after a long journey [he thought], I have found that goodness does not vanish where the Jew stands. I have found a home." He dies at peace, dreaming of this miracle—"that a Jew would be lying dead among strangers and that the night would be filled with compassion."[24]

The distance between *A Jew in Love* and "God Is Good to a Jew" is the territory traveled by an American Jew who has confronted the Holocaust. As Stanley Yedwab said about a whole group of writers of whom Hecht was one, "fascism seemed to force the marginal Jew back to a Jewishness which he no longer possessed."[25] Hecht's "conversion" is stridently mapped out in two autobiographies published during and after the war. Even as he celebrated the opportunities America presented the Jew to live, or die, as a Jew, much as he had once celebrated the opportunity to assimilate, Hecht is filled with contempt for those Americans—Jews and non-Jews—who were prominent in politics and the arts and who did not speak out during the war. Although his credibility is not incontestable, and his abrupt about-face in Jewish sympathies may even be suspect, it is hard to disprove his contention that "the Americanized Jews who ran newspapers and movie studios, who wrote plays and novels, who were high in government and powerful in the financial, industrial and even social life of the nation were silent" while the atrocities were being committed.[26]

The silence of both the Jews and the gentiles during the Holocaust can be seen as a reflection—either in fear or in sympathy—of the specter of anti-Semitism which had haunted prewar America. World War II followed hard on two decades in which some of the most prominent writers in America had voiced opinions more modulated than but not altogether different in kind from those of the more vociferous anti-Semites in Europe. From Wolfe to Dreiser, from Eliot and Pound to Hemingway and Fitzgerald, in fiction, poetry, and polemical journalism,[27] the Jew in America was vilified, often along the very lines in which the traditionally anti-Semitic portraits of Jews had been drawn in European literature: the Jew as Shylock, the Jew as Machiavel, the

Jew as polluter of Western culture. True, only Pound and a few others refused to recant once it became clear what the application of their prejudices in a fascist regime were leading toward. Wolfe wrote a de-nunciatory account of his trip to Nazi Germany, "I Have a Thing to Tell You," and the novel *You Can't Go Home Again,* which included a sympathetic portrait of a Jewish refugee and eventuated in the banning of his books in Hitler's Germany; even Dreiser denied that he as-sociated himself with the values of the Third Reich.[28] But their earlier attitudes, which reflected a certain climate of opinion in America, must have had no small influence on Jewish writers who, in spite of a large number of both realistic and ideological works reflecting American-Jewish life, had not yet acquired the cultural citizenship in American letters that they would eventually enjoy. One typical Jewish response to the religious tolerance embodied in the American ideal on the one hand and to the anti-Semitism manifested in American culture on the other is the self-deprecation or self-denial which can be found in the works of writers from divers periods, ranging from Mary Antin in the second decade of this century to Samuel Ornitz, Ben Hecht, and Budd Schulberg in the thirties and forties, Jerome Weidman in the fifties, and Philip Roth in the sixties. In the thirties and forties especially, the vigorous protestations of faith in America as the last stronghold of liberty and avenger of fascism can be seen, conversely, as a wishful evasion of the dangers inherent in the murky undercurrent of anti-Semitism that flowed through American society.

This undercurrent was brought to the surface in a new way in three novels of the immediate postwar period, Arthur Miller's *Focus* (1945), Laura Z. Hobson's *Gentleman's Agreement* (1946), and Saul Bellow's *The Victim* (1947). These novels, which are not commensurate in quality, illuminate at different levels the subtle and insidious manifestations of anti-Semitism in American society and expose the raw nerves of Holocaust-haunted American Jews. Hobson's novel is not much more than a screenplay strung together by a predictable narrative; Miller's is more substantive, though still a rather callow venture into fiction for the young playwright, while Bellow's novel is important both as an early indicator of thematic and structural directions in his own writing and as a serious attempt at an allegorical, rather than polemic, explo-ration of complex social and psychological issues.

Miller's *Focus* and Hobson's *Gentleman's Agreement* are both predicated on the rather improbable act of assumption of Jewish iden-tity by an American gentile. In the case of Miller's protagonist, Law-rence Newman, it is an involuntary act—his purchase of eyeglasses results in such a change of physiognomy that he is suddenly taken for a Jew by all his associates and acquaintances. The initial response of

Newman (a prototype of Miller's antihero, a man of average stature, whose conformity to prevailing social codes extends to membership in the anti-Semitic Christian Front) is bitter resentment at such mistaken identity, but eventually he comes to accept the burden of martyrdom that accompanies the physical transformation. In Hobson's *Gentleman's Agreement,* in which stick figures enact the pageant of pride and prejudice in inexorable ways which lead toward an agreeable end, the protagonist is a non-Jewish newspaperman, Philip Green, who decides to impersonate a Jew in order to represent from the "inside" the problem of anti-Semitism which he has been assigned to write about for *Smith's Weekly Magazine.* Both Miller and Hobson seem to assume that the "Jewish problem" would be more comprehensible to the American reader if perceived through the eyes of the gentile.

The assumption of Jewish identity on the part of Hobson's Green is, at least on the surface, far more credibly engineered than that of Miller's Newman. The occasion of mistaken identity—the acquisition of a pair of glasses—is improbable to the point of being ludicrous, unless one reads *Focus* as a satire on the myth of physically defined racial features. Ostensibly, the transformation occurs as suddenly and markedly as that experienced by Kafka's Gregor Samsa; Newman returns home with his glasses and stares at himself in the mirror:

> In the mirror in his bathroom, the bathroom he had used for nearly seven years, he was looking at what might very properly be called the face of a Jew. A Jew, in effect, had gotten into his bathroom.... Under such bulbous eyes...[his smile] was a grin, and his teeth which had always been so irregular now seemed to insult the smile and warped it into a cunning, insincere mockery of a smile, an expression whose attempt at simulating joy was belied, in his opinion, by the Semitic prominence of his nose, the bulging set of his eyes, the listening posture of his ears.[29]

This stereotype of racial characteristics, which corresponds to the standard anti-Semitic portrait of the Jew in American and European literature, is a boomerang of the typecasting which Newman himself had indulged in for years in his capacity as personnel manager for a large corporation which did not hire Jews. Just before his own credentials are called into question, he interviews a woman, a Miss Hart who, he is convinced, is a Jewess hiding behind a Christian name. Her appearance, in his eyes, is cheap, gaudy, and lustful; "he could not blot out the sheen of her dress and the dazzling pin she wore between her breasts.... She was overdressed, overpainted" (p. 35). Yet later, after he himself has been mistaken for a Jew, fired from the company for which he has worked for twenty-five years, and forced to look for a job, he encounters the same Miss Hart—*she* is on the hiring and firing end this time—and his realization that she is not Jewish changes his entire perception of her: "As a Jewess she had seemed dressed in cheap taste, too gaudily. But as a Gentile he found her merely colorful in the same dress, a woman who expressed her spirited nature in her clothes" (p. 83).

The arbitrariness of the criteria by which the destiny of a people is carved is nowhere more evident than in the ridiculous misperceptions from which most of the characters in this novel suffer. Even Newman's mother comments that he looks like a Jew with his new glasses, and the others, who notice the same change, waste no time in acting upon their perceptions: after losing his job, Newman is harassed by his neighbors and ostracized from those very exclusive circles from which he had once prided himself on excluding others. Soon, however, outward posture does acquire a corresponding inner dimension and Newman, like Hobson's Green, begins to "focus" on the world through Jewish eyes. At this point, for both men, mankind comes to be divided into Semites and anti-Semites (with a sprinkling of philo-Semites). In fact, since one's attitude toward the Jews becomes the only touchstone of character, most of the people in both novels emerge as one-dimensional characters, and the "Jewish problem" takes on the proportions of an epidemic. Newman's transformation coincides with the "intrusion" of a Jewish family into his neighborhood; as he sits in the subway he notices that a no-smoking sign has "Jew" written above the offensive smoker; the anti-Semitic graffiti scrawled on the pillars of the train station represent, to him, "a secret newspaper publishing what the people"—including himself, up to a point—"really thought" (p. 7). Phil Green suddenly discovers anti-Semites in taxicabs, hotels, offices—and even in his own family. The problem becomes so ubiquitous that an atmosphere of harassment is created which resembles, if only in its psychological effect, the early stages of the persecution of the Jews in Nazi Germany. True, each incident is fairly insignificant in itself. "No big things," Philip realizes after his first few days as a Jew; "no yellow armband, no marked park bench, no Gestapo. Just here a flick and there another . . . . Each to be rejected as unimportant."[30] Yet the Holocaust represents an intensification in degree, not in kind, for the oppressed American Jew. Newman, married now (to Miss Hart), goes to a movie theater which, it turns out, is featuring a film on the treatment of the Jews in Nazi Germany. The sympathies of the audience around him are not clearly with the victims. The parallel is obvious, and yet that scene constitutes the only instance in the novel where the Jews of Europe are specifically mentioned. Where they do appear, then, the victims of the Holocaust function more as a reference than as the center of the novel's concerns; one is, in fact, barely conscious in reading either of these novels that at the very hour that Philip Green is being turned away from a restricted resort and Lawrence Newman is being fired from his job, millions of Jews are being incinerated in Europe for the same "crime" of birth that Newman and Green are accused of. Ludwig Lewisohn wrote a scathing critique of Hobson's book soon after it appeared, in which he charged that "the six million martyrs, the monstrous theft of all Jewish property over half the world, the closed doors of America, these things, and I am speaking from *her* angle, seem not even to be within her grasp of knowledge."[31]

Yet Miller carries the problem one step further than Hobson. Lawrence, a little man trapped in the clichés of suburban living and of a small job in a large corporation, subscribes to all the prejudices that go with such status. As the enforced change produces certain internal adjustments, he abandons these stereotypes for a more ambiguous, autonomous mode of thought and behavior. And as his prejudices fall away, the novel itself develops from a satiric portrait of the mechanical thoughtlessness of the prejudiced man into a more psychologically complex character study. The transition is not altogether successful, and at times Miller's schematic inversions defeat what should be the organic nature of a growth in stature and in subtlety. But the shift is a significant one, and the concluding chapters are convincing enough to drive home the message that the protagonist must become his own adversary, the Christian Fronter must become a Jew, in order to become a man.

Saul Bellow's *The Victim* is a more consistent and penetrating psychological study than either *Focus* or *Gentleman's Agreement*. The victimization of the Jew in this novel takes place in the encounter between only two people, with few of the social supports which made anti-Semitism appear so rampant and so threatening in the novels of Miller and Hobson. Yet, on another level, *The Victim* is a probing allegory of the Holocaust as a process whereby prejudice and delusion take possession of the psyche. Using the Dostoyevskian technique of the "double," whereby the "other" appears as both victimizer and alter ego of the victim, with just a shadow of a doubt about the full reality of his being (like Yakov Golyadkin in *The Double*, Asa Leventhal awakens from sleep into the atmosphere of suspicion and harassment which materialize in the person of his tormentor), Bellow distills the concentrationary system into two of its most basic components: failure which seeks an external scapegoat and fear compounded by a sense of guilt.

Kirby Allbee, a onetime acquaintance of Asa Leventhal's, reenters

Leventhal's life in a state of destitution, blaming him for having willfully caused his downfall. In the course of their succeeding encounters, it emerges that he holds Leventhal initially, and therefore ultimately, responsible for the chain of events which began with a few anti-Semitic remarks that Allbee had made at a party, after which Leventhal, determined, Allbee claims, to seek revenge, brought about the loss of Allbee's job, which in turn drove him to drink and to the loss of his wife.

While Leventhal, who is alone (his wife is visiting her mother) and, like Bellow's other solitary heroes, particularly vulnerable to such an attack, wrestles with whatever the germ of truth may be in this welter of accusations ("he liked to think 'human' meant accountable"),[32] all the while outwardly denying any responsibility, Allbee insists on identifying Leventhal's behavior with that of his "people" (p. 34)— insisting, that is, that in some deterministic sense, one's heritage is one's fate. The Holocaust is mentioned directly only in one scene when, to protect himself against the onslaught of incriminations against himself and his "people," Leventhal responds rather lamely, "I don't see how you can talk that way.... Millions of us have been killed. What about that?" (p. 133). But Bellow's novel delineates, on the individual level, the myth of the Jew which was propagated on the social level as the ideological justification for the extermination of a whole people. As the Nazis, needing a scapegoat to explain their destitute state after World War I, accused the Jews of stealing their jobs, ruining their economy, polluting their culture, defiling their family lives, and conspiring to usurp political power, so Allbee accuses Leventhal of getting him fired, of bringing about his financial ruin, of precipitating his wife's death—and of belonging to a tribe that has violated the purity of American culture ("Last week I saw a book about Thoreau and Emerson by a man named Lipschitz," he sneers [p. 131]). Even the most natural acts take on sinister racial implications in the eyes of the anti-Semite. When Allbee finally meets Mary, Leventhal's wife, years after the series of encounters that eventuate in Allbee's eviction from Leventhal's apartment and from his life, he notices that she is pregnant, and smiling, he says to Leventhal, "Congratulations. I see you're following orders. 'Increase and multiply'" (p. 254). This last encounter is a meeting between the restored victimizer (Allbee in formal dress squiring around a has-been actress) and the restored victim (Leventhal, a prospective father, more secure in his job, protected from loneliness by his devoted wife, free from harassment) which nevertheless reinforces the old relationship. In a statement defining his sense of his own station in life, Allbee explains to Leventhal that he himself is "not the the type that runs things." He disappears as Leventhal, stunned, calls out to him, "Wait a minute, what's your idea of who runs things?" (p. 256). The implication is clear.

In all three of these novels, written just after the war, the Holocaust appears less as a historical event than as a demonic force inherent in Western society. The fear of a potential pogrom on American shores was, evidently, still greater than the empathy for the actual victims of events which had already taken place.

One writer who distilled the Holocaust into components even more basic and further removed from historical events than the substratum of anti-Semitism which Miller, Hobson, and Bellow had exposed was Isaac Rosenfeld. Remaining very much a loner in his literary experiments, yet pointing the way to a symbolic assimilation of the Holocaust as a common cultural heritage generalized beyond its particular historical coordinates, Rosenfeld produced a series of allegories in the postwar years which capture the essence of the concentrationary experience with a power and inexorability that even more accomplished artists have rarely achieved, either before or since. A confessed disciple of Kafka, Rosenfeld reconstructs the terror, if not the *mise-en-scène,* of recent history. "Terror" is in fact the key to an understanding of Rosenfeld's work, a key that he himself provided in two essays published in 1948 and 1949 in which he also revealed the extent to which the Holocaust haunted and informed his imagination. These essays are worth quoting at some length:

> We still don't understand what happened to the Jews of Europe, and perhaps we never will. There have been books, magazine and newspaper articles, eyewitness accounts, letters, diaries, documents certified by the highest authorities on the life in ghettos and concentration camps, slave factories and extermination centers under the Germans. By now we know all there is to know. But it hasn't helped; we still don't understand.... There is no response great enough to equal the facts that provoke it.

And even those people—the "innocent and the indignant, the relatives and coreligionists or friends of the victims"—who may be willing to admit and to try to understand the facts can never really give an accounting for their own "numbness" in the face of the screams that reached them from a distant continent: "When it comes to numbness we are no different from the murderers who went ahead and did their business and paid no attention to the screams," Rosenfeld continues, in one of the earliest and most relentless expressions of self-reproach by an American-Jewish writer.

Faced with such facts and such numbness, Rosenfeld concludes that "the concentration camp is the model educational system and the model form of government. War is the model enterprise." It is into such "models," he maintains, that we must fit all contemporary experience, as the humanistic cultural traditions have been violated and can no longer provide the structure and value system for human events: "There is no more good and evil—if there were, the screams would have been heard. There is only the terror."[33]

Yet even from such desperate pronouncements Rosenfeld emerges as a moralist. A few years earlier, at the height of the war, he had addressed himself to the "situation of the Jewish writer," and had concluded that, in spite of the fact that it is a burden on the artist, who "should first of all have the security of a dignified neutrality," to know that "he may at any time be called to account not for his art, nor even for his life, but for his Jewishness," nevertheless "out of their recent sufferings one may expect Jewish writers to make certain inevitable moral discoveries. These discoveries, enough to indict the world, *may also be crucial to its salvation*" (emphasis mine).[34]

It is, therefore, out of a moral commitment as deep as that of Kafka, as well as out of pessimism as great as that of his mentor, that Rosenfeld constructs his allegories of terror. Several of the stories which were published posthumously in *Alpha and Omega* (Rosenfeld died suddenly in 1956) are parables of the closed society, of which the concentration camp may be seen as the "model." "An Experiment with Tropical Fish" is a humourous fable of helpless beings trapped in a concentrationary system (the aquarium) in which the impulse to understand and influence one's environment is mocked by a total absence of autonomy. "The New Egypt" is an apocalyptic allegory of the totalitarian society in which even death, the surcease of suffering, is denied the enslaved citizens, who have been granted immortality to perform the Sisyphean task of constructing pyramids. The most sinister and uncompromising presentation of the "terror" is the portrait of the oppressor in "The Brigadier," which was part of a novel that was never published. Unsatisfied with the mere defeat of his enemy, the Brigadier-narrator strives to *possess* him by a total understanding of his character, as he is convinced that "victory will be impossible until we gain this knowledge" of the essential nature of the enemy. "What do we know?" he asks concerning his adversary (who bears close resemblance to the two biological groups singled out for extermination during World War II): "The enemy is darker than we, and shorter in stature.... His language...has nothing in common with our own...his religion is an obscenity..."[35] The Brigadier's tactics involve, in the first place, befriending his prisoners and winning their confidence and, when that yields little "knowledge," torturing and finally killing them: "I would feel an overwhelming hatred of the enemy, and become convinced that my hatred had brought me so much farther than love, to the very brink of knowledge" (p. 108). The perverse Nazi preoccupation with defining and labeling Jewish character and culture, exhibited in the careful preservation of a museum of Jewish artifacts in Prague, coupled with the assumption of the impenetrability and foreignness of the Jew, is generalized here into an epistemological drama of group sadism.

Rosenfeld's penetration into the psychology of hatred and the sociology of oppression was coupled with a kind of mystical faith in the redeeming power of "joy" as the obverse of terror, a version of Reichian principles which consists of "love and restoration" and the "creation of a new capacity ... to experience our natural life to the full."[36] His Reichianism was never fully realized in his fiction, and in fact many of his stories appear to have remained in the experimental stage where the fusion between ideas and characters had not yet been perfected. Yet Rosenfeld pointed the way to a radically different absorption of the Holocaust into the imagination of the American writer, and if his writings never matured beyond a promising apprenticeship, he was engaged, like Kafka, in the major enterprise of what Theodore Solotaroff calls the sublimation of "his own and his people's needs and terrors in an absolute statement of the human crisis":

> The ghetto sensibility, which Rosenfeld himself loved, with all its hallucinations and hope and ironies both intact and transformed in Kafka's art, reached out in parables to comprehend and redeem the broken, fearful moral order of Europe.[37]

Kafka's pre-Holocaust statement that the suffering of the Jew is emblematic of the suffering of all mankind—"Man schlagt den Juden und erschlagt den Menschen"[38]—is echoed in Rosenfeld's post-Holocaust declaration: "As a Jew ... I am all Europe."[39]

Salvaging the Voices of the Dead
Rosenfeld was to remain for many years largely without successors. While most writers, and their readers, had not yet emerged from the "numbness" that had prevailed during the war years, and a few others remained preoccupied with the possibility of a fascist threat to American Jews, a small group of writers and critics began to assume a kind of historical imperative by searching throughout Europe to piece together the story of what had happened—only to discover that the endless repetition of horror stories, which should lend them credibility and

even familiarity in the eyes of the American visitor, served but to
reconfirm how great the distance was that separated those who were
there from those who had been spared.

Yet the refugees themselves seemed eager to tell their stories, which,
they thought, must be of interest to American Jews. Rosenfeld
observed that the journalistic reports were valuable because they
merely "set down what [the writer] has seen and heard on a visit to
[Europe's] surviving Jews.... [Such a book] has the courage...to
stay near the thing itself and not to cast about for the usual re-
assurance."[40] For some writers the subject had to be left there, at the
level of bare fact; for others these stories would eventually serve as
resources for their own imaginative retellings. But for many years the
ruthless realism of atrocity was largely avoided or at best transformed
into the remote domain of nightmare or fable more reconcilable with
the American faith in human goodness.

One writer who did not attempt any psychological or artistic incorporation of the European Jewish ordeal into the American experience but who was, unwittingly perhaps, to challenge the sanguine pre-
suppositions underlying the American ideal was Meyer Levin. His
concept of the role of the American writer was, quite simply, that of a
midwife to the authentic recitations of the victims themselves. As a war
correspondent, Levin had asked for "one special assignment—to uncover what had happened to the Jews"—and he had, by his own account, "sought out every survivor I could unearth, from the first who
emerged from the subcellars of Paris, to the living cinders of the
death-camp crematoria."[41] He faithfully collected information and
recorded numerous testimonies, but he felt he would "never be able to
write the story of the Jews of Europe,"[42] for in spite of the cultural
familiarity and sympathy as well as the wealth of knowledge about the
Holocaust reality that he had gained, he too, like the war poets and
novelists, sensed the impenetrable mystery of the experience that he
had not shared: "This tragic epic cannot be written by a stranger to the
experience, for the survivors have an augmented view which we cannot attain; they lived so long so close with death that *on a moral plane
they are like people who have acquired the hearing of a whole range of
tones outside normal human hearing*" (*In Search*, p. 173, emphasis
mine).

Yet when Levin, in his travels, came upon the work that he could
finally regard as the "voice I had been waiting for, the voice from
amongst themselves, the voice from the mass grave" (*The Obsession*,
p. 35), it was in fact a story which *did* remain within the range of
"normal human hearing." *Anne Frank: The Diary of a Young Girl*,
which Levin discovered in its French edition, had not yet been ac-

cepted by any American publisher. Levin was instrumental in finding a publisher, but only after several editors had rejected the book because, as they wrote, "they were personally touched, but professionally they were convinced that the public shied away from such material" (*The Obsession*, p. 35). Later, when Levin discussed with various producers the concept of transposing the diary into a play, the reaction of Herman Shumlin was typical of the sympathetic-but-realistic attitude that he was to encounter repeatedly; as Levin reports in *The Obsession*, Shumlin warned him that "it's impossible. You simply can't expect an audience to come to the theater to watch on the stage people they know to have ended up in the crematorium. It would be too painful. They won't come" (p. 36). And yet this diary, which of course did achieve, both in the original and in the theatrical and cinematic adaptations, popularity unmatched by any other documentary or artistic representation of the Holocaust, had the wide appeal it did not only because of the articulate, sensitive, and candid writing of a precocious thirteen-year-old girl but also, or perhaps especially, because of the sanguine tone which dominates the text, because of the absence of any direct account of the horrors and the loneliness that were the lot of most of the Jews who went into hiding during the war—and of the Franks and Van Daans themselves, after their arrest. Although Levin never acknowledges the fact, it is precisely because the book does *not* record that "whole range of tones outside normal human hearing" that it could be so well received by an audience who shared in what Bettelheim describes as the "general repression of the discovery" of the horrible facts of the concentrationary universe.[43]

Bettelheim claims that all the arrangements made by the Frank family in hiding ran counter to the requirements of self-preservation under such circumstances (he particularly cites their failure to prepare any escape routes to the free world or, while in hiding, to practice survival techniques in anticipation of possible arrest). Yet, while Bettelheim's simplistic assumption that if the Franks had "faced the facts," they would probably have survived, takes very little account of the utterly helpless and unprecedented situation in which the Jews found themselves (and this assumption, that adaptation to "extreme social circumstances"[44] would have been an almost certain guarantee of survival, is a dominant theme throughout *The Informed Heart*), his extension of this psychology of denial does facilitate our understanding of the reasons for the warm reception granted the diary and the play on which it was based: "[Anne Frank's] story found wide acclaim because . . . it denies implicitly that Auschwitz ever existed. If all men are good, there never was an Auschwitz."[45]

The circumstances attending the dramatic adaptation of the diary

tend to confirm Bettelheim's observations. The need to affirm that "all
men are good" and, by extension, that all men are brothers casts the
manuscript that Anne Frank left behind her into the pale afterglow of
the ideals of socialism and universalism that had informed so much of
the American art of the thirties and that were suffering their own political martyrdom in the fifties. By circumventing the impenetrable "terror" that Rosenfeld had defined as the essence of the Holocaust, the
drama of Anne Frank which opened on Broadway and played in
theaters and moviehouses throughout the world succeeded also in
avoiding the issue of Jewish identity which was at the core of the diary
that Anne Frank had abandoned when she was arrested in her "secret
annex." From a moving document of the plight of an assimilated
Jewish family which nonetheless perceives its suffering and its destiny
as part of the particularistic destiny of the Jewish people, the diary was
transformed into a work of art which comprises both a litany of human
suffering and a declaration of ultimate faith in universal goodness. The
playwrights who converted the diary into a commercial drama availed
themselves of a young girl's naive belief in the potential for human
goodness to serve the defense of American liberal optimism against the
evidence of pure evil. In the emphasis on Anne's faith there is an
implicit denial of her fate—either as the innocent victim of demonic
forces or as the Jewish victim of anti-Semitism. The adaptation of *The
Diary of a Young Girl*, while it brought the Holocaust to the forefront
of mass consciousness, did not really seek to dispel the curiously functional "amnesia" toward the events themselves, which was accompanied by a general unwillingness on the part of non-Jews in America
to explore the "Jewish problem" and by a Jewish ambivalence toward
accepting the role of messengers of the reality of evil in a society still
largely animated by faith in the moral order.

Meyer Levin has recorded, fictionalized, litigated, and lamented this
phenomenon for a quarter of a century. His discovery of the diary and
his role in getting it published in America prompted him to bid for a
chance at dramatizing it himself. The ensuing story of manipulation of
the text by many hands not only is a thoroughly documented and
tedious case history of the paranoia of Meyer Levin, but also highlights
an important stage in the evolution of American attitudes toward the
Holocaust.

A few parenthetical comments should be made at this point about the
very act of converting the diary into a play, an act which cannot be
judged independently of the mediocre talents of all those who engaged
in the adaptation, but which also points to a certain inherent resistance
of the original text to any modification. No matter how faithful the
artistic adaptation might have been to the diary, it would necessarily

have betrayed the very nature of the genre—for the numerous diaries which were written by the victims in hiding or in ghettos or camps, and posthumously published, constitute a peculiar genre with a beginning and a middle, but no end. The tragic impact of a diary like Anne's is a product of the interaction between the writer who, even in her last entries, affirms her belief that "it will all come right,"[46] and the post-Holocaust reader who, through the burden of hindsight, knows that it did not come right. The diary ends abruptly, randomly; the various versions of the play, answering to the exigencies of form, have their resolutions and their "moments of truth" that the imagination imposes on reality. Furthermore, the characters lose much of the mystery and complexity combined with the adolescent naiveté with which Anne perceives them when they are translated from the subjectivist perspective of a diary to the autonomy of stage personae. And all of the playwrights who tried their hands at the task failed particularly in the representation of the secret duality of Anne's character, for this "little bundle of contradictions" (p. 280), who could confide her true self only to paper, must suddenly externalize and verbalize feelings which by their very admission violate that realm of privacy which is the diary itself.

But the central issue which Levin raises in documenting the history of his own and the Broadway versions of the play, an issue which reflects on the assessment of American willingness to relate to the particularity of Jewish suffering, remains an important measure of both the popular and the more serious art of the fifties. What is deleted from the original text in the Broadway drama is the engagement with Jewish history (such as Anne's sister's pledge to become a nurse in Palestine) and the affirmation of Jewish destiny (exemplified in Anne's assertion of the uniqueness and purpose of Jewish martyrdom and her declaration of faith). That such omissions are the deliberate expression of an ideology which universalized the Jewish experience may be supported by a passage from Lillian Hellman's autobiography *Pentimento,* in which the writer who was the guiding spirit behind the Broadway play tells of having smuggled a large sum of money into Nazi Germany in 1937 for a friend who was engaged in buying the freedom of endangered persons; when Hellman asked her if the people for whom the money was intended were Jews, the friend answered, in a line which anticipates one of Anne's statements in the Broadway play, "About half. And political people. Socialists, Communists, plain old Catholic dissenters. *Jews aren't the only people who have suffered here*" (emphasis mine).[47]

On such grounds Meyer Levin tries to build a case for the existence of a kind of literary mafia of Communist sympathizers who engaged,

during the McCarthy period, in a counteroffensive against ethnic perspectives and reflected a widespread liberal defensiveness against
elevating Jewish particularism through the enormous emotional lever
of the Holocaust. Through more balanced arguments, Edward
Alexander has demonstrated how "resistant to [the] negative evidence" of recent events were the humanitarian, universalistic ideals
which American Jews, no less than non-Jews, had rescued from the
promise of the Enlightenment.[48] One can shore up this claim with a
consideration of both the scarcity of literature in the fifties dealing with
the Holocaust from a Jewish perspective and the reception given those
works which did appear. A number of writers who participated in a
symposium sponsored by *Congress Weekly* in 1951 told of the resistance with which their books, touching on the Holocaust or other manifestations of anti-Semitism, were greeted.[49] In fact the high degree of
self-consciousness which dominates most of the symposia sponsored
by Jewish literary journals in those years is in itself indicative of the
conflict that Jews perceived between their identity as Americans and as
Jewish writers, and the sense they still had of their own precarious
status in the American literary community. This sense persisted well
into the years that have been hailed as a period of "philo-Semitism"
in America, which began as a belated penitential reaction to the
Holocaust and peaked in the sixties.

The legacy of the thirties, then, which contained the slowly dying
vestiges of gentile anti-Semitism as well as a persistent liberal resistance among Jews and non-Jews to differentiating the Jewish experience, was a recurrent issue which certain writers, such as Hobson,
Miller, and Bellow, had begun to explore directly in their fiction, which
others such as Rosenfeld reflected in their allegorization of the events,
and which a few of the more polemically minded writers and journalists, such as Levin and Hecht, openly challenged in various literary
and extraliterary forums. The publication of Hersey's *The Wall* in 1950
conferred the legitimization of gentile authorship and readership as
well as a heroic perspective on what had been formerly perceived by
Jews and non-Jews alike as a parochial and shameful subject. And if
the drama *The Diary of Anne Frank,* which was first performed in 1955,
did attempt to portray Jewish suffering, it was after purging it of its
particularity. It would take another five to ten years before the cultural
and spiritual requisites for a more specific and personal engagement
with the events of 1933–45 would suffice to generate in American
literature a more straightforward historical relationship on the one
hand and a more profound assimilation of the implications of the
Holocaust for nonsurvivors on the other.

The Man in the Glass Booth

The intensity and scope of the renewed engagement of American writers with the Holocaust were catalyzed by an event which took place sixteen years after the war. The Eichmann trial, coming as it did after a decade and a half of documentation and testimony on the part of scholars and survivors, forcing its entry into the homes of all Americans who committed the minimal act of turning on their television sets, ensued in a spate of literary activity unprecedented at any time since the war. Of course television was far more pervasive and influential in the sixties than it had ever been and, as evidenced by the impact that televised reports of the Vietnamese war were to have on the American people a few years later, could succeed in conveying remote events with unprecedented urgency and immediacy. Much of the literature written in the mid- and late sixties reflects the heightened historical consciousness which the trial precipitated. In some cases the creative mind, compelled to acknowledge the horrors that were now granted the status of higher reality by the legal process itself, responded by seeming to abdicate altogether the task of imposing form; Charles Reznikoff's series, *Holocaust,* which we have already considered, is a long documentary poem based on the records from the Eichmann and Nuremberg trials. Resembling Weiss's *Investigation* in its reproduction of excerpts of legal testimony from the trials of Nazi criminals, it shares with all the documentary art of the Holocaust the premise of minimal intervention in or manipulation of history on the part of the artist.

Other works of the period following the trial are more specifically concerned with the implications for Americans of the discoveries made during the proceedings. Two themes seem to dominate this body of literature: the first, influenced in no small measure by Hannah Arendt's interpretation of the trial, which was the filter through which most Americans were able to conceptualize what was otherwise a morass of indigestible, unintegrable facts,[50] concerns the "banality" and the "bureaucracy" of the Nazi evil. The second theme, which derives from the first, relates to the appropriation of the Holocaust not primarily as a historical event but as a complex of psychological possibilities. The thesis which Arendt and others espoused, which rendered the actions of the oppressor intelligible and even predictable under certain conditions, and which claimed "that this new type of criminal, who is in actual fact *hostis generis humani,* commits his crimes under circumstances that make it well-nigh impossible for him to know or to feel that he is doing wrong,"[51] denies, as it were, the historical circumscription of the Holocaust and engages the writer who did not experience the events in a process of self-scrutiny and speculation on the implications for the human species of the victimization and annihilation of the Jews. Again, as in the case of the immediate postwar literature which distilled the Holocaust into the ubiquity of the anti-Semitic menace, or the stories of Rosenfeld which reduced historic events to parables of the closed society, American writers seemed to avail themselves of the evidence produced at the Eichmann trial to try to possess not the events themselves but the moral options which prevailed in those times and which could be repeated under similar circumstances.

We have seen that a similar process took place at the same time in Israeli literature. The fact that the Eichmann trial proved to be such a watershed can, perhaps, be ascribed to a parallel development in the literary history of the two countries where large concentrations of Jews were removed from what had happened to the Jews of Europe. In a discussion among four Hebrew authors who had responded to the question of why contemporary Israeli writers had not previously given adequate literary expression to the Holocaust, Moshe Shamir is reported as having said:

> as for the catastrophe of European Jewry, it is not quite true to say that our literature has failed to reflect the tragedy, but we are troubled by the feeling that it has not yet found adequate expression. The difficulty is that "just as the catastrophe was something hellish and inconceivable, so we are waiting for a work that will express something of *our inability to grasp the catastrophe, the fact that we confront it with empty hands.*" ... Until Hebrew authors feel the catastrophe as a personal tragedy, they will not be able to write about it. The trouble is that from the cold biological point of view, the Yiddish writers were "*inside* the burning house" while the Hebrew writers saw it from the outside . . . .
>
> There is . . . a recent event which has brought the subject home to the younger generation "as a personal, moral problem." That is the Eichmann Trial, not only in itself but against the background of the affluent society—Israeli version, in the Sixties of this century: the dramatic and shattering contrast between the world that the trial presented with such terrific force, and the life that surrounded the courthouse (emphases mine).[52]

Dalia Ravikovitz, a poet who represents the younger generation of Israeli writers, is quoted as saying that "especially after the Eichmann trial, . . . 'the Holocaust is like an exploding hand grenade; each of us has been struck by his private splinter, which he carries in his own body.'"[53]

Many American writers might have said what Shamir and Ravikovitz did about their former inability to personalize or internalize the Holocaust, and the thawing impact of the Eichmann trial which transformed the Holocaust into a "personal, moral problem." Denise Levertov wrote a trilogy of poems, "During the Eichmann Trial," which explores the challenge presented to Everyman by evil impulse, and Eichmann's failure to meet the challenge to look into the faces of his victims and pity them. The reflection in the glass booth, then, is our own reflection, and Eichmann becomes the example of a lesson not learned:

> He stands
>
> isolate in a bulletproof
> witness-stand of glass,
> a cage, where we may view
> ourselves, an apparition
>
> telling us something he does not know: we are members
>
> one of another.[54]

In the second poem in the trilogy, Levertov presents Eichmann as the agent of death in an inversion of the Edenic myth; a Jewish boy who is lured into Eichmann's orchard ("the Devil's garden") by the sight of one "yellow and ripe" peach is pounced on by "mister death . . . / who wanted that yellow peach / for himself." The anecdote is consistent with the previous portrait of Eichmann, the demon-as-technocrat, "mister death who signs papers / then eats" (p. 64). Levertov admits in a note that her poem, though based on an incident reported at the trial, is not an exact "report of what happened but of what I envisioned" (p. 65). The trial and the person of Eichmann become, then, triggers for the poetic imagination.

The literary fascination with this character as the embodiment of the human potential for blind obedience and criminal pitilessness[55] is significant in that it reflects an implicit acceptance of Eichmann's defense of himself as a mere cog in the machinery of Nazism and an implicit rejection of the prosecution's charge, echoed by Jacob Robinson, that "he was no average man and possessed no ordinary criminal skills."[56] The temptation of compliance with the dictates of the impersonal bureaucratic systems which control the lives of individuals in both totalitarian and democratic states is, perhaps, more familiar and more threatening to the American writer than the elusive ideology of evil on which the Third Reich was founded.[57]

One writer for whom the Eichmann trial provided a personal link not so much with the oppressors or the oppressive impulse as with the

victims of Nazism is Norma Rosen. Her novel *Touching Evil* is a portrait of the intrusion of monstrous evil into the domestic realm, and of
the incompatibility, to which Shamir alluded, between the concentrationary universe reconstructed at the trial and the "affluent society"
beyond the courthouse doors. The narrative comprises a series of letters written by Jean Lamb to her absent lover, describing her own
activities and those of her friend Hattie during the period that the
Eichmann trial is being serialized on television. The premise by which
historical experience is appropriated by these nonparticipants (and
non-Jews) is one which honestly acknowledges the gap in experience
and struggles with the need to repossess the events vicariously. Each
of these two women has "extracted [her] private symbols of horror
from the welter of horror symbols."[58] Jean, in her letters, reveals that
the Holocaust has so invaded her personal life that her initial discovery
of the concentration camps, just after the war, generated in her a
pledge to withdraw from the pursuit of a normal life. Though she has
retained the outward appearance of normalcy, she has remained un-
married and, of course, childless; the Holocaust has become her "personal catastrophe" (p. 78), and whenever she hears her name called—
"Miss Lamb"—she feels, she says, "a tugging of the rope. 'Miss Lamb
to the slaughter!' Not as victim, I never thought that, but as witness"
(p. 97). The ultimate knowledge of the twentieth century is contained
for her in the sum of the experience of the victim and the one who has
touched evil through the imagination: "Between those who were there
and those who dreamed they were there we've been through everything, haven't we? Between the survivors and the ones who didn't
survive we know it all" (p. 57).

Jean's younger friend, Hattie, has learned of the Holocaust through
the Eichmann trial, and Jean relives her initial reactions to the discovery of the concentrationary universe through her. Hattie, in an
advanced state of pregnancy, is extraordinarily vulnerable to the
onslaught of morbid facts that are reported at the trial and not only
empathizes with all those pregnant women who, together with their
fetuses or newborn infants, were tortured and killed by the Nazis, but
in some mystical sense tries to internalize—and redeem—their plight.
Her struggle culminates, after the birth of her own daughter, in a
metempsychotic vision of the death and rebirth of children, which she
relates to Jean as a possible scenario for a play:

> "the children talk about their happiness to be alive at first,
> and then each tells how he or she died. After each war, each
> atrocity, each death, the children fly down to their mothers'
> beds and disappear in them. Then the whole thing is re-
> peated, and the children fly up again. New children . . . .

> New births.... New times.... New joys.... Centuries
> and centuries and centuries of joyful births and terrible
> deaths.... After a while we begin to see similarities... we
> see the same children over and over... those children
> haven't been lost...." [P. 237]

Hattie's own child, then, becomes the reincarnation of one of those infantile victims of the Holocaust, and the act of parturition is, for her, an act of resurrection.

The discovery of the Holocaust, imparted through the Eichmann trial, invades and transforms, in one way or another, the lives of all the characters in this novel who have followed the proceedings on television. The sign of contemporary civilization, which Jean compares to the monuments of other eras—to Stonehenge, the Parthenon, and the Great Pyramid at Giza—is the "piled up stick bodies at the bottom of a lime pit" (p. 73).

In an essay, Norma Rosen says her novel was conceived out of Bertolt Brecht's pronouncement that "he who can still smile has not yet heard the terrible news," and was shaped by the realization that the only role that she could adopt for herself as an American writer was the vicarious one of "witness—through the imagination," of "documenter of the responses of those who had (merely) 'heard the terrible news.'" The Holocaust, Rosen writes, is the "central occurrence of the twentieth century. It is the central human occurrence. It cannot therefore be more so for Jews and Jewish writers. But it ought, at least, to be that."It is, then, as a Jewish writer that she would convey in fiction not the "meaning of the Holocaust for Jewish history," but the "meaning to human life and aspiration of the knowledge that human beings—in great numbers—could do what had been done."[59] Again it is the Jewish experience yielding some lesson about the behavior and destiny of the species which is preeminent and, as in the novels of Hobson and Miller, the center of consciousness is a non-Jew. Finally, in an act reminiscent of the sacramental resolutions in Wallant's novels and consistent with a perspective that assimilates the Holocaust into prevailing religious or social codes in America, Jean, in her last letter to her lover, pledges herself to a search for "Jesús," a destitute Puerto Rican boy whom she has befriended and cared for and who has now disappeared.

As so often happens in these novels, the burden of the "terrible news" weighs too heavily on the frail shoulders of the well-meaning American protagonists, and their actions in a sane society can never be commensurate with their "knowledge" of the madness that prevailed under Nazism. The novel is, therefore, not altogether convincing on the psychological level; nevertheless, Rosen does achieve a partial balance between the narrative of commonplace events in the lives of a

few people living in New York in 1961 and the subterranean forces of
Holocaust evil and suffering which constantly threaten to subvert those
events.

Imagination in Place of History

Norma Rosen's assumption of the role of "witness-through-the-
imagination" resembles in certain respects that of Irving Feldman in
two Holocaust poems which appeared in his collection of poetry *The
Pripet Marshes,* published in 1965. Directly acknowledging, as Rosen
does, the gap between survivors and those who were not there,
Feldman attempts to make the experience his own in one poem, "The
Pripet Marshes," through a leap of the historical imagination, and in
another, "To the Six Million," through a mystical act of erotic
possession.

In "The Pripet Marshes," Feldman transforms historical remove
into historical prerogative. Unlike the survivor-writer, whose imagination is ultimately accountable to history—who, like Wiesel, for example, may suspend history momentarily in order to resurrect his friends
and family but who must in the end surrender them to their historical
deaths—the liberated fantasies of Irving Feldman allow him to manip-
ulate history freely. The poem is a visionary transplantation of
Feldman's own, American, family and friends into the ghetto in the
Pripet Marshes (northwestern Ukraine) at the moment before the Germans are to arrive:

> Often I think of my Jewish friends and seize them
> as they are and transport them in my mind to the
> shtetlach and ghettos.[60]

As in Yeats's "Easter 1916," the speaker names the victims ("Maury
is there, uncomfortable and pigeon-toed.... And Frank who is
goodhearted.... And my mother.... And my brown-eyed son" [pp.
44, 45]), but unlike the elegist, he is spared the necessity of eulogizing
them—for, after all, they are only the understudies for the real victims,
whom the poet never knew. Only minutes before their martyrdom is to
be enacted ("in the moment when the Germans are beginning to enter./
the town"), the speaker snatches them back—for, freed from historical
necessity, he has the divine power of the creator:

> But there isn't a second to lose, I snatch them all back,
> For, when I want to, I can be a God.
> No, the Germans won't have one of them!
> This is my people, they are mine.
>
> [P. 146]

In the second poem, "To the Six Million," the autobiographical
"exemption" which the speaker invoked in order to save lives in the
first poem is transformed into a tragic mission. Through an act of the
imagination no less radical than that exercised in "The Pripet
Marshes," the poet takes upon himself the burden of the death of the
six million—a burden imposed on him because he is a survivor ("survivor" here as one who was spared, was not touched by the events).
Here, as in the first poem, the speaker does not eulogize the real
victims, whom he never knew personally—and eulogy, it should be
recalled, is one of the major tasks in nearly every work of art by a
survivor of the Holocaust. He would appropriate the victims, then, not
in their lives, but in their deaths. Again, like the soldier-writers who
came upon the traces of death but could never reconstruct the lives of
the victims, the American writer here relates only to the corpses and
the desolation.

In the central part of the poem the speaker is alone in a ghost town,
without either divine or human supports, and he asks himself, "survivor, who are you?" (p. 49). The terrible loneliness which underlies
that question generates the search for historical coordinates by which
the "I" can possess and merge with the dead victims. And here the
historical exemption which the poet invoked to rescue Jews in "The
Pripet Marshes" becomes an imperative to relive "the agony of the
absence" (p. 51), for he who dies, dies only once, but he who remains
must relive the death of the millions, over and over.

In the last section of the poem, the speaker persists in his attempt to
possess the death of the six million, to merge with the collective destiny. In this section biblical images, mostly from Song of Songs, predominate, sanctifying, as it were, the erotic vision. Yet several of these
images takes on an additional meaning, transforming the portrait of
divinely sanctioned love into a vision of grotesque, concentrationary
death. "And your necks that are towers, / Your temples that are as
pieces / Of pomegranate within your locks" (p. 52), a direct quote from
the Song of Solomon, can be construed not simply as the physiognomy
of the beloved but also as the sight of mutilated corpses: "necks as
towers" can also be decapitated necks; "temples...as pieces of
pomegranate" can also be bleeding skulls.

The speaker's search for a way into this death leads him through all
the possible relationships to the dead ones; he appears alternately as
mother, as child, as father, as brother, and as friend: "I must possess
you, befriend you, / ...and be your brother and your son" (p. 53).
And, finally, the speaker appears as the bridegroom, and through a
necrophilic act of love, succeeds in possessing—and reviving—the

beloved dead, who is simultaneously widow and stillborn child:

> Sweetness, my soul's bride,
> Come to the feast I have made,
> My bone and my flesh of me,
> Broken and touched,
> Come in your widow's raiment of dust and ashes,
> Bereaved, newborn, gasping for
> The breath that was torn from you,
> That is returned to you.
>
> [Pp. 53–54]

Despite the grotesqueness of the imagery, the concluding lines of the poem carry a serene resolution which the act of love and the liturgical tone of the poem have evoked: "My heart is full, only the speech / Of the ritual can express it" (p. 54).

Feldman's poems are among the most daring examples of the attempt of the creative writer to overcome what Shamir calls "the fact that we confront [the Holocaust] with empty hands," what the writers of A-bomb literature call, in relation to the events at Hiroshima and Nagasaki, "the differences between those who went through this historical experience and those who did not."[61] Both Feldman and Rosen, freed from historical imperative, perform an act of mystical transference in an effort to engage history. Another writer, Arthur A. Cohen, has appropriated the symbols of the Holocaust through a more radical fiat of the historical imagination. *In the Days of Simon Stern*,[62] which is a complex and diffuse but philosophically provocative novel by a contemporary American-Jewish thinker, is an apocalyptic legend of the founding of a secret "Society for the Rescue and Resurrection of Jews." The Society's compound, on the Lower East Side of New York, is inhabited by one thousand survivors of the Holocaust who have been gathered from the liberated camps in Europe. The story, narrated by blind Nathan Gaza (such symbols as Nathan's name, borrowed from the Sabbatean and other contexts, are overly transparent), focuses on the career of one Simon Stern, an American-born millionaire real-estate dealer who receives an annunciation of his mission as Messiah and tries to fulfill it by establishing the Society and reconstructing the broken lives of a collection of survivors. Based on the traditional belief that the Messiah will come in the wake of terrible cataclysm, the narrative is a concatenation of biblical and cabbalistic legends, theological discourses, and homilies loosely held together by an improbable narrative. The two themes which dominate the novel are the theme of rescue and rehabilitation, in America, of the survivors of the European Holocaust, and the related process by which Jewish history is reenacted—and thereby authenticated for the historically "deprived" American Jew—on American soil. Within the Society's compound a replica of the Temple of Solomon is constructed, and the narrative concludes with an emblematic holocaustic conflagration which destroys the Temple and the compound and scatters the inhabitants all over land. Cohen's novel is an ambitious, at times engaging, but seriously flawed attempt on the one hand to render the Holocaust theologically meaningful, and on the other hand to possess the Holocaust by means of a kind of shadow-play recapitulation of history.

In addition to the existential leaps of imagination by which writers such as Norma Rosen, Irving Feldman, and Arthur Cohen have attempted to appropriate the Holocaust in fiction and poetry, two distinct attitudes seem to characterize the Holocaust literature that has appeared in America in the years since the Eichmann trial. The first, which may be associated with the universalistic perspective of writers such as Rosenfeld and Levertov, attempts to extract the moral and emotional options from the extreme conditions of a holocaust and to explore their implications for post-Holocaust man. The second mode, which matured only with the accumulation of documentation that conferred a kind of familiarity on events totally outside the realm of the authors' experience, and which is formally derivative from the European literature, is a version of the historical novel.

There is a group of writers who can be said to have borrowed the loaded symbols and scenarios of the Holocaust in order either to achieve a kind of instantaneous emotional pitch or to demonstrate the misery of the human condition by reference to the most abject of its victims. Arthur Miller, who graduated from *Focus* to more explicit uses of the concentrationary experience, literally places the ruins of a death camp as a backdrop to the personal drama in *After the Fall;*[63] in the words of A. Alvarez, Miller "thumbed an emotional lift from Dachau"[64] in that play, invoking the horror of violent and anonymous death as a kind of atmospheric prop surrounding the death of Marilyn Monroe. Miller's *Incident at Vichy* is more specifically related to the Holocaust, but even here, in the interrogation room in Vichy, where a group of Jews and one German nobleman are gathered, the drama is enacted between abstract moral forces which assume, for the occasion, a variety of stereotyped identities. "Jew," says the psychiatrist Leduc, "is only the name we give to that stranger, that agony we cannot feel, that death we look at like a cold abstraction. Each man has his Jew; it is the other. And the Jews have their Jews . . ."[65] This play, according to Miller himself, is an "attempt to understand the fundamental . . . forces . . . operating in us today."[66]

A far more serious experiment with the emotional load of Holocaust symbols appears in some of the later poetry of the non-Jewish poet Sylvia Plath. The images of her skin as a Nazi lampshade, of ashes, a cake of soap, a gold filling to invoke visions of her own death ("Lady Lazarus"); the fantasy of her German-born father as a Nazi and herself as a Jewish victim, meant to represent the problematic father-daughter relationship ("Daddy"); the kitchen oven emblematic of the crematory ovens and the fat of the Sunday lamb recalling the fat of the Jews, while the speaker's "heart" is entered like a "holocaust" ("Mary's Song"),[67] are manifestations of the process by which Sylvia Plath came to regard herself as "an imaginary Jew from the concentration camps of the mind."[68] Irving Howe makes a strong moral and literary judgment about Plath's use of these images and raises some provocative questions relating to a major trend which we have identified in some of the Holocaust literature of the sixties in America:

> That dreadful events in the individual's psyche may approximate the sufferings of a people is indeed possible, but again it might be good to remember that Jews in the camps didn't merely "suffer": they were gassed and burned. Anyone—poet, novelist, commentator—who uses images of the camps in order to evoke personal traumas ought to have a very precise sense of the enormity of what he or she is suggesting. He or she ought to have enough moral awareness and literary control to ask whether the object and the image have any congruence . . . .
>
> Is it possible that the condition of the Jews in the camps can be duplicated? Yes . . . . But it is decidedly unlikely that it was duplicated in a middle-class family living in Wellesley, Massachusetts, even if it had a very bad daddy indeed . . . .
>
> To condone such a confusion is to delude ourselves as to the nature of our personal miseries and their relationship to—or relative magnitude when placed against—the most dreadful event in the history of mankind.[69]

Howe's critique of Plath touches on the question of the rightful and credible claims which can be made upon the memory and the images of the Holocaust. On the one hand, Plath's use of those symbols is a testimony to the widespread diffusion of the Holocaust images, their common currency, so to speak, in Western culture. On the other hand, it represents a kind of devaluation of the particularity as well as the monstrosity of the historical experience. Of course those who regard themselves as the guardians of the culture and destiny of a martyred people and who insist on considering the Holocaust as a nonanalogous horror, totally unrelated to any other acts of organized brutality or to any form of personal suffering, are in fact denying the process by which the events of the past become the shared heritage of humanity. Yet when James Baldwin compares black militant Angela Davis to the "Jewish housewife in the boxcar headed for Dachau,"[70] when the vocabulary of the events of 1933–45 is applied to any situation of intense emotional or social privation, the enormity and the moral inadmissibility of the concentrationary experience are diluted even as the widespread symbolic assimilation of the experience is achieved.

One group of American writers who cannot be accused of the "solipsistic fallacy" are the authors of the realistic fiction which proliferated in the sixties and seventies. Written for the most part by Jews, this fiction is one attempt to recoup the double loss experienced by American Jews: the loss of continuity with their communal origins as a result of the emigration from Europe, and the loss of the remaining bearers of the past as a result of the Holocaust. The latter loss renders the former irremediable and thus the search for avenues into the past becomes so difficult and, often, so guilt-ridden. Susan Fromberg Schaeffer's novel *Anya*[71] is a consummate example of the appropriation of the Holocaust and of the pre-Holocaust heritage through the vicarious acquisition of the details that constituted the events. The author's research into the period is so extensively displayed that it is almost as if she were making a bid for entry into unknown territory through an astounding command of maps and charts. It is a novel which could hardly have been written before scholarship and testimony had provided compensation for the existential distance and a novel like Ilona Karmel's *An Estate of Memory* had provided the literary model. *Anya* centers on one young woman's struggle to preserve her own and her daughter's lives, and traces her journey from the plenitude of life in a wealthy Polish-Jewish home through the scarcity of the ghetto, the eventual disappearance and death of the other members of her family, and her incarceration in the Kaiserwald camp, from which she ultimately escapes and is reunited with her daughter; Anya lives out the rest of her life as a "refugee" in New York. The authenticity achieved by a plethora of details is, nevertheless, undermined by occasional gaps in acquired knowledge—such as glimpses of Hasidic life which reveal a lack of familiarity with the subject—and the integrity of the narrative is violated by speculation on the "meaning" of survival in the last chapter. The novel is a good example of impressive erudition and a sensitive exploration of brutal experience, as well as of the lapses which are probably inevitable in the vicarious reconstruction of cataclysmic history.

In their reliance on meticulous reconstruction based on research, such novels exemplify a form of realism or naturalism which posits as morally acceptable the appropriation of the Holocaust through the autonomy and primacy of facts and the function of those facts in constraining imagination and personal fantasy. The tension between internal accountability to the imagination and external accountability to the victims expresses the heart of the dilemma of Holocaust literature in America. In the decades that have ensued since the liberation of the camps, American writers have engaged history vicariously through several avenues, the different stages and trends in literature revealing changing perspectives on the events and on their relevance to the American experience. The insular response of postwar Jewish writers to the events in Europe was the first indication of a tendency to extract a universal moral message out of the particularistic experience and to explore the relevance of such experience for post-Holocaust man. A parallel response which has become more prominent over the years derives from the impulse to possess the experience itself, either through a form of witness or historical reconstruction, or through a leap into fantasy charged with historical possibilities.

Afterword

All sorrows can be borne if you put them into a story.

Isak Dinesen

S.S. Lieutenant Schillinger of Auschwitz was killed by a young Jewish dancer on her way to the gas chamber only once, but the story has been told again and again—by two Jewish clinicians trying to penetrate the psyche of the rebellious prisoner; by a Czech-Jewish novelist who invests the act with dimensions of bravery and self-sacrifice befitting the heroine in a classic tragedy; and by a Polish storyteller who highlights not the momentary triumph of the rebel but the craven submissiveness of her fellow inmate who drives her into the gas chamber.

The claims of the imagination as it circles around the corpse of six million Jews are infinite. While attempting to draw critical distinctions between the works of art discussed in the preceding chapters, I have tried to avoid the kind of evaluation which borders on moral judgment, the speculation on whether any literary expression can be considered "adequate" to the enormity of the reality it represents. In the end, however, it is a question that cannot be dismissed; it is the heart of the matter.

Does Tadeusz Borowski capture the Holocaust experience because he makes no concessions to hope or faith, in literature or in life— because for him Auschwitz has obliterated the past and preempted the future? Or is Ilona Karmel more valuable because in her story the imagination provides a retreat from and a defiance of reality? Are we still searching for redemption in literature? Or do we rather condemn the writer who finds it in the darkest regions?

Is there a book or a song where this tragedy finds its proper voice? Perhaps it is the failure of classic tragic possibilities in the drama of mass mechanized death, but in America a kind of sentimentality has covered the victims with a thick haze dispelled only by the pious

217

formulas of popular culture, while a certain indulgent fascination with the potential for evil in Everyman has largely replaced the outrage and the empathy that suffering traditionally commands. All the facts of human behavior are admissible in a kind of neutral effort to classify all the news that's fit to print. Whether Auschwitz is regarded as the cause or just the symptom of a diminished heroics, there is a timidity about exploring the spirit from its heights to its depths, and a preference for psychological codes over moral agonies. It is possible that when all the races of this century are run, history will show that where there was less posturing, there was more decency, that the demotion of the towering hero, the lightning rod of tragedy, elevated the common man and the sense of common responsibility; but the literary record shows a deflation of passion as of rhetoric. Saul Bellow, America's laureate storyteller, perhaps comes closest to formulating the challenge—and the limits—of his own art in *Humboldt's Gift:* in America "we weren't starving, we weren't bugged by the police, locked up in madhouses for our ideas, arrested, deported, slave laborers sent to die in concentration camps. We were spared the holocausts and nights of terror. With our advantages we should be formulating the new basic questions for mankind. But instead we sleep. Just sleep and sleep, and eat and play and fuss and sleep again."[1] The impulse that would have driven Dostoevski or Mann to transcend reality in the search for a metaphysics of existence becomes in America a minuet between the inherited impulse to rage and to chastise and the contemporary skepticism about the ultimate sense of things that breeds irony, indulgence, and complacency.

In Europe, where the reality of the concentration camps and the nights of terror is more compelling, the traditions of the past also prove insufficient. Unlike the medieval Inferno, the concentration camp can hardly be imagined as the punitive realm of a larger moral order; nor, without a vision of beatitude, can it be integrated into a symmetry of human deeds and divine rewards. Yet even in the absence of the systems that once sustained the spirit, art is still expected to salvage the voices of the dying. The poem is summoned to replace the disrupted ceremonies of mourning, to give dignity and form to ignominious, unmarked death; and the novel to resurrect private destiny from the heaps of bone and ash. The modern imagination struggles to assimilate the modern forms of death. Some of the genres of this literature have parallels in other literatures of catastrophe, such as those produced by the A-bomb survivors and Soviet prison camp inmates. Where the historical matter is a fixed and total devastation, the versions of history reflected in art reveal each artist's struggle between continuity and discontinuity with his cultural and private past. Narrative or symbolic distance from the brutalizing facts is often a function of the effort to maintain the bridges. Much of the documentary literature and the fiction of the concentrationary realists obscure past and future by adhering to the self-limiting facts of the experience; following a different route, the myth-makers foreclose escape by extending the boundaries of the camp to encompass all of existence. The survivalist perspective clings to memory and hope as the possible threads which will lead out of the abyss.

These are great narratives that invent out of spent lives the fictitious struggle of the lonely individual for survival and identity, but it may be that the real story of the Holocaust is the story of Israel's death and can be told only by one of her spokesmen. For the Hebraic writer, who alone writes out of a collective body of memory and inherited faith, the deeper the commitment to traditional Jewish norms and beliefs, the more shattering is the impact of the Holocaust. For such a writer, groping for the proper form, time is running out. Though the facts may be passed on from generation to generation like a mutated gene that lodges ineradicably in the collective body, it seems that only the personally afflicted can measure the words against the sharp edge of their pain. Or is it rather that, as with the ancient epics composed by the light of dimly remembered events, the symbolic transfiguration achieved over time and distance will secure a more lasting place in the human imagination for yesterday's catastrophe?

Cemeteries confine death itself. But where the enormity and senselessness of death defy confinement, the wandering souls of the unburied permeate the entire universe, and may reappear anywhere at any time. They infuse the words of the poet with a restlessness that finds no resolution in any art form, that can never fully engage or relinquish history. Bialik observed that the speech of the poet is born of the "magnitude of his fear of remaining even one moment in the . . . unmediated nothingness" of a speechless encounter with reality.[2] Ultimately a literature of the Holocaust may require a monumental act of creation inducing form and order into a universe unformed and void, where darkness is upon the face of the deep and the clouds from the chimneys hover over the earth.

Notes

One: Introduction

1. Jean-Paul Sartre, *What Is Literature?* p. 211.

2. The Yiddish word that has come to designate the Nazi genocide, *ḥurbn,* resonates etymologically with memories of the destruction of the two Temples in Jerusalem, carrying with it no sacral associations but rather connoting the *violation* of the continuity of sanctified life within the community. The Hebrew word *shoah* is a biblical synonym for widespread, even cosmic disaster—again, with no necessary association of the victims with ritual sacrifice: "they are gaunt with want and famine; they gnaw the dry ground, in the gloom of wasteness (*shoah*) and desolation" (Job 30:3).

3. *The Gates of Horn: A Study of Five French Realists* (New York: Oxford University Press, 1963), p. 468.

4. As Paul Fussell writes in his study of the literature of World War I, "the Great War was perhaps the last to be conceived as taking place within a seamless, purposeful 'history' involving a coherent stream of time running from past through present to future.... The literary scene [at the outbreak of the war] is hard to imagine. There was no *Waste Land,* with its rats' alleys, dull canals, and dead men who have lost their bones: it would take four years of trench warfare to bring those to consciousness [and] it was not until eleven years after the war that Hemingway could declare in *A Farewell to Arms* that 'abstract words such as glory, honor, courage or hallow were obscene beside the concrete names of villages, the numbers of roads, the names of rivers, the numbers of regiments and the dates.' " (*The Great War and Modern Memory* [London: Oxford University Press, 1975], pp. 21, 23).

5. The term used by Harry Levin in *The Gates of Horn* to describe twentieth-century reality which "has been eventful to the point of becoming millennial, where truth has been stranger than fiction and fiction more dangerous than ever because no clear-cut line has divided it from the truth" (p. 46).

6. In *The Holocaust and the Literary Imagination* Lawrence Langer analyzes the perversions and inversions of traditional literary images and themes as reflections of the distortions of human experience in the concentration camp.

7. The firsthand accounts of life in the camps by Bruno Bettelheim and

Viktor Frankl (*The Informed Heart* and *From Death Camp to Existentialism,* respectively) have come to serve as major guidelines for the student of concentrationary behavior, and their very different conclusions constitute the basis for opposing theories of individual responses to the pressures of mass society. And, like Bettelheim, Hannah Arendt, in her study of the responses of the victims and the victimizers under Nazism, *Eichmann in Jerusalem: A Report on the Banality of Evil,* has shaped the artistic responses of many writers to Eichmann in particular and to the Jews and the Nazis in general; the effect of her interpretation of the Eichmann trial on American writers will be discussed in chapter 8. The influence of these works cannot be overstated, though it is often challenged on both scientific and ethical grounds. See, for example, Gershom Scholem's charge that Hannah Arendt lacks "ahabath Israel" (love of the Jewish people). In an exchange of letters after the appearance of Arendt's book on the Eichmann trial, he condemned her failure to "mourn the fate of your own people—this is not the way to approach the scene of that tragedy" ("Eichmann in Jerusalem: An Exchange of Letters between Gershom Scholem and Hannah Arendt," pp. 51–52). See also Sammler's argument in Saul Bellow's novel *Mr. Sammler's Planet,* that "banality is the adopted disguise of a very powerful will to abolish conscience" (p. 18).

Even literary philosophers and critics defer at times to the authority of the social scientist; George Steiner writes that "none of the numerous novels or poems that have taken on the dread theme of the concentration camps rivals the truth, the controlled poetic mercy of Bruno Bettelheim's factual analysis, *The Informed Heart*" (*Language and Silence,* p. 25). I suspect that it is not the "poetic mercy" that engages Steiner—mercy and poetry are not the predominant attributes of Bettelheim's study—but rather *the very presentation of systematic explanation.* Similarly, Frederick Hoffman, in a chapter on the concentration camps in his monumental work on death and the imagination, *The Mortal No,* which mentions briefly a number of reports, memoirs, diaries, and novels that reflect the camp experience, singles out the work of Bruno Bettelheim as going "beyond the recital of details and provid[ing] serious analyses of meaning" (p. 278).

8. Jean Cayrol, "Pour un romanesque lazaréen," in *Les Corps étrangers,* p. 203.

9. *Mimesis: The Representation of Reality in Western Literature,* trans. Willard Trask (New York: Doubleday, 1953), p. 482.

10. Mario Praz writes that "each epoch has its peculiar handwriting or handwritings, which, if one could interpret them, would reveal a character, even a physical appearance, as from the fragment of a fossil paleontologists can reconstruct the entire animal" (*Mnemosyne: The Parallel between Literature and the Visual Arts* [Princeton: Princeton University Press, 1970], p. 24).

11. *The Mortal No,* p. 37. See also Lawrence Langer's discussion of the literature of atrocity in *The Age of Atrocity.*

12. *The Mortal No,* p. 287.

13. Ibid., p. 288. The quote is from Stevens's "The Noble Rider and the Sound of Words" (1948).

14. "A Dissenting Opinion on Kafka," *New Yorker,* July 26, 1947, pp. 63, 61, 64.

15. "Engagement," in *Noten zur Literatur,* vol. 3, pp. 125–27, 130.

16. "The Literature of the Holocaust," p. 23.

17. *What Is Literature?* p. 216.

18. *The Rebel: An Essay on Man in Revolt,* trans. Anthony Bower (New York: Knopf, 1957), p. 263n.

19. *The Sense of an Ending* (New York: Oxford University Press, 1967), p. 102.

20. *Death in Life: Survivors of Hiroshima,* p. 473.

21. *The Shop on Main Street,* p. 89.

22. *A Prayer for Katerina Horovitzova,* p. 129.

23. "The Massacre of the Boys," in *Lest We Forget,* ed. Adolf Rudnicki, p. 94.

24. *The Other Kingdom,* trans. Ramon Guthrie (New York: Reynal and Hitchcock, 1947). The phrase was translated into English as "the concentrationary universe."

25. See, for example, Nachman Blumenthal, "On the Nazi Vocabulary," *Yad Vashem Studies,* vol. 1, 1957; Shaul Esh, "Words and their Meanings: 25 Examples of Nazi Idiom," *Yad Vashem Studies,* vol. 5, 1963; George Steiner, *Language and Silence,* pp. 136–51; and the work of Victor Klemperer and Henry Friedlander.

26. See below, chap. 5. See also Ann L. Mason's discussions of the literary expiation of such writers as Günter Grass and Rolf Hochhuth, and the unique function of the artist in Nazi propaganda ("Günter Grass and the Artist in History"; "Nazism and Postwar German Literary Style").

27. Although he does not refer to events as recent as the Holocaust, Uriel Weinreich, in his textbook of the Yiddish language, refers to the "status of Yiddish as a record of Jewish history." He cites idiomatic expressions that have their origins in ancient persecutions, such as the phrase "men zol ihm afile brenen un brotn" ("even if he should be burned and roasted"), which alludes to the tortures to which the victims of the Inquisition were subjected and connotes a firm resolution (*College Yiddish: An Introduction to the Yiddish Language and to Jewish Life and Culture* [New York: YIVO Institute for Jewish Research, 1971], p. 35).

28. To some extent, postwar Polish literature can also be studied with regard to the defilement of the landscape and the values of a people who had coexisted with Jews for a thousand years and, with negligible exceptions, were at best spectators and at worst willing collaborators in their murder. Writers who have explored this theme include Różewicz, Miłosz, Borowski, Rudnicki, Jastrun, and Krasiński. With the principal exception of Rudnicki, the prevailing concern in this literature is with the implications of the Holocaust for the Pole or for Poland, rather than for the victim, who often appears more as a mythical echo of the past than as a real, suffering Jew. Nevertheless there was, particularly in the years right after the war and in later years following the partial thaw in the political manipulation of art, a collective preoccupation with the subject which reflects the unique position of a community of writers in Poland. See Jadwiga Maurer, "The Jew in Contemporary Polish Writing." See also George Gömöri, Introduction to *The New Writing of East Europe,* ed. George Gömöri and Charles Newman, p. 17.

29. "John Brown and His Little Indians," in *Times Literary Supplement,* May 25, 1973, pp. 589, 590.

30. *The Liberation of the Jew,* p. 185. Linguistic dislocation may be typical of, but is of course not restricted to, the Jewish experience. George Steiner refers to some of the great writers of our century, such as Nabokov and Beckett, writers "driven from language to language by social upheaval and war," as "an apt symbol for the age of the refugee" (*Extraterritorial,* p. 11).

31. "Survol d'une littératur de Juifs," in Isaac Schneersohn, ed., *D'Auschwitz à Israel,* p. 356.

32. *Anatomy of Criticism: Four Essays* (Princeton: Princeton University Press, 1957), p. 25.

33. See the growing body of research on "exile literature," including Robert Boyers, ed., *The Legacy of the German Refugee Intellectuals, Salmagundi,* special issue, no. 10–11 (Fall 1969–Winter 1970); W. K. Pfeileer, *German Literature in Exile: The Concern of the Poets* (Lincoln: University of Nebraska Press, 1957); *Colloquia Germanica* (University of Kentucky), no. 1/2, special issue devoted to exile literature (1971).

34. One such story is related by Yanina Hesheles, who at the age of twelve was discovered to be such a talented poet that members of the underground decided to smuggle her out of the Janowska camp (*Yaldei ha-Shoah Mesaprim,* ed. Y. Goldschmidt, C. Viesel, A. Malamed, Y. Shaked [Tel Aviv: Ahduth, 1966], pp. 9–18).

35. *I Never Saw Another Butterfly,* ed. Hana Volavková.

36. "Les Rêves lazaréens," in *Lazare parmi nous,* pp. 19–20.

37. Quoted in Léon Poliakov, *Harvest of Hate,* with forewords by François Mauriac and Reinhold Niebuhr (London: Elek, 1956), p. 98.

38. *Forest of the Dead,* p. 120.

39. *The Theory and Practice of Hell: The German Concentration Camps and the System behind Them,* trans. Heinz Norden (New York: Berkely, 1958), p. 140.

40. *Survival in Auschwitz: The Nazi Assault on Humanity,* p. 22.

41. Josef Bor, *The Terezin Requiem,* pp. 8, 9.

42. "The Literature of the Holocaust," p. 65.

43. *In Bluebeard's Castle,* pp. 77, 56; see also Irving Howe's rejoinder, "Auschwitz and High Mandarin," in *The Critical Point: On Literature and Culture,* pp. 182 ff.

44. *Kaputt,* p. 338.

45. "La Littérature yiddish après la catastrophe," in Schneersohn, ed., *D'Auschwitz à Israel,* p. 375.

46. *L'Arche,* September–October 1965, quoted by W. Rabi in "Vingt ans de littérature," in Schneersohn, ed., *D'Auschwitz à Israel,* pp. 363–64.

47. *Sefer ha-Dema'ot,* ed. Shime'on Bernfeld, vol. 2, p. 89.

48. *Blood from the Sky,* p. 34.

49. Both in the volume *Child of the Shadows.*

50. *The Destruction of the Dutch Jews,* trans. Arnold Pomerans (New York: Dutton, 1969).

51. Neither the first novel, which appeared in Hebrew as *Be-Damayyikh*

Ḥayyi, nor the second, *Be-za'adim Sumim al Penei ha-Adamah,* has been translated into English.

52. Introduction to Abraham Sutzkever, *Green Aquarium* (Tel Aviv: Shamgar, 1975), p. vii. Sutzkever is another writer who wrote both memoirs and poetry reflecting the Holocaust experience.

53. *The Great War and Modern Memory,* p. 310.

Two: Documentation as Art

1. "American Apocalypse: Notes on the Bomb and the Failure of Imagination," in *The Forties: Fiction, Poetry, Drama,* ed. Warren French (Deland, Fla.: Everett/Edwards, 1969), p. 142.

2. "The Art of Fiction, 1884," in *The House of Fiction,* ed. Leon Edel (London: Rupert Hart Davis, 1957), p. 32.

3. *Block 26: Sabotage at Buchenwald,* p. viii.

4. *Babi Yar,* pp. 17, 13.

5. Phillip K. Tompkins, "In Cold Fact," *Esquire,* June 1966, p. 171.

6. *The Theory and Practice of Hell,* p. 70.

7. "The Memories," *New York Times Book Review,* April 9, 1967, p. 45.

8. "The Memoir," *New York Times Book Review,* April 9, 1967, pp. 5, 28.

9. "I had been trying to write a straightforward novel in accordance with the rules of 'socialist realism'—the only guide to writing which I knew and which I had been taught ever since my schooldays," writes Kuznetsov in the unexpurgated version; "but the truth of real life, which cried out from every line written in my child's notebook, immediately lost all its vividness and became trite, flat, false and finally dishonest when it was turned into 'artistic truth'" (p. 14).

10. *The Gulag Archipelago,* I–II, trans. Thomas P. Whitney (New York: Harper and Row, 1974), pp. vi, iii.

11. Preface to *Treblinka,* trans. Helen Weaver (New York: Simon and Schuster, 1967), p. 8.

12. *History and Human Survival,* p. 206.

13. "Adolf Rudnicki et 'Les Fenêtres d'or,'" p. 11.

14. "Newer Emphases in Jewish History," in *History and Jewish Historians* (Philadelphia: Jewish Publication Society of America, 1964), pp. 96, 94.

15. "Fiction of the Holocaust," *Midstream,* June/July 1970, p. 16.

16. "The Story That Must Build Itself," in *Mid-Century,* ed. Harold U. Ribalow, p. 233.

17. "Book Week," *New York Herald Tribune,* March 1, 1964, repr. in *The Storm over the Deputy,* ed. Eric Bentley, p. 118.

18. "Silence," in *This Way for the Gas, Ladies and Gentlemen,* pp. 142–43.

19. *The Investigation,* trans. Jon Swan and Ulu Grosbard (New York: Atheneum, 1966), p. xi.

20. Oliver Clausen, "Weiss/Propagandist and Weiss/Playwright," *New York Times Magazine,* October 2, 1966, p. 132.

21. Ibid., p. 128.

22. Ibid., p. 132.

23. Ibid., p. 128.

24. *Dr. Korczak and the Children,* in *Postwar German Theatre,* ed. and trans. Michael Benedikt and George E. Wellwarth, p. 116.

25. Introduction to Benedikt and Wellwarth, eds., *Postwar German Theatre,* p. xvii. The similarity with the famous "Millgram experiment" at Yale is striking.

26. Ibid., p. xviii.

27. So claims Eric Bentley, in the preface to *The Storm over the Deputy,* p. 8.

28. *The Deputy,* p. 12.

29. Friedlander places at the center of the moral consideration of Gerstein's case the "paradox" which is "inherent in any opposition carried on from within against a system such as Nazism, to the extent that it enforces participation in its crimes as a condition of being able to act against them." Friedlander asks whether a "resister" such as Gerstein is therefore "*less,* or *more* 'guilty' of the crime than the passive spectator who tolerates it without moving against it" (*Counterfeit Nazi: The Ambiguity of Good,* trans. Charles Pullman [London: Weidenfeld and Nicolson, 1969], p. 227). See also Pierre Joffroy, *A Spy for God* (New York: Harcourt, Brace, 1961).

30. *What Is Literature?* p. 211.

31. "Drama or Pamphlet: Hochhuth's *The Deputy* and the Tradition of Polemical Literature," trans. Abe Farstein, repr. in Bentley, ed., *The Storm over the Deputy,* pp. 127–28.

32. Ibid., p. 129.

33. Quoted in Ann L. Mason, "Nazism and Postwar German Style," p. 70.

34. Quoted in Milton Hindus, *Charles Reznikoff: A Critical Essay* (Santa Barbara: Black Sparrow, 1977), pp. 56 ff.

35. *The Twenty-eighth Day of Elul,* p. vii.

36. *The Reckoning: The Daily Ledgers of Newman Yagodah, Advokat and Factor,* p. 173.

37. Quoted in *The Gates of Horn,* p. 459.

38. Compare, for example, Sylvanus's play with other artistic references to Korczak in the fiction of Manès Sperber or Adolf Rudnicki, or with an eyewitness account such as that of Hanna Mortkowicz-Olczakowa, "Yanosz Korczak's Last Walk" (repr. in *Anthology of Holocaust Literature,* ed. Jacob Glatstein, Israel Knox, Samuel Margoshes). Miss Mortkowicz-Olczakowa is very careful to distinguish between the *"known" facts* ("The day was Wednesday, 5th August, 1942, in the morning. The gendarmes close [*sic*] off the streets..."); *conflicting facts* ("According to eye-witnesses, the children were dressed in their holiday clothes, as though they were going for a trip.... Some say they wore their ordinary clothes, while others say they had blue knapsacks with them. Another version says that their arms were folded on their breasts..."); *deductive facts* ("However, those who have personally seen a deportation day or who have personally made their fearful way to a Nazi assembly place, assure us that those times were not particularly suited to special sartorial effects..."); and *legend* ("[The legend is] long and many-sided. There are many versions... of the last trip which was taken by the children educated by Yanosz Korczak.... Did Korczak tell them they were

going for a picnic, to the country? We cannot know . . . . Did they sing? Possibly, yes . . .'') (pp. 134–35).

39. *Blood from the Sky*, p. 316.

Three: "Concentrationary Realism" and the Landscape of Death

1. *Mimesis*, p. 488. See also Harry Levin, *The Gates of Horn*, pp. 468, 469.

2. *The Tower and the Abyss: An Inquiry into the Transformation of Man* (New York: Viking, 1957), p. 98.

3. *The Captive Mind*, p. 41.

4. Ibid.

5. Borowski was, according to Adolf Rudnicki, an "ardent partisan des Américains et de leur littérature"; "American literature" inevitably meant Hemingway, first and foremost, as Rudnicki demonstrates in a later discussion of the subject ("Voyage en Occident," pp. 322, 329–30).

6. Quoted in Kahler, *The Tower and the Abyss*, p. 99. See also p. 102.

7. Translated from *Les Temps Modernes*, October 1947, reprinted in Nathalie Sarraute, *The Age of Suspicion: Essays on the Novel* (New York: Braziller, 1963), p. 50.

8. Examples of fiction which reaches only the threshold of the concentration camp include most of the novels of Elie Wiesel; Piotr Rawicz, *Blood from the Sky;* Jean Bloch-Michel, *The Witness;* Elżbieta Ettinger, *Kindergarten;* Henia Karmel-Wolfe, *The Baders of Jacob Street;* Richard Elman, *The Twenty-eighth Day of Elul;* Arthur Miller, *Incident at Vichy;* Jacob Presser, *Breaking Point;* Ilse Aichinger, *Herod's Children;* Giorgio Bassani, *The Garden of the Finzi-Continis*.

9. See, for example, Edward Lewis Wallant, *The Pawnbroker;* Saul Bellow, *Mr. Sammler's Planet;* Ladislav Fuks, *Mr. Theodore Mundstock*.

10. "Auschwitz, Our Home," in *This Way for the Gas, Ladies and Gentlemen*, p. 152.

11. *Noten zur Literatur*, pp. 126–27.

12. *The Truth of Poetry: Tensions in Modern Poetry from Baudelaire to the 1960's* (New York: Harcourt Brace Jovanovich, 1969), p. 247.

13. Quoted in ibid., pp. 247, 249. Miłosz once wrote that Różewicz's poetry embodies "la nudité de l'homme sur la terre impitoyable" (quoted by Gömöri, "Literature Deprophetized: New Trends in East European Literature," in Gömöri and Newman, eds., *The New Writing of East Europe*, p. 254).

14. "Orwell: History as Nightmare," in *Politics and the Novel* (London: Stevens, 1961), pp. 237, 238.

15. *The Informed Heart*, p. 243.

16. *The Watch*, pp. 70–71.

17. Harry Levin talks of the "ultimate reification" of the human being into matter (*The Gates of Horn*, p. 454). George Steiner, Frederick Hoffman, Lawrence Langer, and Alvin Rosenfeld have also touched on this subject.

18. *Blood from the Sky*, p. 22.

19. *The Captive Mind*, p. 123. Miłosz discreetly refers to Borowski, who was still alive at the time the essay was written, as "Beta." In 1951, at the age of twenty-nine, Borowski committed suicide.

20. Ibid., p. 119.

21. In 1974, survivors of an Andes plane crash published a book detailing their experiences, which included the systematic consumption of their dead companions (Piers Paul Read, *Alive: A Story of the Andes Survivors* [Philadelphia: Lippincott, 1974])—and they were on the whole more praised for their ingenuity than condemned for their cannibalism.

22. *Kaputt*, p. 244.

23. This filicide recalls the ancient vision of a cursed world which Moses invoked as the alternative to a society governed by divine law: "The Lord will bring a nation against thee from far, from the end of the earth, as the vulture swoopeth down; . . . a nation of fierce countenance . . . . And thou shalt eat the fruit of thine own body, the flesh of thy sons and of thy daughters whom the Lord thy God hath given thee; in the siege and in the straitness, wherewith thine enemies shall straiten thee" [Deut. 28:49–53].

24. The detail in charge of unloading the transports of people as they arrived at Auschwitz—so named because they often grew rich on the possessions which they appropriated from the new arrivals.

25. *Night*, p. 348. In Hilsenrath's second novel, *The Nazi and the Barber*, irony replaces brute reality as the lens through which the Nazi period is filtered. An improbable satire reminiscent of Romain Gary's *The Dance of Genghis Cohn* and Robert Shaw's *The Man in the Glass Booth* (see below, ch. 4, n. 27 and ch. 8, n. 57) the novel portrays the victim as the victimizer's alter ego and nemesis. Moral and metaphysical issues such as human guilt and divine silence, which find no resonance in the bare narrative in *Night*, are explored here with a cynicism that gives way to despair and creates in the end a compelling morality tale for our times.

26. Piotr Rawicz presents a similar image in his novel; Boris, the protagonist who is to be the sole survivor of his home town in the Ukraine, looks back on the town, which has just been emptied of its Jews:

> "I directed my eyes toward the plain. I was seeing it from a
> very long way off, as though through the wrong end of a
> telescope. A pair of children's shoes, a doll that had come
> through unscathed, a silk brassiere . . . . There lay the foun-
> tainhead. In the interlude between the slamming of the gates
> just now and the opening of a museum at some future date,
> this brassiere lifted and rustled like a butterfly in no man's
> land." [*Blood from the Sky*, p. 13]

27. "Les Rêves lazaréens," *Lazare parmi nous*, p. 16.

28. Euripides, *The Trojan Women*, trans. Richmond Lattimore, in *Euripides III*, ed. David Grene and Richmond Lattimore (Chicago: University of Chicago Press, 1958), p. 141 (ll. 376–79).

29. Hiroko Takenishi, *Ceremony* (1963), quoted by Lifton, *Death in Life*, p. 477.

30. *Ancun de nous ne reviendra*, p. 109.

31. Introduction to *Selected Poems: Abba Kovner and Nelly Sachs*, p. 9.

32. Another example is the fiction of Israeli writer Yehiel Dinur, who writes under the pseudonym Katzetnik (see especially *House of Dolls* [New

York: Simon and Schuster, 1955] and *Atrocity* [New York: Lyle Stuart, 1963]).

33. On schizophrenic language, see Kurt Goldstein, "Methodological Approach to the Study of Schizophrenic Thought Disorder," in *Language and Thought in Schizophrenia,* ed. J. S. Kasanin (Berkeley: University of California Press, 1951), pp. 28–29. Enlarging on Goldstein's observations, Silvano Arieti explains that "in a certain way the universe of the schizophrenic, of the primitive and of the child is closer to the immediate perception, to the phenomenological world, and at the same time it is farther from the truth than ours because of its extreme subjectivity. [Adherence to] denotation prevents the schizophrenic from using figurative or metaphorical language, contrary to what it may seem...at first impression" (*Interpretation of Schizophrenia* [New York: Robert Brunner, 1955], p. 213; see also pp. 308 ff.).

In an early study of both concentration camp prisoners and schizophrenics, Bettelheim went so far as to claim that the symptomatology is so similar that "a description of prisoner behavior would be tantamount to a catalogue of schizophrenic reactions" ("Schizophrenia as Reaction to Extreme Situations," *American Journal of Orthopsychiatry* 26, no. 3 [July 1956]: 512). R. J. Lifton is another psychoanalyst who has drawn comparisons between the behavioral syndrome of A-bomb and concentration camp victims, which he calls "psychic numbing," and schizophrenia, particularly as regards the "tendencies toward concretization of ideas and extreme desymbolization" (*Death in Life,* pp. 507–8).

34. "Symbolization and Fiction-Making," from a taped presentation at the "Wellfleet Meetings," as presented in *Explorations in Psychohistory: The Wellfleet Papers,* ed. Robert Jay Lifton with Eric Olson (New York: Simon and Schuster, 1954), pp. 217, 219.

35. *The Rebel,* p. 268.

36. See George Lukács's contrast of what he calls Camus's "lack of perspective" with Thomas Mann's "critical realism," which he attributes to Mann's recognition of "the subjective character of the modern experience of time" (*The Meaning of Contemporary Realism,* trans. John and Necke Mander [London: Merlin, 1962], pp. 59, 51). Lukács's distinction, however, is too rigid and fails to take into account those characters in Camus's novel who manage to maintain their spiritual detachment, and those in Mann's novel who do not. Of Castorp's stay on the mountain, the narrator says that "it was neither short nor long, but hermetic," and when he "saw himself released, freed from enchantment [it was] not of his own motion...but by the operation of exterior powers" (*The Magic Mountain* [New York: Vintage, 1955], pp. 715, 711).

37. In responding to the imprisonment enforced by disease or oppressive penal systems, Arthur Koestler's Rubashov (*Darkness at Noon*) and Bernard Malamud's Yakov Bok (*The Fixer*) exhibit the same tenacious independence in the face of attempts to break their spirit as Kostoglotov, Tarrou, and Rieux do.

Four: Literature of Survival

1. On the high proportion of female writers in A-bomb literature, see Lifton, *Death in Life,* p. 474.

2. "The Survivor: On the Ethos of Survival in Extremity," pp. 6, 5. A

revised version of this article later appeared as the first chapter in Des Pres's book *The Survivor: An Anatomy of Life in the Death Camps.*

3. *The First Circle,* quoted by Des Pres, "The Survivor," p. 5.

4. I use Des Pres's term, "Darwinian," to suggest the individual's struggle for survival at the expense of others—although the evolutionary process of selection by which the "fittest" survive is, of course, not necessarily synonymous with cannibalism.

5. William G. Niederland, "Psychiatric Disorders among Persecution Victims," *Journal of Nervous and Mental Disease* 139 (1964): 468, quoted in Lifton, *Death in Life,* p. 457.

6. Introduction to *Selected Poems: Abba Kovner and Nelly Sachs,* p. 7. This theme also figures in the literature we are about to consider; the narrator of Anna Langfus's *The Whole Land Brimstone* looks up at the stained-glass windows of the church located within the walls of the ghetto and sees Mary Magdalen "wiping up the blood and spittle with her hair. And she reflected that, outside, there were too many people against the walls for even a whore to show them pity" (p. 32).

7. "The Survivor," p. 4.

8. See, for example, Arnošt Lustig, *A Prayer for Katerina Horovitzova,* or André Schwarz-Bart, *The Last of the Just.*

9. *The Mortal No,* pp. 15, 493.

10. Malamud's novel is the fictionalized story of the Beiliss trial.

11. *An Estate of Memory,* p. 3.

12. *The Long Voyage,* p. 9. For a discussion of Semprun, see below, chap. 7.

13. Zdena Berger, *Tell Me Another Morning,* p. 8.

14. We noted a similar phenomenon in Hochhuth's refusal to identify the Doctor in *The Deputy;* in both cases the reference is, presumably, to the infamous Dr. Mengele of Auschwitz.

15. A short novel which shares many of the characteristics of this genre, Jacob Presser's *Breaking Point,* dramatizes such a moment of truth and its consequences for spiritual as well as physical survival. It is interesting to note that Presser, in the manner of the documentary writers we have considered, insists throughout that his story is the "whole truth" (p. 13). This is no doubt the case—as historian of the Holocaust, Presser came across many dramatic testimonies (he himself was in hiding during the Nazi roundup of the Jews of Holland, but his wife was deported and killed) and his scholarly study is studded with personal anecdotes—but it also reveals the extent to which the gifted artist (Presser also wrote poetry on the Holocaust) bows to the "authority" of the careful historian.

Bettelheim, who ascribes to the inmates the potential for a higher degree of self-awareness and rational, premeditated behavior than was normally possible in the camps, defines the significance of the "point of no return" in a manner relevant to the quality of, if not the actual opportunities for, human survival:

> To survive as a man, not a walking corpse, as a debased and degraded but still human being, one had first and foremost to remain informed and aware of what made up one's personal point of no return, the point beyond which one would never,

under any circumstances, give in to the oppressor, even if it meant risking and losing one's life. It meant being aware that if one survived at the price of over-reaching this point, one would be holding on to a life that had lost all its meaning. It would mean surviving—not with a lowered self-respect but without any (*The Informed Heart*, p. 157).

16. Quoted in Kahler, *The Tower and the Abyss*, p. 88.

17. *From Death Camp to Existentialism: A Psychiatrist's Path to New Therapy*, p. 38. Other psychiatrists who have worked with survivors, such as Hillel Klein in Israel, demonstrate the life-preserving function of memory or fantasy in the context of the concentration camps.

18. *The Rebel*, p. 186. See also the chapter "Metaphysical Rebellion," pp. 23–104.

19. The phrase "survivor of the concentration camp of the mind" is borrowed, out of context, from A. Alvarez's representation of Sylvia Plath's conviction that to be an adult in the twentieth century meant to be a "survivor, an imaginary Jew from the concentration camps of the mind" (*The Savage God: A Study of Suicide* [New York: Random House, 1970], p. 19).

20. *Mr. Theodore Mundstock*, pp. 111–12.

21. Lawrence Langer suggests that there is a current of irony which undercuts the pretense of "method" that Mundstock adopts to cope with the Nazi madness (*The Holocaust and the Literary Imagination*, pp. 94 ff.). The irony resides not in the text, which is a warm testimony of human faith against overwhelming odds, but rather in the historical retrospect, in the reader's knowledge of how paltry and futile were any individual acts of defiance against the machinery of mass murder. Another work of deception built on faith and the nay-saying of the spirit to the body's degradation is Jurek Becker's *Jacob the Liar*.

22. Berger, *Tell Me Another Morning*, p. 227.

23. Ibid., p. 229.

24. Tola, on the other hand, was granted the dubious privilege, at an early stage of her incarceration, of a glimpse into a future devoid even of the window dressings: as she is marched from the camp near Cracow through the streets of her hometown, she notices that "chintz curtains" had already replaced her family's "embroidered tulle" (Karmel, *An Estate of Memory*, p. 10). That may have been one of the factors which contributed to her repression of fantasy and loss of hope from the very beginning.

25. Quoted in Des Pres, "The Survivor," p. 18.

26. Ibid., pp. 18, 19.

27. Romain Gary's novel *The Dance of Genghis Cohn* is a satiric version of the popular legend, in which the spirit of one Genghis Cohn haunts the body of the Nazi official who shot him in a mass execution.

28. Lifton, *Death in Life*, p. 492.

29. In *Les Corps étrangers*, pp. 201–20.

30. *The Lost Shore*, p. 9.

31. *The Pawnbroker*, p. 183.

32. "Le temps, pour moi, s'est arrêté. Je n'ai aucune raison de le remettre en

marche" (Langfus, *Saute, Barbara*, p. 95). The two characters in Ḥaim Gouri's Hebrew novel *The Chocolate Deal* inhabit the same airless twilight zone that separates "surviving" from "living." They meet after the war in an unnamed town in Europe and go through the motions of activity in a sort of pantomime which leaves no trace in reality.

33. *The Lost Shore*, p. 255.
34. *Saute, Barbara*, p. 260.
35. *Herzog* (Harmondsworth: Penguin, 1964), pp. 97, 183, 275.
36. *Mr. Sammler's Planet*, p. 313.

Five: The Holocaust as a Jewish Tragedy 1

1. A. Leyeless, quoted in Joseph Leftwich, *Abraham Sutzkever: Partisan Poet*, p. 112.
2. Jacob Glatstein accused Leyeless of betraying the Introspectivist detachment from communal concerns; see David Roskies, "The Apocalyptic Theme in Yiddish Narrative Poetry," *Working papers in Yiddish and East European Jewish Studies* (New York: YIVO Institute for Jewish Research, 1977), pp. 1, 11.
3. *World of Our Fathers*, pp. 451, 455.
4. Quoted in the introduction to *A Treasury of Yiddish Poetry*, ed. Irving Howe and Eliezer Greenberg, p. 52.
5. Wiesel's first book, an autobiography, was originally published in 1956 in Yiddish under the title, *Un di Velt Hot Geshvigen* [And the world was silent], and two years later appeared in French as *La Nuit* [Night].
6. *The Oath*, p. 238.
7. *L'Exil de la parole*, pp. 228 ff.
8. "Gilui ve-Kisui be-Lashon" [The revealed and the concealed in language], in *Kol Kitvei Bialik* [Complete writings of Bialik] (Tel Aviv: Dvir, 1971), pp. 202–4.
9. "Yehoash," quoted in Yeshurun Keshet, "Al Shirato Shel Avraham Sutzkever" [On the poetry of Abraham Sutzkever], *Molad* (Winter 1975): 188. Translation mine.
10. "Under the Earth," in *An Anthology of Modern Yiddish Poetry*, selected and translated by Ruth Whitman (New York: October House, 1966), p. 127.
11. The *seliḥot* are prayers recited during the month of Elul and variations on the dirge "El Malei Raḥamim." The *kinah* was originally recited when an important person had died (Jer. 22:18, Gen. 23:2); later it was recited over a whole community that had suffered catastrophe. The Book of Lamentations is referred to in rabbinic literature as *kinot*. The Talmud preserved many of the early *kinot*. The first collection of *kinot*, in the Ashkenazic tradition, was published in 1585. Since then many versions have been published. In 1923, Shime'on Bernfeld published the three-volume Hebrew anthology *Sefer ha-Dema'ot* [The book of tears], which included representative stories and poems generated by the major catastrophes that the Jews had endured since the days of Antiochus Epiphanes. As an aside, one may note the rather intense interest in martyrology among European Jewish scholars in the 1920s and 1930s, especially when compared with the relative lack of interest by American-Jewish

scholars in the subject. Bernfeld strikes an ominous note when he writes, in the introduction to his work, "we are fearful that what will come after us will be more terrible than that which we have witnessed" (vol. 1, p. 77).

12. The historiographical function of the *midrash* as well as of the *kinah* can be discerned even in the etymology of the word *midrash* which, as translated in the Septuagint, suggests "an account . . . the result of inquiry . . . of the events of the time" (*Encyclopaedia Judaica*, s.v. "Midrash").

13. Quoted in Jacob Lestschinsky, "For a Survey of the Jewish Tragedy," *Chicago Forum* 4, no. 3 (Spring 1946): 151. A few fledgling historians did overcome this apparent resistance to historiography. But for the most part they too shared the poet's vocabulary and sacred perspective on history (see, for example, *Shevet Yehudah, Emek ha-Bakha,* and *Yeven Mezulah,* accounts of Jewish persecution written in the sixteenth and seventeenth centuries). It was not until the pogroms of 1903–5 in Russia that thorough documentation provided reliable sources for secular historical evaluation of collective Jewish catastrophe.

14. A glance at some of the discussions among medieval rabbis and scholars on the subject reveals the extent to which the aversion to historiography was a matter of principle, not of oversight. Chronicles of the deeds of men may, it is argued, be enlightening for the gentiles "who have not seen the light of Torah and must stumble through the darkness of human records" to find some sparks of virtue after which they may pattern their lives (Azariyah Min ha-Adumim, *Me'or Einayyim,* ed. Yitzhak Ben-Ya'akov, vol. 1 [Vilna, 1863], p. 254). Translation mine.

15. In devising forms of desecration of Scriptures, the Nazis, it turns out, were not always original; a seventeenth-century Italian poet, recounting the brutal acts committed by Chmielnicki's Cossacks, describes how "the Torah came into their hands / They made of it shoes for the soles of their feet" ("Let the Heart of Man be Sickened . . ." by the Italian poet R. Ya'akov Bar Moshe ha-Levi, in Bernfeld, *Sefer ha-Dema'ot,* vol. 3, p. 167). The desecration of the Holy Scrolls was a recurrent theme in the most impassioned lamentations of the Middle Ages.

16. Selihah prayer by R. Shabbetai Cohen Ba'al ha-Shah; in Bernfeld, *Sefer ha-Dema'ot,* vol. 3, p. 172. The same was true of the *kinot* written in commemoration of the martyrs of Ancona, which were recited for generations thereafter as part of the Tishah be-Av service in the local community.

17. See Second Book of Maccabees, 6:21–7:41; Lamentations Rabbah, 1:16; and a Sephardic *kinah* for Tishah be-Av in Bernfeld, *Sefer ha-Dema'ot,* vol. 1, pp. 91–95. For a discussion of the versions of this legend in the contemporary martyrological literature, see Gershon David Cohen, "Ma'aseh Hannah ve-Shivat Baneha be-Sifrut ha-Ivrit," in *Mordecai Kaplan Jubilee Volume,* Hebrew section (New York: Jewish Theological Seminary of America, 1953), pp. 109–22.

18. For a discussion of the general climate of consensus out of which the *paytan* wrote, see Yitzhak Be'er's introduction to *Sefer Gezerot Ashkenaz ve-Zarefat,* ed. A. M. Habermann, pp. 1–7.

19. In repeated *midrashim* on the destruction of the Temple, for example,

the disaster is attributed to the unworthiness of and the fraternal strife among the Jews themselves: "Had you been worthy, you would be dwelling in Jerusalem, uttering songs and praises to the Holy One, Blessed be He; but now that you are unworthy, you are exiled to Babylon where you utter lamentations. Alas!" (Proem 19 to *Midrash Rabbah: Lamentations*, trans. and ed. H. Freedman and Maurice Simon [London: Soncino, 1939], p. 24).

20. See, for example, the phrase, "who is like unto Thee among the speechless, O God, / Who can be compared with Thee in Thy silence?" in the twelfth-century *kinah* by Menaḥem ben Jacob ("Allelai Li," published in *Kovetz Al Yad* and quoted in Israel Zinberg, *A History of Jewish Literature* [Cleveland: Case Western Reserve University Press, 1972], vol. 2, p. 26). The antecedents of this inversion ("who is like unto Thee among the mighty [*elim,* "mighty"] into "who is like unto Thee among the speechless [*ilmim,* "speechless"]) are Tannaitic (see Mekhilta of R. Ishmael).

21. Introduction to Habermann, ed., *Sefer Gezerot Ashkenaz ve-Zarefat,* p. x. Translation mine.

22. "Shaha Nafshi" [My soul bowed down], in *Kol Kitvei Bialik,* p. 61.

23. See "Ha-Matmid" [The scholar] and "Be-Ir ha-Haregah" [In the city of the slaughter], in ibid., pp. 89, 98.

24. See "Akhen Ḥazir ha-Am" [Surely the people is grass] and "Lifnei Aron ha-Sefarim" [In front of the bookcase], as well as "Al ha-Sheḥitah" [On the slaughter], in ibid., pp. 17–18, 54–55, 41.

25. See "Be-Ir ha-Haregah," especially the scene in which the women are raped while their men cower in dark corners, watching, and then run to the rabbi to inquire whether they are allowed to sleep with their defiled wives (ibid., pp. 95 ff.).

26. See, for example, his invocation of the ritual act of animal slaughter in the context of human massacre—an inversion which is an indictment of the divine powers that would countenance such a slaughter ("Al ha-Sheḥitah," in ibid., p. 41).

27. *The Warsaw Diary of Chaim Kaplan,* trans. and ed. Abraham I. Katsh (New York: Collier, 1973), p. 79. (Originally published as *The Scroll of Agony* [Macmillan, n.d.].)

28. Quoted in the introduction to *Ha-Shoah be-Shira ha-Ivrit: Mivḥar* [The Holocaust in Hebrew poetry, an anthology], ed. Natan Gross, p. 7.

29. *Modern Hebrew Literature: From the Enlightenment to the Birth of the State of Israel: Trends and Values* (New York: Schocken, 1970), p. 148.

30. "Keter Kinah le-Khol Beit Yisrael" [Crown of lamentation for the whole house of Israel], in *Reḥovot ha-Nahar,* p. 55.

31. "A Poet of the Holocaust," p. 57; see also Alter's "Confronting the Holocaust," in *After the Tradition: Essays on Modern Jewish Writing,* p. 164.

32. Gershon Shaked, *Gal Ḥadash ba-Siporet ha-Ivrit* [A new trend in Hebrew fiction], p. 75 and passim. This chapter appeared in English translation as "Childhood Lost: Studies in the Holocaust Theme in Contemporary Israeli Fiction," in *Literature East and West,* March 1970.

33. "On the Boy Avram," in Gross, ed., *Ha-Shoah be-Shira ha-Ivrit,* p. 152.

34. "Isaac," trans. Arieh Sachs, in *The Hebrew Poem Itself,* ed. Stanley

Burnshaw, T. Carmi, Ezra Spicehandler (New York: Schocken, 1965), p. 137.

35. "My Little Sister," trans. Shirley Kaufman and Nurit Orchan, in *Selected Poems: Abba Kovner and Nelly Sachs*.

36. From a speech delivered in San Francisco on January 20, 1972, and translated by Shirley Kaufman; quoted in the introduction to *A Canopy in the Desert: Selected Poems by Abba Kovner*, p. xiii.

37. Introduction to *Selected Poems: Abba Kovner and Nelly Sachs*, pp. 16, 17.

38. David Vogel, *Kol ha-Shirim* [Collected poems], ed. Dan Pagis, Ha-Kibbutz ha-Me'uḥad, 1975), p. 261. Translation mine.

39. Quoted by Léon Poliakov in *Harvest of Hate*, pp. 232–33.

40. "La Littérature yiddish après la catastrophe," in Schneersohn, ed., *D'Auschwitz à Israel*, p. 374.

41. Quoted in Memmi, *The Liberation of the Jew*, p. 185.

42. Quoted in Alter, *After the Tradition*, pp. 28–29.

43. "Vingt ans de littérature," in Schneersohn, ed., *D'Auschwitz à Israel*, p. 361.

44. Quoted in Cynthia Haft, *The Theme of the Nazi Concentration Camp in French Literature* (The Hague: Mouton, 1973), p. 78.

45. *One Generation After*, p. 82.

46. "My Quarrel with Hersh Rasseyner," from the collection *Mother's Sabbath*, reprinted in *A Treasury of Yiddish Stories*, ed. Irving Howe and Eliezer Greenberg (New York: Viking, 1954), p. 598.

47. Elie Wiesel, *A Beggar in Jerusalem*, p. 113.

48. *. . . Than a Tear in the Sea*, p. 9.

49. "Katuv be-Iparon ba-Karon he-Ḥatum" [Written in pencil in a sealed boxcar], in *Gilgul* [Transformation] (Ramat Gan: Sifriat Makor, 1970), p. 22. Translation mine.

50. "A Letter from Menahem-Mendel," in Gross, ed., *ha-Shoah be-Shira ha-Ivrit*, p. 148. Translation mine.

51. Sachs's play *Eli* is subtitled "ein Mysterienspiel vom Leiden Israels" (in *O the Chimneys*).

52. Ernst Wiechert, speech given in Germany in 1945, printed in *The Poet and His Time*, p. 31.

53. Ibid., p. 41. See also Wiechert's autobiographical novel of life in Buchenwald, *Forest of the Dead*, which, he writes in the prologue, is "meant to be no more than a prelude to the great Symphony of Death which will someday be written by hands more competent than mine" (p. 1).

54. See, for example, Heinrich Böll's short novels *And Where Were You, Adam?* and *The Train Was on Time*. In the first novel, a German soldier, Feinhals, falls in love with Ilona, a Jewish girl who is about to be deported to a concentration camp and killed. The main thrust of the novel is the absurdity of war—but there is a kind of sentimental logic to the relationship between the soldier and the Jewess (as Theodore Frankel wrote, in a discussion of several other German war novels, "it is always a Jewish woman, never a man, for whose sake the taboo is violated" ["The Unredeemed," p. 80]). Feinhals himself muses as he waits for the rendezvous that is never to take place:

"Perhaps it was asking too much to love a Jewish girl while this war was on and to hope she would come back . . ." (pp. 75–76). Feinhals is, of course, innocent of any knowledge of the ultimate destination of the deported Jews—this again is a shared quality among the soldiers in German fiction. Böll, however, is one of the few contemporary writers who goes so far as to dramatize a scene in a concentration camp, although the existence of the camp remains on the periphery of the action of the novel. Similar treatment of this theme can be found in *The Train Was on Time,* in which another German soldier, Andreas, on a train bringing him to the front, has premonitions about his own imminent death—and in his prayers for himself and those closest to him he includes a prayer for the Jews of the towns he is passing (pp. 186, 195).

55. See, for example, Carl Zuckmayer's early anti-Nazi play *The Devil's General,* written in exile from 1942 to 1946. The play deals primarily with the activities of the SS, but although it was concerned only indirectly with the fate of the Jews it created a furor in postwar Germany, so recently "denazified" that it could not yet confront the enormity of its own crimes. But the dilemma and the resolution are evoked in such conventional terms, and catharsis is so easily come by, that the unresolved nature of the real conflict and the mystery of human behavior in extremity all but disappear. The ambiguities of the actual events are diminished and distanced by clear-cut distinctions between good and evil, by soothing rhetoric and, finally, by the expiatory suicide of the hero.

A clearly melodramatic, though moving, portrayal of expiatory suicide deriving from an assumption of guilt by association for the fate of the Jewish victims is Albrecht Goes's *The Burnt Offering.* It is the story of a simple German woman who comes to understand what awaits the Jews who are being deported from her town, and who immolates herself and just barely escapes death by refusing to escape from her bombed and burning house—as a "burnt offering" to God. The narrator poses the ultimate question at the end as to "whether there is one who can balance the terrible guilt of the age against the wild self-immolation of a butcher's wife, against this readiness to crawl into the fiery furnace" (pp. 88, 92).

56. See, for example, references to the Holocaust in Heinrich Böll's *The Clown* and *Billiards at Half-Past Nine.*

57. The master of satire on Nazi inhumanity is Günter Grass; see his *The Tin Drum* and *Dog Years* (the latter is especially relevant in any consideration of Nazi-Jewish relations in contemporary German literature). Grass's brilliant execution of the form suggests that it is through surrealistic satire or parable, rather than realistic fiction, that the madness of the Nazi years can be most effectively translated into art.

Six: The Holocaust as a Jewish Tragedy 2

1. *One Generation After,* p. 78.

2. *God's Presence in History: Jewish Affirmations and Philosophical Reflections.*

3. Shalom Spiegel, introduction to Louis Ginzberg, *Legends of the Bible* (New York: Simon and Schuster, 1956), p. xxii.

4. Fackenheim, *God's Presence in History,* pp. 67–69, 77.

5. Quoted in Jerome R. Mintz, *Legends of the Hasidim: An Introduction to Hasidic Culture and Oral Tradition in the New World* (Chicago: University of Chicago Press, 1968), p. 250.

6. "After Such Knowledge . . . ," p. 108.

7. This is an inhibition which many of the *paytanim* who wrote poetic lamentations commemorating centuries of suffering did not share; see the *selihah* prayer by R. Shabbetai Cohen Ba'al ha-Shah in memory of the victims of Chmielnicki: "Their feet and hands they severed / and cut the corpse in half" (Bernfeld, *Sefer ha-Dema'ot*, vol. 3, p. 172). The elevation of reality to the level of legend or myth in the poetry of another Hebraic writer, Uri Zvi Greenberg, functions, as it does in Wiesel, as a prism through which otherwise intolerable reality can be filtered.

8. *The Town beyond the Wall*, p. 73.

9. Ginzberg, *Legends of the Bible*, p. 382.

10. *Mimesis*, p. 17.

11. "Ki ze Kevar Bekhi" [A time for tears], in *Rehovot ha-Nahar*, p. 80.

12. "Shir Min ha-Ya'ar: Haya Zoheket" [Song of the forest, an animal laughs], in ibid., p. 95.

13. Ephraim Oshry, *She'eilot u-Teshuvot mi-Ma'amakim* (New York, 1959).

14. *Night*, p. 47.

15. Wiesel, *Legends of Our Time*, p. 61.

16. "I. B. Singer," p. 60.

17. "The Slaughterer," in *The Seance*, p. 29.

18. Wiesel, *The Accident*, p. 72.

19. *After the Tradition*, p. 160.

20. "The Last Demon," in *Short Friday* (New York: Noonday Press, 1964), pp. 119, 129.

21. "Esthétique du Mal," in *The Collected Poems of Wallace Stevens* (New York: Knopf, 1954), p. 320.

22. "The Letter Writer," in *The Seance*, pp. 262–63.

23. *One Generation After*, p. 166.

24. *Ani Ma'amim*.

25. "Crown of Lamentation for the Whole House of Israel," in *Rehovot ha-Nahar*, p. 62.

26. *Not of This Time, Not of This Place*, p. 254.

27. "Ha-Mafte'ah Zalal," in *Mi-Kol ha-Ahavot*, p. 178. Translation mine.

28. Recorded by Nathan Eck in *Wandering on the Roads of Death* [Hebrew], quoted by Shaul Esh, "The Dignity of the Destroyed," *Judaism* 11, no. 2 (Spring 1962): 106–7.

29. *The Last of the Just*, p. 4.

30. "The Tradition of the Hidden Just Men," in *The Messianic Idea in Judaism* (New York: Schocken, 1971), p. 251.

31. Ibid., p. 256.

32. Paraphrased by Lothar Kahn, *Mirrors of the Jewish Mind: A Gallery of Portraits of European Jewish Writers of Our Time*, p. 215. See also Lisa Billig, "Voices out of the Holocaust," *Reconstructionist* 26, no. 15 (December 2, 1960): 24.

33. *World of Our Fathers,* pp. 450–51.

34. *One Destiny: An Epistle to the Christians,* trans. Milton Hindus (New York: Putnam, 1945), p. 26.

35. Megillah, 29a.

36. *A Woman Named Solitude,* trans. Ralph Manheim (New York: Bantam, 1973), p. 150. As moving as this passage is, it should be recalled that even the "ruins" of the Warsaw Ghetto were quickly obliterated and the city rebuilt.

37. "Across Different Cultures," *Midstream,* March 1973, p. 77.

38. Quoted in Marie Syrkin, "Nelly Sachs—Poet of the Holocaust," p. 15.

39. Letter dated January 27, 1946, which appeared in *Aufbau,* November 4, 1966, p. 22, quoted in David Bronsen, "The Dead among the Living: Nelly Sachs' 'Eli,'" p. 126.

40. Ibid., p. 121.

41. "Der Kheshbon Is Nokh Alts mit Dir, Bashefer" [The reckoning is only with You, Creator of the Universe], in *In Treblinka Bin Ikh Nit Geven,* p. 17.

42. "Ani Ma'amin," in Howe and Greenberg, eds., *A Treasury of Yiddish Poetry,* pp. 323–24.

43. *Aufbau,* October 28, 1966, quoted in Syrkin, "Nelly Sachs—Poet of the Holocaust," pp. 16–17.

44. Postscript to *Eli,* in *O the Chimneys,* pp. 387, 386.

45. "Paul Celan," p. 77.

46. Quoted in ibid., p. 76.

47. "There Was Earth in Them," in *Speech-Grille and Selected Poems,* p. 173.

48. *Paul Celan* (New York: Twayne, 1973), p. 121.

49. "Todesfuge," in Karl S. Weimar, "Paul Celan's 'Todesfuge': Translation and Interpretation," p. 85.

50. For a recounting of this *midrash,* see Louis Ginzberg, *Legends of the Jews,* vol. 4 (Philadelphia: Jewish Publication Society of America, 1946), pp. 303 ff.

51. Howe and Greenberg, eds., *A Treasury of Yiddish Poetry,* p. 322.

52. "I'll Find My Self-Belief," in Whitman, ed., *An Anthology of Modern Yiddish Poetry,* pp. 5–7.

Seven: The Holocaust Mythologized

1. *London Magazine,* January 1971, quoted in Stephen Spender, "The Last Ditch," *New York Review of Books,* July 22, 1971, p. 3.

2. *The Sense of an Ending,* p. 39.

3. For an extensive discussion of the identification of the Jews with the demonic forces in traditional Christian mythology, see Joshua Trachtenberg, *The Devil and the Jews* (New Haven: Yale University Press, 1943).

4. Certain writers of the prewar period may, of course, wittingly or not, have been pointing in that direction, and Kermode adds to the great debate over the implications for subsequent reality of the "apocalyptic" anti-Semitism and totalitarianism in the aestnetics and politics of modernist writers such as Pound and Eliot (*The Sense of an Ending,* p. 109).

5. *After the Tradition,* pp. 50, 60.

6. *Second Treatise of Government,* Secs. 87 and 57, quoted in and discussed by Martin Seliger, *The Liberal Politics of John Locke* (London: George Allen and Unwin, 1968), pp. 105, 167.

7. *The Author on "The Painted Bird,"* pamphlet written to be translated for the German version of *The Painted Bird.*

8. *The Painted Bird,* p. 11.

9. See especially "The Children" and "Moral Education," in *Night and Hope* and "Michael and the Boy with the Dagger," "A Bite to Eat," "The White One," and "The Last Day of the Flames," in *Diamonds in the Night.*

10. *Herod's Children,* p. 111.

11. *The Author on "The Painted Bird,"* pp. 26, 20.

12. *The Raft of the Medusa,* in Benedikt and Wellwarth, eds., *Postwar German Theatre,* pp. 48–49.

13. *The Author on "The Painted Bird,"* p. 19.

14. Ibid., p. 25.

15. In his *explication de texte,* Kosinski demonstrates the use and significance of the two train incidents (ibid., p. 26).

16. For Lind's own account of his appropriation of a succession of languages in his wanderings, see above, chap. 1.

17. *The Sense of an Ending,* p. 25.

18. "Soul of Wood," in *Soul of Wood and Other Stories,* p. 98.

19. *The Holocaust and the Literary Imagination,* p. 237.

20. "American Apocalypse: Notes on the Bomb and the Failure of Imagination," in French, ed., *The Forties,* p. 149.

21. *Anatomy of Criticism,* p. 41. See also pp. 147–50.

22. "A Poor Christian Looks at the Ghetto," in *Selected Poems,* pp. 49–50.

23. "Adolf Rudnicki et 'Les Fenêtres d'or,'" p. 11. Translation mine.

24. Ibid.

25. "Voyage en Occident," pp. 307, 326, 734. Translation mine.

26. Quoted in Rawicz, "Adolf Rudnicki et 'Les Fenêtres d'or,'" p. 11.

27. Adolf Rudnicki, "The Crystal Stream," in *Ascent to Heaven,* p. 78.

28. The culpability of the silent witnesses is the focus of the "inquest" in Wiesel's *The Town beyond the Wall;* it is also the substance of Jean Bloch-Michel's short allegorical novel *The Witness.*

29. *Survie et réinterprétation de la forme proustienne: Proust, Déry, Semprun* (Debrecen: Kossuth Lajos Tudomanyegyetem, 1969), pp. 72–73, 141.

30. Langer refers to this narrative technique as "anticipative memory" (*The Holocaust and the Literary Imagination,* p. 288).

31. *Survie et réinterprétation de la forme proustienne,* pp. 144, 157. Translation mine.

32. "The Season of the Dead," in *Beasts and Men,* pp. 163, 162.

33. *The Mortal No,* p. 286.

34. *The Holocaust and the Literary Imagination,* pp. 64–65, 66.

35. *The Garden of the Finzi-Continis,* pp. 11–13.

36. *The Mortal No,* p. 286.

37. *Blood from the Sky,* p. 57.

38. See "Elleh Ezkerah," an alphabetical acrostic incorporated into the

Yom Kippur *Musaf* prayer which recalls the Ten Martyrs of the Roman period.
39. *Blood from the Sky*, pp. 57–59.

Eight: History Imagined

1. Introduction to Wiesel, *Night*, p. 7.
2. "Some Notes on Recent American Fiction," in *The American Novel Since World War II*, ed. Marcus Klein (Conn.: Fawcett, 1969), p. 160.
3. The phrase is from A. Alvarez, "The Literature of the Holocaust," p. 69.
4. Shlomo Katz, "What Should We Write?" p. 16.
5. *Thieves in the Night: Chronicle of an Experiment* (London: Macmillan, 1946), p. 351.
6. "L'univers concentrationnaire" remained peripheral during the war because the ghettos and camps did not fit into the strategic calculations of either side; on the rare occasions when camps such as Buchenwald were attacked by the Allied forces, it was the weapons-manufacturing plants which were adjacent and not the camps themselves that were the target of the bombing. The camp administrators did not in any way consider themselves subject to the regulations of international warfare and treatment of prisoners. Hitler's policy of genocide was carried out by special units set up for that purpose and was avoided by both the Axis and the Allied powers as an issue of belligerency. The extermination of the Jews of Europe seems almost coincidentally to have been carried out during the Second World War.
7. Stefan Heym, *The Crusaders*, vol. 2, p. 630.
8. In our discussion of the documentary reconstruction of Nazi trials, it will be recalled, we mentioned a related story by Borowski which dramatizes, from the perspective of the *katzetnik*, the incongruities between the pretenses of law to redress the crimes of Auschwitz and the lawless forces which had been unleashed. See above, chapter 2.
9. *The Trumpet Unblown*, p. 200.
10. *The Mortal No*, pp. 258, 257.
11. In the German war literature, on the other hand, the subject seems to be deliberately avoided. Theodore Frankel draws the portrait of the German soldier who fights heroically on the Russian and Polish fronts but never comes across or acknowledges the concentration camps which dot the countryside of Europe. Walter Dirks, who was an editor of the *Frankfurter Hefte*, is quoted in that essay as having forthrightly admitted: "My brother who died on the side of the road during the retreat from the Caucasus knew what was happening in Buchenwald and Dachau . . . . Of course, he was only a Landser [simple German G.I.], and possibly for that reason he had a better chance to learn what went on" ("The Unredeemed," p. 79). But, as Frankel points out, most of the fictional characters, also "Landsers," who appear in these novels never acknowledge knowing about and certainly never participate in, those atrocities. For that matter, hardly a Nazi appears in these novels. As I have already noted, the most detailed fictionalized account of the Holocaust circulating in Germany as late as 1954 was a translation of John Hersey's *The Wall*.
12. *Randall Jarrell* (Minneapolis: University of Minnesota Press, 1972), p. 6.

13. Introduction to "In the Camp There Was One Alive," in *The Complete Poems,* p. 405.

14. The same image, with somewhat altered meaning but the same effect, appears in another of Jarrell's Holocaust poems, "Protocals"; a child who died in Birkenau describes her death in the gas chamber where "the water drank me" (*The Complete Poems,* p. 193).

15. Jarrell's concern for the Jews of Eastern Europe does go beyond the confines of the camps; two poems on the plight of Jewish refugees, "To the New World (For an Emigrant of 1939)" and "Jews at Haifa," probe a more familiar human condition than that which was so inaccessible to the imagination of the liberator of the concentration camps.

16. Malcolm Cowley, *The Literary Situation,* quoted in Stanley Cooperman, *World War I and the American Novel* (Baltimore: Johns Hopkins Press, 1967), p. 221n.

17. Frederick Hoffman, *The Mortal No,* pp. 236–37.

18. *The Young Lions,* p. 680.

19. *Face of a Hero,* pp. 189–90.

20. "Till the Day I Die," p. 154.

21. *Starting out in the Thirties,* pp. 82–83, 166.

22. "Under Forty: A Symposium in American Literature and the Younger Generation of American Jews," *Contemporary Jewish Record,* February 1944, pp. 22–23.

23. "Passport to Nowhere," in Harold U. Ribalow, ed., *A Treasury of American Jewish Stories,* p. 570.

24. "God Is Good to a Jew," in ibid., pp. 419, 420.

25. "The Jews as Portrayed in American Jewish Novels of the 1930's," *American Jewish Archives* 10, no. 2 (October 1959): 152.

26. *A Child of the Century* (New York: Simon and Schuster, 1954), pp. 519–20.

27. See, for example, the polemic that was generated by the "Editorial Conference" in which the editors of the *American Spectator*—Theodore Dreiser, George Jean Nathan, Ernest Boyd, James Cabell, and Eugene O'Neill—participated in September 1933, and the responses to it from Michael Gold ("The Gun is Loaded, Dreiser," *New Masses,* May 7, 1935, p. 13), Hutchins Hapgood, and others.

28. "I have no hatred for the Jew and nothing to do with Hitler or fascism," Dreiser insisted when interviewed in the *New Masses* (April 30, 1935, p. 10).

29. *Focus,* pp. 24–25.

30. Laura Z. Hobson, *Gentleman's Agreement,* p. 97.

31. "Comment on Writing," *New Palestine* 37, no. 14 (April 14, 1947): 118.

32. *The Victim,* p. 139.

33. "Terror Beyond Evil," *New Leader,* February 1948, and "The Meaning of Terror," *Partisan Review,* January 1949, both reprinted in *An Age of Enormity: Life and Writing in the Forties and Fifties,* pp. 197, 198, 199, 206, 207.

34. "The Situation of the Jewish Writer," in *An Age of Enormity,* pp. 67, 69.

35. "The Brigadier," in *Alpha and Omega,* p. 104.

36. Rosenfeld, "The Meaning of Terror," in *An Age of Enormity*, p. 209.

37. Introduction to Rosenfeld, *An Age of Enormity*, p. 32.

38. Quoted in George Steiner, *Language and Silence*, p. 166.

39. "The Hand That Fed Me," in *Alpha and Omega*, p. 9.

40. "Terror beyond Evil," in *An Age of Enormity*, p. 198.

41. *The Obsession*, p. 28.

42. *In Search*, p. 173.

43. *The Informed Heart*, pp. 252–53.

44. Ibid., pp. 252–54.

45. Ibid., p. 254.

46. *Anne Frank: The Diary of a Young Girl*, trans. B. M. Mooyaart (Garden City: Doubleday, 1952), pp. 278–79.

47. *Pentimento: A Book of Portraits* (New York: New American Library, 1973), p. 113.

48. "The Holocaust in American-Jewish Fiction: A Slow Awakening," in *Judaism* 25, no. 2 (Spring 1976): 322. Alfred Kazin characterizes the same trends when he writes that in the postwar period "the left had nothing to say, did not even include the gas in its summary view of Hitlerism as the 'last decadent stage of capitalism'" (*New York Jew*, p. 195).

49. "Why I Wrote a Jewish Novel," symposium in *Congress Weekly*, November 26, 1951, reprinted in Ribalow, ed., *Mid-Century*, pp. 316–32.

50. As an example, Mary McCarthy, contributing to the polemic that developed over Arendt's book, wrote that for her, *Eichmann in Jerusalem* was "morally exhilarating," that the chaos and the suffering of those times were shaped in the book into "a plot and a lesson" ("The Hue and Cry," in *The Writing on the Wall and Other Literary Essays* [London: Weidenfeld and Nicolson, 1970], pp. 66, 67).

For another gauge of Arendt's widespread influence on American writers, see the numerous works which were dedicated to her, including Anthony Hecht's poem "More Light, More Light" (reprinted in *Norton Anthology of Modern Poetry*, ed. Richard Ellmann and Robert O'Clair [New York: Norton, 1973], p. 1026).

51. Arendt, *Eichmann in Jerusalem: A Report on the Banality of Evil*, p. 253. That this interpretation of the trial is not the only possible one, and that, therefore, those writers who reflect it are probably reflecting Arendt's hypothesis rather than their direct perception of what took place at the trial, may be deduced from Jacob Robinson's quite different analysis of the trial and the character of Eichmann in *And the Crooked Shall Be Made Straight* (Philadelphia: Jewish Publication Society of America, 1965).

52. Moshe Bar Nathan, "The Authors and the Party," *Jewish Frontier*, November 1963, pp. 4–7. This analysis of a discussion which originally appeared in Hebrew in *Ma'ariv* is quoted in Robinson, *And the Crooked Shall Be Made Straight*, p. 138.

53. Ibid., p. 139.

54. "During the Eichmann Trial," in *The Jacob's Ladder*, p. 63.

55. Michael Hamburger, who despite his German origins and prolonged periods of residence in the United States should probably be considered a

British poet, wrote a poem which reflects the same attitudes toward Eichmann and toward the threat to humanity that the devil-as-technocrat represents:

Yet, Muse of the IN-trays, OUT-trays,
Shall he be left uncelebrated
For lack of resonant numbers calculated
To denote your hero, and our abstract age?
Rather in the appropriate vocabulary
Let a memorandum now be drawn up—
Carbon copies to all whom it may concern—
. . . Adolf Eichmann, civil servant (retired):
A mild man, meticulous in his ways,
As distinctly averse to violence
As to all other irregularities
. . . with a head for figures, a stable family life.
No abnormalities.
Never lost his temper on duty
Even with subordinates, even with elements earmarked
For liquidation.

Hamburger, like Levertov, calls upon mankind to find within itself the quality of "pity" which Eichmann lacked and which can save "man," "woman," and "child" from the cold, calculated hatred that kills remorselessly ("In a Cold Season," pp. 67–70). Along these lines, see also Muriel Spark, *The Mandelbaum Gate* (New York: Knopf, 1966), pp. 210—12.

56. *And the Crooked Shall Be Made Straight*, p. 58.

57. Even the occasional departure from the portrait of Eichmann as bureaucrat, as Everyman gone astray, such as Robert Shaw's novel and drama *The Man in the Glass Booth*, seems difficult to sustain. Shaw's exploration of the insane, criminal Nazi as "no average man" disintegrates under the revelation that the presumed Nazi is actually a Jew masquerading as Nazi masquerading as Jew. It is perhaps a confession of an evil so opaque that the outsider can only trace its shadows. The sharper features of Eichmann as "the enemy" are delineated by Italian-Jewish writer Primo Levi. His poetic address to Eichmann as "our precious / enemy, / You, forsaken creature, man ringed / with death," who came to disrupt the natural order of the universe is more consonant with the attitude of most survivors ("For Adolf Eichmann," trans. Ruth Feldman and Brian Swann, in the *Jewish Quarterly* 21, nos. 1 & 2 [1973]: 216).

58. *Touching Evil*, p. 55.

59. Norma Rosen, "The Holocaust and the American-Jewish Novelist," pp. 57–60.

60. "The Pripet Marshes," in *The Pripet Marshes and Other Poems*, p. 44.

61. The statement, made by a "nonhibakusha" writer named Kim Kokubo in a discussion with R. J. Lifton, reflects the opinions of many Japanese writers, both survivors and nonsurvivors (*Death in Life*, pp. 433 and 414 ff.).

62. *In the Days of Simon Stern* (New York: Random House, 1973).

63. *After the Fall* (London: Secker and Warburg, 1964).

64. "The Literature of the Holocaust," p. 67.

65. *Incident at Vichy,* p. 84.

66. Comment made in the course of a conversation with Norman Lloyd after the production of *Incident at Vichy* on "Hollywood Television Theatre" on NET, 1974.

67. The poems are from Plath's last collection, *Ariel.*

68. Alvarez, *The Savage God,* p. 19. See above, chapter 4.

69. Irving Howe, letter to the editor, *Commentary,* October 1974, p. 12.

70. Quoted by Shlomo Katz in "An Open Letter to James Baldwin," *Midstream,* April 1971, p. 3: see Baldwin's reply and Katz's rejoinder in the June/July issue of the journal, pp. 3–10.

71. *Anya* (New York: Macmillan, 1974).

Afterword

1. *Humboldt's Gift* (New York: Viking, 1975) pp. 226–27.

2. "Gilui ve-Kisui Be-lashon," *Kol Kitvei Bialik,* p. 202.

Bibliography

.

Imaginative Literature

Aichinger, Ilse. *Herod's Children*. Trans. Cornelia Schaeffer. New York: Atheneum, 1963.

Amichai, Yehuda. *Not of This Time, Not of This Place*. Trans. Shlomo Katz. New York: Harper and Row, 1963.

Appelfeld, Aharon. *Ashan* [Smoke]. Jerusalem: Marcus, 1969.

———. *Shanim ve-Sha'ot* [Years and hours]. Ha-Kibbutz ha-Me'uḥad, 1975.

———. *Tor ha-Pela'ot* [The age of miracles]. Ha-Kibbutz ha-Me'uḥad, 1978.

Asch, Sholem. *Tales of My People*. Trans. Meyer Levin. New York: Putnam, 1948.

Bartov, Ḥanoch. *The Brigade*. Trans. David Segal. Philadelphia: Jewish Publication Society of America, 1967.

Bassani, Giorgio. *The Garden of the Finzi-Continis*. Trans. Isabel Quigly. New York: Atheneum, 1965.

Becker, Jurek. *Jacob the Liar*. Trans. Melvin Kornfeld. New York: Harcourt Brace Jovanovich, 1975.

Bellow, Saul. *Dangling Man*. New York: New American Library, 1944.

———. *Mr. Sammler's Planet*. New York: Viking, 1970.

———. *The Victim*. New York: New American Library, 1947.

Benedikt, Michael, and Wellwarth, George, eds. and trans. *Postwar German Theatre*. New York: Dutton, 1967.

Berger, Zdena. *Tell Me Another Morning*. New York: Harper, 1961.

Bloch-Michel, Jean. *The Witness*. Trans. Eithne Wilkins. New York, 1949.

Böll, Heinrich. *The Train Was on Time. And Where Were You Adam?* Two novels. Trans. Leila Vennewitz. New York: McGraw-Hill, 1970.

Bor, Josef. *The Terezin Requiem*. Trans. Edith Pargeter. New York: Knopf, 1963.

Borowski, Tadeusz. *This Way for the Gas, Ladies and Gentlemen*. Trans. Barbara Vedder. New York: Viking, 1967.

Carmi, T., and Pagis, Dan. *Selected Poems*. Trans. Stephen Mitchell. Harmondsworth: Penguin, 1976.

Celan, Paul. *Paul Celan: Selected Poems*. Harmondsworth: Penguin, 1972.

————. *Speech-Grille and Selected Poems*. Trans. Joachim Neugrochel. New York: Dutton, 1971.

Child, Philip. *Day of Wrath*. Toronto: Ryerson, 1945.

Cohen, Arthur A. *In the Days of Simon Stern*. New York: Random House, 1973.

Cohen, Leonard. "All There Is to Know about Adolf Eichmann." *Poems 1956–1968*. London: Jonathan Cape, 1969.

Delbo, Charlotte. *Aucun de nous ne reviendra*. Paris: Éditions de Minuit, 1970.

————. *Une Connaissance inutile*. Paris: Éditions de Minuit, 1970.

————. *Mesure de nos jours*. Paris: Éditions de Minuit, 1971.

Del Castillo, Michel. *Child of Our Time*. Trans. Peter Green. New York: Knopf, 1959.

Elman, Richard. *Lilo's Diary*. New York: Scribner, 1968.

————. *The Reckoning: The Daily Ledgers of Newman Yagodah, Advokat and Factor*. New York: Scribner, 1969.

————. *The Twenty-eighth Day of Elul*. New York: Scribner, 1967.

Ettinger, Elżbieta. *Kindergarten*. Boston: Houghton Mifflin, 1970.

Falstein, Louis. *Face of a Hero*. New York: Harcourt, Brace, 1950.

Feldman, Irving. *The Pripet Marshes and Other Poems*. New York: Viking, 1965.

Friedlander, Albert H., ed. *Out of the Whirlwind: A Reader of Holocaust Literature*. New York: Union of American Hebrew Congregations, 1968.

Fuks, Ladislav. *Mr. Theodore Mundstock*. Trans. Iris Urwin. London: Jonathan Cape, 1969.

Gary, Romain. *The Dance of Genghis Cohn*. Translated by the author with the assistance of Camilla Sykes. New York: New American Library, 1968.

Gascar, Pierre. *Beasts and Men*. Trans. Jean Stewart. London: Methuen, 1956.

Glatstein, Jacob; Knox, Israel; Margoshes, Samuel, eds. *Anthology of Holocaust Literature*. New York: Atheneum, 1973.

Goes, Albrecht. *The Burnt Offering*. Trans. Michael Hamburger. New York: Pantheon, 1956.

Goodrich, Frances, and Hackett, Albert. *The Diary of Anne Frank*. Based upon the book, *Anne Frank: Diary of a Young Girl*. New York: Random House, 1956.

Gouri, Ḥaim. *The Chocolate Deal*. Trans. Seymour Simckes. New York: Holt, Rinehart, and Winston, 1968.

Grade, Chaim. *Seven Little Lanes*. Trans. Curt Leviant. New York: Bergen Belsen Memorial Press, 1972.

Greenberg, Uri Ẓvi. *Reḥovot ha-Nahar* [Streets of the river]. Jerusalem: Schocken, 1954.

Gross, Natan; Yaoz-Kest, Itamar; Klinov, Rinah, eds. *Ha-Shoah be-Shirah ha-Ivrit: Mivhar* [The Holocaust in Hebrew poetry, an anthology]. Introduction by Hillel Barzel. Ha-Kibbutz ha-Me'uhad, 1974.

Grossman, Ladislav. *The Shop on Main Street*. Trans. Iris Urwin. New York: Doubleday, 1970.

Grynberg, Henryk. *Child of the Shadows*. Trans. Celina Wieniewoka.

Hartford, Conn.: Hartmore House, 1969.

Hamburger, Michael. "In a Cold Season." *Ownerless Earth, New Selected Poems*. New York: Dutton, 1973.

Hecht, Anthony. *The Hard Hours*. New York: Atheneum, 1967.

Hersey, John. *The Wall*. New York: Knopf, 1950.

Heym, Stefan. *The Crusaders*. 2 vols. Berlin: Seven Seas, 1958.

Hilsenrath, Edgar. *The Nazi and the Barber*. Trans. Andrew White. New York: Doubleday, 1971.

———. *Night*. Trans. Michael Roloff. London: W. H. Allen, 1967.

Hobson, Laura Z. *Gentleman's Agreement*. New York: Simon and Schuster, 1946.

Hochhuth, Rolf. *The Deputy*. Trans. Richard and Clara Winston. Preface by Albert Schweitzer. New York: Grove, 1964.

Hoffman, William. *The Trumpet Unblown*. New York: Doubleday, 1955.

Jarrell, Randall. *The Complete Poems*. New York: Farrar, Straus and Giroux, 1969.

Julitte, Pierre. *Block 26: Sabotage at Buchenwald*. Trans. Francis Price. New York: Doubleday, 1971.

Karmel, Ilona. *An Estate of Memory*. Boston: Houghton Mifflin, 1969.

Karmel-Wolfe, Henia. *The Baders of Jacob Street*. Philadelphia: Lippincott, 1970.

Kosinski, Jerzy. *The Painted Bird*. New York: Pocket Books, 1965.

Kovner, Abba. *A Canopy in the Desert: Selected Poems by Abba Kovner*. Ed. Shirley Kaufman. Pittsburgh: University of Pittsburgh Press, 1973.

———. *Mi-Kol ha-Ahavot*. Merḥavia: Sifri'at ha-Po'alim, 1970.

Kovner, Abba, and Sachs, Nelly. *Selected Poems: Abba Kovner and Nelly Sachs*. Introduction by Stephen Spender. Harmondsworth. Penguin, 1971.

Kuznetsov, Anatoli. *Babi Yar*. Trans. David Floyd. Rev. ed. London: Jonathan Cape, 1970.

Langfus, Anna. *The Lost Shore*. Trans. Peter Wiles. New York: Pantheon, 1963.

———. *Saute, Barbara*. Paris: Gallimard, 1965.

———. *The Whole Land Brimstone*. Trans. Peter Wiles. New York: Pantheon, 1962.

Leivick, H. *In Treblinka Bin Ikh Nit Geven* [In Treblinka I never was]. Cyco Press, 1945.

Levertov, Denise. *The Jacob's Ladder*. New York: New Directions, 1958.

Levi, Carlo. *The Watch*. New York: Farrar, Strauss and Young, 1951.

Levin, Meyer. *Anne Frank*. Adapted from *The Diary of Anne Frank*. Published privately by Meyer Levin, Herzliya-on-Sea, Israel.

———. *Eva*. New York: Simon and Schuster, 1959.

Lind, Jakov. *Landscape in Concrete*. Trans. Ralph Manheim. New York: Grove, 1966.

———. *Soul of Wood and Other Stories*. Trans. Ralph Manheim. New York: Grove, 1964.

Lustig, Arnošt. *Diamonds in the Night*. Trans. Iris Urwin. Prague: Artia, 1962.

————. *Night and Hope*. Trans. George Theiner. New York: Dutton, 1962.

————. *A Prayer for Katerina Horovitzova*. Trans. Jeanne Němcová. New York: Harper and Row, 1973.

Maladowska, Kadia, ed. *Leider fun Ḥurbn* [Songs from the ruins]. Tel Aviv: I. L. Peretz, 1962.

Malamud, Bernard. "The German Refugee." *Idiots First*. New York: Delta, 1963.

————. "The Lady of the Lake." *The Magic Barrel*. New York: Farrar, Straus and Cudahy, 1953.

Malaparte, Curzio. *Kaputt*. Trans. Cesare Foligno. New York: Dutton, 1946.

Mezey, Robert. "Theresienstadt Poems." In Stephen Berg and Robert Mezey, eds., *Naked Poetry*. Indianapolis: Bobbs-Merrill, 1969.

Miller, Arthur. *After the Fall*. London: Secker and Warburg, 1964.

————. *Focus*. New York: Reynal and Hitchcock, 1945.

————. *Incident at Vichy*. London: Secker and Warburg, 1964.

Miłosz, Czeslaw. *Selected Poems*. New York: Seabury, 1973.

Modiano, Patrick. *La Place de l'Etoile*. Paris: Gallimard, 1968.

Moss, Stanley. "A Valentine's Day Sketch of Negro Slaves, Jews in Concentration Camps, and Unhappy Lovers." *The Wrong Angel: Poems*. New York: Macmillan, 1966.

Odets, Clifford. "Till the Day I Die." *Six Plays*. New York: Modern Library, 1939.

Plath, Sylvia. *Ariel*. New York: Harper and Row, 1965.

Presser, Jacob. *Breaking Point*. Trans. Barrows Mussey. Cleveland: World, 1958.

Rawicz, Piotr. *Blood from the Sky*. Trans. Peter Wiles. New York: Harcourt, Brace and World, 1964.

Reznikoff, Charles. *Holocaust. By the Well of Living and Seeing: New and Selected Poems*. Edited with an introduction by Seamus Cooney. Los Angeles: Black Sparrow, 1974. Printed in a limited edition.

Ribalow, Harold U., ed. *Mid-Century*. New York: Beechhurst, 1955.

————, ed. *A Treasury of American Jewish Stories*. New York: Thomas Yoseloff, 1958.

Rokhman, Leib. *Be-Za'adim Sumim al Penei ha-Adamah*. Tel Aviv: Am Oved, 1976.

Rosen, Norma. *Touching Evil*. New York: Harcourt, Brace and World, 1969.

Rosenfeld, Isaac. *Alpha and Omega*. New York: Viking, 1966.

Rudnicki, Adolf. *Ascent to Heaven*. Trans. H. C. Stevens. London: Dennis Dobson, 1951.

————, ed. *Lest We Forget*. Warsaw: Polonia Foreign Language Publishing House, 1955.

Sachs, Nelly. *O the Chimneys*. New York: Farrar, Straus and Giroux, 1967.

Schaeffer, Susan Fromberg. *Anya*. New York: Macmillan, 1974.

Schwarz-Bart, André. *The Last of the Just*. Trans. Stephen Becker. London: Secker and Warburg, 1961.

Semprun, Jorge. *The Long Voyage*. Trans. Richard Seaver. New York: Grove, 1964.

Shaw, Irwin. *Mixed Company*. New York: Random House, 1947.

———. *The Young Lions*. New York: Random House, 1948.

Shaw, Robert. *The Man in the Glass Booth*. New York: Harcourt, Brace and World, 1967.

Silberstang, Edwin. *Nightmare of the Dark*. New York: Knopf, 1967.

Singer, Isaac Bashevis. *A Crown of Feathers and Other Stories*. New York: Farrar, Straus and Giroux, 1973.

———. *Enemies, A Love Story*. New York: Farrar, Straus and Giroux, 1972.

———. *The Seance*. New York: Farrar, Straus and Giroux, 1968.

———. *Shosha*. New York: Farrar, Straus and Giroux, 1978.

Sperber, Manès. ... *Than a Tear in the Sea*. Trans. Constantine Fitzgibbon. New York: Bergen Belsen Memorial Press, 1967.

Steiner, Jean-François. *Treblinka*. Trans. Helen Weaver. New York: Simon and Schuster, 1967.

Uris, Leon. *Mila 18*. New York: Doubleday, 1961.

Volaková, Hana, ed. *I Never Saw Another Butterfly*. Trans. Jeanne Němcová. New York: McGraw-Hill, 1962.

Wallant, Edward Lewis. *The Pawnbroker*. New York: Macfadden-Bartell, 1961.

Wiechert, Ernst, *Forest of the Dead*. Trans. Ursula Stechow. New York: Greenberg, 1947.

Wiesel, Elie. *The Accident*. Trans. Anne Borchardt. New York: Avon, 1962.

———. *Ani Ma'amin*. Trans. Marion Wiesel. New York: Random House, 1973.

———. *A Beggar in Jerusalem*. Trans. Lily Edelman and the author. New York: Random House, 1970.

———. *Gates of the Forest*. Trans. Frances Frenaye. New York: Avon, 1966.

———*Legends of Our Time*. New York: Avon, 1968.

———. *Night*. Trans. Stella Rodway. Introduction by François Mauriac. New York: Hill and Wang, 1960.

———. *The Oath*. Trans. Marion Wiesel. New York: Random House, 1973.

———. *One Generation After*. Trans. Lily Edelman and the author. London: Weidenfeld and Nicolson, 1970.

———. *The Town beyond the Wall*. Trans. Stephen Becker. New York: Avon, 1964.

Zuckmayer, Carl. *The Devil's General*. In Haskell M. Bloch and Robert G. Shedd, eds., *Masters of Modern Drama*. New York: Random House, 1962.

Critical Literature

Many bibliographies of Holocaust studies have been published in recent years. Essays or books of philosophical, psychological, or historical nature are listed here only as they bear on the imaginative literature.

Adorno, T. W. "Engagement." *Noten zur Literatur*. Vol. 3. Frankfurt: Suhrkamp Verlag, 1963.

Alter, Robert. *After the Tradition: Essays on Modern Jewish Writing*. New York: Dutton, 1971.

———. "A Poet of the Holocaust." *Commentary*, November 1973, pp. 57–63.

Alvarez, A. "The Literature of the Holocaust." *Commentary*, November 1964.

Arendt, Hannah. *Eichmann in Jerusalem: A Report on the Banality of Evil.* New York: Viking, 1963.

———, and Scholem, Gershom. "Eichmann in Jerusalem: An Exchange of Letters between Gershom Scholem and Hannah Arendt." *Encounter 22*, no. 1 (January 1964): 51–56.

Bellow, Saul. "Some Notes on Recent American Fiction." In Marcus Klein, ed., *The American Novel since World War II.* Greenwich, Conn.: Fawcett, 1969.

Bentley, Eric, ed. *The Storm Over the Deputy.* New York: Grove, 1964.

Bernfeld, Shime'on, ed. *Sefer ha-Dema'ot.* 3 vols. Berlin: Eschkol, 1923.

Bettelheim, Bruno. *The Informed Heart: Autonomy in a Mass Age.* Glencoe: Free Press, 1960.

Boas, Henriette. "Jewish Figures in Post-War Dutch Literature." *Jewish Journal of Sociology* 5, no. 1 (June 1963): 55–83.

Bronsen, David. "The Dead among the Living: Nelly Sachs' 'Eli.'" *Judaism* 16, no. 1 (Winter 1967): 120–28.

Cayrol, Jean. *Les Corps étrangers.* Paris: Éditions du Seuil, 1964.

———. *Lazare parmi nous.* Neuchâtel: Éditions de la Baconnière, n.d.

Daiches, David. "After Such Knowledge . . ." *Commentary*, December 1965, pp. 105–10.

Dawidowicz, Lucy. "Epic of the Warsaw Ghetto." *Menorah Journal* 38, no. 1 (Winter 1950): 88–103.

Des Pres, Terrence. "The Survivor: On the Ethos of Survival in Extremity." *Encounter*, September 1971, pp. 3–19.

———. *The Survivor.* New York: Pocket Books, 1977.

Ezrahi, Sidra. "Holocaust Literature in European Languages." *Encyclopaedia Judaica.* 1973 Yearbook, pp. 106–19.

———. "The Holocaust Writer and the Lamentation Tradition: Responses to Catastrophe in Jewish Literature." In Alvin H. Rosenfeld and Irving Greenberg, eds., *Confronting the Holocaust: The Impact of Elie Wiesel.* Bloomington: Indiana University Press, 1978.

Fackenheim, Emil. *God's Presence in History: Jewish Affirmations and Philosophical Reflections.* New York: New York University Press, 1970.

Frankel, Theodore. "The Unredeemed: Postwar German Writing." *Midstream* 3, no. 2 (Spring 1957): 78–83.

Frankl, Viktor. *From Death Camp to Existentialism: A Psychiatrist's Path to New Therapy.* Boston: Beacon, n.d.

Freeden, Herbert. "Jewish Theater under the Swastika." *Leo Baeck Institute Yearbook I.* London: E. and W. Library, 1956.

Gömöri, George, and Newman, Charles, eds. *The New Writing of East Europe.* Chicago: Quadrangle, 1968.

Habermann, A. M., ed. *Sefer Gezerot Ashkenaz ve-Ẓarefat* [Chronicle of the persecutions in Germany and France]. Jerusalem: Tarshish, 1946.

Hoffman, Frederick. *The Mortal No: Death and the Modern Imagination.* Princeton: Princeton University Press, 1964.

Howe, Irving. "Auschwitz and High Mandarin." *The Critical Point: On Literature and Culture*. New York: Horizon, 1973.

———. "I. B. Singer." *Encounter,* March 1966, pp. 60–70.

———. Letter to the Editor. *Commentary,* October 1974, pp. 12–13.

———. *World of Our Fathers*. New York: Harcourt Brace Jovanovich, 1976.

———, and Greenberg, Eliezer, eds. *A Treasury of Yiddish Poetry*. New York: Schocken, 1969.

Hupka, Herbert. "Out of the Darkness." *Wiener Library Bulletin* 3, no. 1–2 (January-April 1954): 9.

Kahn, Lothar. *Mirrors of the Jewish Mind: A Gallery of Portraits of European Jewish Writers of Our Time*. New York: Thomas Yoseloff, 1968.

Katz, Shlomo. "What Should We Write?" *Jewish Frontier* 7, no. 5 (May 1940): 15–17.

Kazin, Alfred. *New York Jew*. New York: Knopf, 1978.

———. *Starting Out in the Thirties*. London: Secker and Warburg, 1966.

Kosinski, Jerzy. *The Author on 'The Painted Bird'*. Pamphlet written to be translated for the German version of *The Painted Bird*. Boston: Houghton Mifflin, 1965.

Langer, Lawrence. *The Age of Atrocity: Death in Modern Literature*. Boston: Beacon, 1978.

———. *The Holocaust and the Literary Imagination*. New Haven: Yale University Press, 1975.

Leftwich, Joseph. *Abraham Suzkever: Partisan Poet*. New York: Thomas Yoseloff, 1971.

Levi, Primo. *Survival in Auschwitz: The Nazi Assault on Humanity*. Trans. Stuart Woolf. New York: Collier, 1959.

Levin, Meyer. *The Fanatic*. New York: Simon and Schuster, 1964.

———. *In Search*. New York: Horizon, 1950.

———. *The Obsession*. New York: Simon and Schuster, 1973.

Lifton, Robert Jay. *Death in Life: Survivors of Hiroshima*. New York: Vintage, 1967.

———. *History and Human Survival*. New York: Vintage, 1971.

Lind, Jakov. "John Brown and His Little Indians." *Times Literary Supplement,* May 25, 1973, pp. 589, 590.

Mason, Ann L. "Gunter Grass and the Artist in History." *Contemporary Literature* 14, no. 3 (Summer 1973): 347–62.

———. "Nazism and Postwar German Literary Style." *Contemporary Literature* 17, no. 1 (Winter 1976): 63–83.

Maurer, Jadwiga. "The Jew in Contemporary Polish Writing." *Wiener Library Bulletin* 21, no. 4 (1967): 26–30.

Memmi, Albert. *The Liberation of the Jew*. Trans. Judy Hyun. New York: Orion, 1966.

Miłosz, Czeslaw. *The Captive Mind*. New York: Knopf, 1953.

Neher, André. *L'Exil de la parole: du silence biblique au silence d'Auschwitz*. Paris: Éditions du Seuil, 1970.

Rawicz, Piotr. "Adolf Rudnicki et 'Les Fenêtres d'Or.'" *Le Monde,* June 18, 1966, p. 11.

Rosen, Norma. "The Holocaust and the American-Jewish Novelist." *Midstream*, October 1974, pp. 54–62.

Rosenfeld, Alvin. "Arthur Cohen's Messiah." *Midstream*, August-September 1973, pp. 72–75.

———. "Jakov Lind and the Trial of Jewishness." *Midstream*, February 1974, pp. 71–75.

———. "Paul Celan." *Midstream*, November 1971, pp. 75–80.

Rosenfeld, Isaac. *An Age of Enormity: Life and Writing in the Forties and Fifties*. Ed. Theodore Solotaroff. Cleveland: World, 1957.

Roskies, David. "The Pogrom Poem and the Literature of Destruction." *Notre Dame English Journal* 11, no. 2 (April 1979): 89–113.

Rousset, David. *The Other Kingdom*. Trans. Ramon Guthrie. New York: Reynal and Hitchcock, 1947.

Rudnicki, Adolf. "Voyage en occident." *Les Temps Modernes* 14, no. 150–51 (August-September 1958): 305–40; and no. 152 (October 1958): 717–47.

Sartre, Jean-Paul. *What Is Literature?* Trans. Bernard Frechtman. New York: Harper and Row, 1949.

Schneersohn, Isaac, ed. *D'Auschwitz à Israel: vingt ans après la libération*. Paris: Centre de documentation juive contemporaine, 1968.

Shaked, Gershon. *Gal Ḥadash ba-Siporet ha-Ivrit* [A new trend in Hebrew fiction]. Tel Aviv: Sifri'at ha-Po'alim, 1971.

Steiner, George. *Extraterritorial: Papers on Literature and the Language Revolution*. New York: Atheneum, 1971.

———. *In Bluebeard's Castle: Some Notes Towards the Redefinition of Culture*. New Haven: Yale University Press, 1975.

———. *Language and Silence: Essays on Language, Literature and the Inhuman*. Harmondsworth: Penguin, 1969.

Stern, Guy. "Exile Literature: Designation or Misnomer?" *Colloquia Germanica*, January 1972, pp. 167–78.

Syrkin, Marie. "Nelly Sachs—Poet of the Holocaust." *Midstream*, March 1967, pp. 13–23.

"Under Forty: A Symposium in American Literature and the Younger Generation of American Jews." *Contemporary Jewish Record* 7, no. 1 (February 1944): 3–36.

Weimar, Karl S. "Paul Celan's 'Todesfuge': Translation and Interpretation." *PMLA* 89, no. 1 (January 1974): 85–89.

Wiechert, Ernst. *The Poet and His Time*. Trans: Irene Tauber. Hinsdale, Ill.: Regnery, 1948.

Index